THE OTHER SIDE OF TENKO

A scream of rage filled the air as the Jap came rushing over. A teak two-handled practice sword was raised high over his head, and in his fury he sounded like a madman. The heavy log I was carrying made it impossible to dodge as the weapon came crashing down on my skull. Again and again it landed, half the blows missing my head and cutting pieces of bark off the log. I felt little pain, but as each blow landed I felt as though my brain were soft, and was gently being pressed in while everything became dark. The Jap stopped hitting me and stepped back, dazed with the shock of not seeing me fall though looking as though my head were bashed in. Blood by this time was everywhere. The Thai women covered their faces. My friends told me later that they thought I was like a chicken still standing after losing its head, and they were waiting to see me fall.

THE OTHER SIDE OF TENKO

L. L. Baynes

A STAR BOOK

published by

the Paperback Division of
W. H. Allen & Co. PLC

A Star Book
Published in 1985
by the Paperback Division of
W. H. Allen & Co. PLC
44 Hill Street, London W1X 8LB

First published in Great Britain by The Book Guild Ltd in 1984
under the title *Kept – The Other Side of Tenko*

Printed and bound in Great Britain by
Anchor Brendon Ltd, Tiptree, Essex

ISBN 0 352 31721 3

Verses taken from the Living Bible

Foreword

'A terrifyingly authentic document that brought back much too vividly (for me) the miseries of those years of captivity under the Japanese. Len Baynes has added some fine detail to the memorial honouring those who were not so fortunate as we, and did not survive to tell the tale – a tale of suffering, courage and soldierly cunning, in the face of medieval, oriental cruelty.'

RONALD SEARLE

Preface

For years I have jibbed at the thought of writing this book. A torn-up, defaced diary of life under the Imperial Japanese Army has lain, undeciphered at the bottom of a drawer. Our captors had regarded it as a crime for us to record our treatment during the years they held us prisoner, and to have been caught with a diary would have meant severe punishment. Therefore I had to tear up the pages as I wrote them, smudging each one so that no-one but myself would realize that it was anything other than a scrap of toilet paper.

Chapter 1

'Though a thousand fall at my side,
Though ten thousand are dying around me,
The evil will not touch me.'

It began when, at four o'clock on a misty afternoon we boarded SS Orcades in Liverpool harbour. Most of us were pleased and excited at the prospect of seeing the world; after many false alarms and three 'embarkation leaves' we were now itching to go. Although we had not been informed of our destination, as we had been trained for open warfare and were now issued with tropical kit we assumed we were off to North Africa. On the thirteenth of October, 1941 at 7.30 a.m. after remaining in harbour for three days, we at last heart the rattle of anchors weighed, and our ship nosed slowly out of the harbour. At the age of twenty-two I was leaving England (lovely name) for the first time.

The Americans had not at this time entered the war. Halfway over the Atlantic nevertheless, their navy joined our convoy, and we saw our own warships disappear over the skyline in the direction of home. Our navy had only been able to spare two or three small ships in those difficult days, but the Yanks did the job in style. Their escort included an aircraft carrier, Catalina flying-boat and several more warships. We said 'Good old Roosevelt', and felt much safer.

After calling at Halifax (Canada), Trinidad, Cape Town and Bombay we were still without any idea as to where we were to finish up as we steamed south yet again. Then, on the twenty-eighth of January, 1942, twelve days after leaving Bombay, we saw land on the horizon, off the starboard bow. One of the

American crew told us that the land we could see was Java. We knew at last into which theatre of war we were probably about to enter.

During that day, when we came under attack from several Japanese planes, all the British troops were sent below the waterline. We heard the heavy thud of bombs exploding, and the lighter bangs of anti-aircraft fire but had no idea as to how the attack was going. When it was over and we were at last allowed back on deck we found that our ship had not been hit, although we later discovered that several others in our widely spread-out convoy had not fared so well. This was our introduction to the Japanese.

As we pulled into a quayside the next day three Hurricanes passed over our heads and we cheered at the sight of those friendly bullseye markings. That was the only opportunity we were to have of seeing them; they were the last of our airforce to be evacuated from the area. We had arrived in Singapore.

During our long voyage the world situation had completely changed. Pearl Harbour had intervened, and America was now in the war with us. We were in the war with them too, having just lost two of our best battleships off Malaya; they had been sent to attempt to scare the Japs off.

Disembarking, we marched away, and were housed in temporary billets at Bournemouth Road, in the Katang District of Singapore City. Singapore itself is an island about twenty miles long separated from the Johore province of the Malayan mainland, which is an isthmus, by a narrow channel known as the Straits of Johore. A causeway existed joining Singapore Island to the mainland, and carried both road and rail traffic.

That first day was spent in manoeuvres among the trees of local rubber plantations. Next day we marched off along the North-bound highway, to go into action for the first time. We were dive-bombed by Japanese Stuka planes as we went, and were glad of the drainage ditches that ran most of the way beside the road. After the Stukas dropped their one big bomb, they returned again and again machine-gunning us.

We crammed so much into those first few days that my first impression of Singapore remains very hazy, but it is the smell of that oriental city that first comes into my mind. It is made up, as I later discovered, from a mixture of garlic, fish, joss-sticks, frying oil, charcoal and probably much more; I came to like the smell, and now think of it with some nostalgia. Next I recall bamboo poles poking out of windows, hung with beautifully clean washing. The Chinese women seemed to carry on with their daily chores right through the battle for Singapore, philosophically drawing their water, cooking outside their houses over their little buckets of charcoal, even when there were bullets flying. I think also of the wealthy Chinese gentlemen who passed by. We were told how to tell their wealth by the number of their wives. These preceded their husband, each one with a springy bamboo pole over her shoulder, baskets suspended at each end of the pole carrying various kinds of merchandise. The women moved with strange bouncy steps which made them appear to move forward in a series of jerks. There were on average five or six wives per husband. I was told that once a man acquired enough cash to purchase a couple of wives he need work no more, only supervise; from then on the profit on their labour would enable him to go on purchasing wives at an ever increasing rate! If true, no wonder the young men in China have turned to communism; probably more to establish an equal distribution of wives than cash!

Old Chinese ladies passed us, with tiny feet only three or four inches long. Their big toes had been tightly bound under their feet in childhood until they became dislocated and were forced into the sole. Their tiny shoes had the heel in the centre so that they had to balance on two points, and were consequently only able to take six-inch steps, travelling at a snail's pace.

Four days digging trenches, moving on, being machine-gunned and dive-bombed, more moves – trenches – bombs, and all the time without a clue as to what was happening. We knew not whether the enemy were a thousand, a hundred, or maybe only ten miles distant; but on the fifth of February, we came under direct shellfire for the first time, and knew that the Japs were indeed close at hand. We had just dug in under rubber trees, near the Straits of Johore.) As we heard later, they had moved down the mainland so rapidly by leapfrogging sea-borne landings continually behind our front line. Now all that separated us was a narrow strip of water. Our sappers had blown up the causeway, but how long would that delay the enemy?

During that night, without our knowledge, our own brigade artillery unit dug their twenty-five pounders in not far behind us. With first light they fired their opening salvo, and I thought for the moment that our end had come as the ground rocked and the shells whistled low over our heads; but once I realized that it was our own battery firing, it seemed an auspicious beginning to my twenty-third birthday. The guns across the water were soon silenced; what a pity our boys had so few targets; with our camouflaged enemy dispersed among the heavily wooded landscape, we had very little to fire at. Our well-trained gun teams were knocked out one by one by Stukas over the coming days.

We were moved around many more times during the next two days, each time digging fresh trenches, and always under air attack. At dawn the next morning we vacated our newly dug trenches yet again, and dug in near an evacuated RAF camp, around the foot of a wooded hill. This was the neighbourhood we were to hold for the next four days while the Japs tried their best to dislodge us. Our CO was decorated, he later told us, for our stand.

During that day we were constantly moved as the situation developed, and by the time four o'clock came, and having already dug ourselves in three times, we were too tired to do much more than scratch the surface of the sun-baked ground in the place where we were to need protection the most.

Our new position was close to the RAF hutments, and there was only barbed wire separating us. Looking across I saw the interesting initials NAAFI over one of the buildings, and it was a long time since we had eaten. I made my way over and entered the building through the unlocked door. It appeared that our airmen did not use their canteen for eating, as not a single comestible could I find, but literally thousands of bottles of everything from exotic Cherry Brandy and Creme de

Menthe, to whisky and beer. As I left a machine gun opened fire on me from a position a couple of hundred yards away. I moved much faster than I had done when I came, and knew for certain now that the Japs had crossed the water. That evening we all came under small-arms fire; the enemy was now infiltrating the woods all round us.

Looking back on the day's events as I peered out that night, I thought with shame of my actions earlier on. I professed to be a Christian, yet when a small half-naked Malayan boy had approached me, holding out a little hand smashed by shrapnel, I sent him off un-aided. As he wandered slowly away, one of our stretcher-bearers saw him and dressed his wound.

The sun rose on Friday the thirteenth of February; I am not superstitious, but this was to prove a very unlucky day for us all, even though it started off well with some breakfast arriving from our base camp before eight o'clock. I decided to take the food round to each section position myself, finally sitting on the edge of Cpl Malin's trench to eat my own. As Malin had cracked up under fire, I had to spend most of my time with his section as they would otherwise have been leaderless.

Growing out of the trench side, a few inches from my head, was a sapling about two inches thick. As I was about to bite my first sandwich, a volley of machine-gun fire came from the RAF campsite, and before I could dive into the trench the sapling disappeared, leaving a shaving-brush-like stump. That first volley caught many of our company out of their trenches, and many were killed and wounded.

The small-arms fire continued for some time, keeping our heads down; then we heard the deeper sounds of mortars as they were brought to bear, and the bombs began to fall, closer and closer to our trench. We soon realized that it was only a matter of time before we received a direct hit. Suddenly there was an extra loud whine, and a thud followed by a small bang right beside me. Looking round I saw the tail of a mortar bomb sticking out of the trench wall, a wisp of smoke percolating through the earth. We had had our bomb, and it was a dud. We knew of course that bombs never fall twice in the same place! In fact the Japs now cut down their rate of firing, the furious bombardment having probably used up their forward ammunition supply.

As this trench was only half-dug when the bombing started, we tried to deepen it by scratching furiously away with our entrenching tools. Every time a head showed bullets whistled by. Knowing that the adversary could rush us at any time, we popped up our heads at different places every few seconds, and by this means lost no more men for the time being. There were seven of us in the trench and it was by no means easy to deepen it at this stage; nevertheless when about four hours later Capt Stick came along some dead ground to visit us, we were nearly deep enough. 'You are to hold that position to the last man, or until you receive other orders,' he shouted.

Some time later, Tommy Beatty, our Company Sergeant Major came along the same route. He called out a few words of encouragement telling us that he was on his way to try to find out what was wrong at our Company HQ. I told him that the open space he would need to cross to get there was under heavy enemy fire, but he carried on with a cheerful grin. He was only twenty-one or two, having obtained rapid promotion through keenness and hard work. When it came to the test he did his job at least as bravely as the oldest in our ranks. A few hours later we discovered that when he ran the gauntlet of that open space he was hit in the abdomen by a burst of fire. He lay where he fell, conscious all that day in the blistering sun with his bowels exposed to the heat and flies, yet refraining from calling for help lest he cause further casualties. (Two days later, a captain from another company took refuge in our trench having lost his own company. After receiving a harmless neck wound he roared loud enough to be heard at our Regimental Aid Post (RAP) a quarter of a mile away, insisting that stretcher bearers come and carry him over the bullet swept ground. He got off and walked when he reached safety).

There was at this time much wrong at our Company HQ as our Company Commander had been killed along with one of his officers. Poor Tommy was hors de combat, and my own officer had left us at the commencement of the action; so with many NCOs also dead, command was sadly depleted. Late that night a party of our brave stretcher-bearers crept out and rescued Tommy and got him away to base hospital.

The two sections which formed our centre and left positions, had open ground all around them, and were therefore quite unapproachable under fire. This was one of the many mistakes we made in our introduction to jungle warfare. We had been taught that it was essential to give each section a good clear field of fire, which was probably right in the desert, but here where a high degree of mobility, infiltration and sniping were the order of the day, the field of fire made us sitting ducks for the enemy all around.

Later, L/Cpl Kelly, one of our company runners, brought me an order to leave our trenches and take the platoon up the hill behind us to ferret out snipers who were firing at Battn. HQ from the hilltop. (It was then thought that a few snipers had infiltrated through our lines under cover of darkness.) I drew up a plan of action; upon my giving the order, all were to jump out of the trench together, spreading out and making for the cover of the trees. Pte Hoskins was to crawl along the dead ground to take the same message to our two other sections. Advancing up the hill, we were to meet under the water tower, which was situated on the hilltop.

When I gave the order all obeyed (except Cpl Malin who decided to keep the trench warm for us pending our return); we proceeded up the hill and heard the click of bullets hitting trees as Japs across the valley caught glimpses of us. We reached the water tower, and found that it had been hit by a bomb which had knocked it partly on its side. I counted ten dead men from another regiment around the area; they were part of a party send earlier to 'remove the snipers'. We lay quietly under cover for a few minutes, awaiting the arrival of our other two sections, but we waited in vain. We did not then know that Hoskins had been shot dead long before he could pass on any message. Carrying on up the hill, we reached the crest. Heavy firing from the other side of the hill indicated that a very large force was over there, and not just a few snipers for the five of us to deal with. I gave the order to toss one hand grenade each over the top, intending to pop up while the enemy's heads were down to gather what information we could. This failed to work, and the bullets came faster than ever, accompanied by a few mortar bombs. Then we heard a different sound as a salvo of three inch mortar bombs landed just behind us. A few seconds later another salvo passed over our heads, and landed in front; we then knew that we were watching the handywork of our own mortar platoon. BHQ had realised by now that instead of snipers up here a major attack was developing on our rear. I had a very healthy regard for our Mortar Platoon. I yelled for the men to follow, broke cover and ran as fast as I could go back down the hill.

We returned by way of the next section trench, to find out why the others had not rendezvoused with us. I got as close as possible and called out but received no reply and saw no-one. A machine gun opened up on us from a hundred yards away however, and we knew that we had been heard by the wrong people. Later we discovered that our boys were in the trench but could not put out their heads as a machine gun was trained on them. On the way back to our trench we passed Company HQ which was also situated in the centre of an open space. We could see no sign of life there either, and returned to our own position; I landed feet first on Cpl Malin.

All this time we had continued to hear the mortar barrage our boys were laying down and it proved successful in preventing the Japs from breaking through until we had redeployed to face our rear. Our platoon area was separated from the rest of the battalion by triple dannert. This consists of coils of springy barbed wire about three feet in diameter, two stretched out on the ground closely wired together, with the third coil on top of the other two. We had not been back very long when an officer from another platoon, Lt Doans, called to us from the other side of the wire, saying that he did not think that BHQ realized that we were still holding out on this side, and suggested that I bring my men across to join his company. I told him that Capt Stick had told us to stay put, so he went off shouting that he would see Stick and get his instruction confirmed.

About an hour later Capt Stick appeared from among the trees the other side of the wire, shouting and waving his arms. The firing prevented us from hearing what he was shouting, but we took it for granted that he was confirming Doan's earlier instruction to cross over. Triple dannert is no mean obstacle, and this was under direct small-arms fire, so I knew that we should be very lucky to get over unscathed. I instructed each man where he was to cross, so that we should be widely separated targets and then gave the order to go.

I have always been a very poor jumper, and back home in shorts and sports shoes no reward could have enabled me to clear even four feet. Now I was in heavy army boots, carrying full equipment loaded with ammunition and with a short Lee-Enfield rifle in my hand. As I charged across open ground towards the wire, I silently prayed wordless prayers, and felt something pour through my veins as I sailed through the air to clear the wire. Reaching the cover of the bushes we gathered together panting; miraculously we were all there.

Capt Stick came striding up, face black as thunder. 'Is this what you call defending your position to the last man?' he growled. 'I suppose you realize this means a court martial?' He would not listen when I tried to explain why we had returned, and for the moment I hated him more than I feared the bullets out in No Man's Land. My men had been standing around listening to the one-sided conversation; I turned my back on Stick and shouted, 'Come on boys, it's back over the wire'. A terrible groan went up, and Beacon, who was close to breaking point, breathed 'Oh Sarge' in a way that said all. Stick looked back over the wire, and said grudgingly 'You'd better stay over here now and dig yourselves in.' 'You did hear me say that I am prepared to take the men back didn't you, Sir,' I said. 'I'm ordering you to stay where you are now, so don't argue,' was the reply.

So we wearily dug ourselves yet another trench; but by now we had learned a little more and our new position was the best so far. We were in the edge of the trees, with a good field of fire, and with barbed wire between us and the enemy. There was even a lull in the firing to enable us to dig a good trench; however, the firing had stopped only to enable the Japs to re-deploy so that they could try to find a softer spot. During this lull also, the men from our other two sections, who had been pinned down all day, were able to leave their trenches and join us – those of them who were left.

Thus we found ourselves under the direct command of an officer for the first time since the fighting had started. It was good now to have someone to look to for direction with so many lives at stake. Capt Stick came round again at four thirty that afternoon, asking for volunteers to return over the barbed wire to look for wounded. The firing had more or less died down now so Sgt Hanton and I decided to go ourselves.

We found a gap cut in the wire a few hundred yards away, and made a dash through. A short distance along we found three of our boys lying in the grass with bullet wounds. I examined them and found out that they all had flesh wounds, so after binding them up with their own field dressings, we shouted for some of our men to come over and assist them to our RAP (Regimental Aid Post). Before the action, and back at home, I had been very apprehensive as to how I would react to torn flesh. When the crunch came I was surprised how calmly and competently I was able to carry out first-aid, and indeed found that I had a definite gift for this work.

Next we found dear old Simpkin. He was a Gloucester man, slow speaking and thinking, but the salt of the earth. Although both of his legs were badly smashed he had managed to drag himself all that way through the scrub, until stopped by the barbed wire. He had lost much blood and was in considerable pain. there was unspeakable joy in his eyes as he saw that we had returned to help him. I had always found it rather difficult to understand his rich brogue; now as I heard him croaking I put my head close to his face in order to catch what he as trying to say. 'Zorry, oi've laast me bombs zarge, but oi've still got me rifle'. It lay in the grass beside him; it had been drilled into us all never to part from our rifles, and he had dragged it along with him. I thought then of Colour Sergeant Whiskin, old soldier who had left the reserve troops he was leading earlier that day, dumped his rifle and made a dash for our trench; he lay in the bottom of it through the firing. He later persuaded the stretcher bearers that he had dysentery and was carried to safety. His reserves lay useless in the grass where he had left them.

I stayed with Simpkin while Hanton returned over the wire for help, and a few minutes later a party appeared carrying an old charpoy. (Indian bed, made from wood and string.) Gently we lifted Simpkin on to the bed, and he was taken back to our RAP where our doctor sent him off to base hospital.

Hanton and I next found Parkhurst, who was also wounded in the legs, but was without broken bones. We decided to carry him fireman's lift, back to the RAP rather than risk waiting for stretchers, and I took first turn, Hanton carrying both our rifles. We got through the wire and were half-way up the hill that was between us and our destination. I was just about to exchange roles with Hanton as I was beginning to tire, when I noticed spurts of dust rising from the ground as a machine gun opened fire on us. Tired or not, I managed to run flat out up the steepest part of the hill, staggering with my burden into the RAP. Although it was some time before I was to have an opportunity to remove my clothes, when I did I was to discover that I had sweated blood. Until then I had thought it to have been a figure of speech, that our Lord had sweated blood in the garden at Gethsemane. During the whole of the battle I seemed to bear a charmed life, having been missed so many times. Towards the end I began to realize that I was not going to be hit, and consequently became a little less frightened. We rested only a few minutes, then made the return trip through the world of bullets to rejoin our comrades, finding that our positions had not yet come under fire again. Right through the fighting the enemy were so well camouflaged and made such good use of cover that we scarcely saw them. Firing from fresh positions was always our first indication that we had a new front to face. We were eventually able to discuss what had been happening during this stage of the fighting, and heard that BHQ were continually receiving conflicting reports. No sooner had they given orders for one of our companies to dig in to face a given front than another report would come in to say that the Japs had been seen on one of the flanks which should have been covered by another regiment, and each exposed flank would mean re-deployment; to us, digging yet another lot of trenches. We started this battle as a regiment, part of a brigade, defending a section of a continuous front; when the fighting ended, we were defending an island around our Headquarters.

Thus, at a quarter past five, when he was facing what we thought was our front, Sgt Hanton received a bullet in his bottom. I bandaged him up and sent him off to the RAP. The enemy was again behind us, so we turned each alternate trench in our section of the front to face the other way.

All hell seemed to break loose again at ten o'clock that night as about a dozen mortars were brought to bear on us. The Japs made very good use of mortars right through the action; if we dug in where small arms could not reach us, a concentration of mortars was patiently brought up and quickly brought to bear. At the height of this bombardment a message was received that I was to leave my position and take my men to Mr Beardman who was situated a few hundred yards away on our left flank. It was thought that the bombardment might be a decoy to enable the enemy to make the main attempt at penetration there, so off we went. We were given a stretch of the road to defend, and as there was no time to dig trenches we spread ourselves out in the anti-malarial ditch which ran alongside the road.

It was quite dark now, and we could hear the Japs not many yards away across the road. Every now and then we would think we saw a movement, or a glow among the trees, and released a few rounds. Three-quarters of an hour later scouts reported that the enemy had withdrawn, so we returned to our last position.

As dawn broke we were ordered out of our well-dug trenches again. The regiment on our left had gone, either wiped out or withdrawn, so our whole battalion was to be re-deployed. Although it had not occurred to our CO to withdraw, it would have been no easier for us if we had, since, as we later discovered, there were as many Japs behind us as there were in front.

We now found ourselves on a stony hillside opposite our Battalion Headquarters, situated among dozens of bamboo huts which had earlier been used as a transit camp. It seemed the main body of the enemy had moved on, leaving a smaller party to keep our heads down. We dug in therefore as quickly as we could, under only sporadic firing, which lasted all day. As we were unable to see where it was coming from we had virtually no targets ourselves.

That evening, at six o'clock, our platoon officer returned, and almost immediately there followed the worst attack of the campaign. From a quarter mile away a large force opened fire on us with small arms and mortars, and they kept it up until darkness fell. Then the enemy began to advance on us, and at last, through the gloom, we were able to see them and to let them have it. Three tanks pulled out from among the trees. (Our tanks had all been left behind in India as Command had thought them to be unsuited to this type of terrain.) These opened fire on us with their two-pounders, but our trenches were now deep and well-placed so little harm was done. The Jap infantry moved in behind the tanks as they started to advance on us, and we gave them all we had. From over on our left we heard our mortar platoon go into action, the deep thud of their three inch weapons mingling with the other sounds of battle, and we began also to see the flashes as their bombs exploded among the enemy. We clearly heard for the first time the strange sound of Japanese voices as they shouted their orders; heard for the first time also the screams of *their* wounded. I recall the satisfaction we derived from killing off those enemy fathers, husbands, sons.

Pte Martin was in charge of our heavy anti-tank rifle, and when the tanks appeared I crawled over to his trench. Being a weapon-training instructor, I felt that I could probably make the most effective use of this, our only anti-tank weapon, and said so. Martin, however, suffered from no such illusions; having carried it up hill and down dale on our route marches back home, he had no intention of missing out on this, the very first opportunity of firing it in anger. 'Not b..... likely Sarge . . .'. I decided to overlook the insubordination. As had been drilled into him, Martin aimed for the joint between the turret and the main body of the tank, and with a fearsome explosion the first tank disappeared in a flash followed by a cloud of smoke. We heard later that the mortars had claimed this success, but Martin and the rest of us had at that time no doubts about it. As the smoke cleared away we saw that the other two tanks and the infantry were withdrawing to the trees from which they had emerged. The firing petered out, and a strange stillness fell over the land.

Dawn saw us alert, and confident, awaiting the next attack; but that sun rose on our last day of freedom. I had remained awake all that night, and had by now had virtually no sleep for many days, so when no attack had materialised by 8 o'clock, I told my officer that I was going to lie down in one of the huts, and was soon sound asleep on a charpoy in the nearest one. At twelve, noon, I awoke to the sound of bullets tearing through the thin hut walls, and lost no time in diving back into the trench. Now the earlier bombardment resumed, but this time accompanied by heavy fire from our rear as well, as the snipers who had passed through our thinly held lines in the darkness the night before, opened fire unseen from close at hand. Firing into our trenches from the rear they were able to take heavier toll than the main barrage.

Cpl Ginn was standing beside me as we searched the trees behind for a glimpse of the snipers, who had by this time killed two of our men and wounded several more. 'I reckon there's one of the b.....s up that palm tree', he said. Standing on the step he took aim with his rifle, muttering that he would put in a couple of rounds and see what fell out of the tree. As his finger squeezed the trigger, he gasped, and slowly sank to the ground. I quickly knelt down beside him, but he was beyond help, and another section was without a leader. During the next hour we lost several more in a similar way. Although the firing did not let up, the enemy remained invisible, and all we could see was the shell of the one tank we had destroyed; we were again in that most unsatisfactory position of being targets without ourselves having anything to fire at. When we took pot shots at likely hide-outs for snipers in the palm trees, none fell out. It later transpired that Jap snipers tie themselves in the trees, so that if hit they remain suspended, thus not giving the satisfaction of knowledge of success.

A party of Australian troops now retreated through our lines. They were weaponless and very dishevelled, just about all-in. They told us that they had withdrawn from up country, where fighting had virtually ceased. This was our first intimation of the way things were going. To our surprise after this depressing news, we heard cheering, and saw what seemed to be RAF barrage balloons rising into the sky. Our planes must be coming back then, if they were putting balloons up round the aerodrome. Shortly after we saw a plane approaching from the direction of the balloons, and risking the bullets, took off our tin hats to wave. We soon put them back as we recognized the Stuka entering its dive, and a large crater appeared immediately in front of our Battn. HQ. We were soon to learn that Japanese observation balloons look very similar to ours.

Shells from field guns the enemy had in position behind us now began to fall more accurately, as the balloons directed their fire. The next few hours were a nightmare. Men fell to right and left; the huts all caught fire, and some fell burning into our trenches. Many who were not burned to death died later of their terrible burns, including my old friend Sgt Wilson, who in his agony, asked me to shoot him. When on watch together on board ship, I remembered how, as he held his fiancée's picture in his hand, he had told me that he had the certain conviction that he would never see her alive again in this world. Dear God, I breathed as I looked into that awful burned face, let it all be a dream . . . I shouted for the stretcher-bearers, and faithful as ever, they ran over and collected him. I hope they were able to ease the pain of the few days he had yet to live.

As the fire burnt itself out, Mr Doans came running over, telling me that we must now shorten our lines, so I was to take the men to new positions in front of BHQ. We were well dug in, but I knew that the open ground we were now to traverse was covered by a Jap machine gun placed only a hundred yards away in a burnt-out hut. I asked for a couple of volunteers to stay behind with our Bren gun and fire at the Jap while the rest of us broke cover. Utting and Winton instantly claimed the job, although we all knew that they were unlikely to survive. As their gun began to chatter we left our trenches and ran for our lives. Three-quarters of the way across I halted to signal our rearguard to follow, but I saw that they were already on their way, Winton firing his gun from the hip as he ran. We lay down and opened fire with our rifles, and kept the enemy's heads down long enough for the two to reach us. Who could have guessed that so many of us would reach our new position in safety. Mr Doans and my officer had crossed over with us, and both were wounded in the dash; there were also half-a-dozen other ranks missing, we knew not whether they were killed. It is certain that those of us who did get through owed our lives to Utting and Winton. Like most war heroes they received no medal for their valour.

After taking stock, I found that I now appeared to be in sole charge of the remains of two platoons, as neither officer returned from the RAP where they had gone to have their wounds dressed. I had no instructions at this point, so deployed the men in temporary fire positions, dashed into BHQ to try to obtain firm orders and found the Old Man and the Adjutant in the basement. I told them that I had the men available and asked where I should place them; they seemed to be in a daze, and I received no answer. 'Shall we remain where we are then and defend HQ?' I asked, and this time received a nod from the Adjutant. Returning we all found ourselves craters to occupy as there was no chance now to dig in, and wearily awaited the next attack.

At a quarter to three I received what I hope will be the greatest shock of my life as a messenger came with the order to lay our weapons down in front of us and surrender. I find it quite impossible to describe my feelings. Up to now we had felt that we were holding our own, and anticipated pushing the Japs back off the island before many more days had passed. Our wildest guesses did not take into account the possibility of abandoning the territory to the enemy; we had been told that the island must be retained at all costs, since it was an essential link in our communications with Australasia. In any case we did not think of throwing in the sponge while any of us remained alive, that was not the British way. I crept round the position passing on the order, adding the instruction to remove the rifle bolts and bury or otherwise hide them.

Pte Tanner stood six feet two, and had proved himself in the fighting to be a very brave soldier. He stood there unashamedly with tears streaming down his cheeks; his were not the only tears that sad day. I felt as though my bowels had been painlessly removed, my mind refused to work properly and was unable to grapple with the situation. Hardly a word was exchanged between us as we silently remained there awaiting further orders. Talking about this afterwards, we agreed that we were all undergoing a feeling of bitter shame at our arms lying useless on the ground with our country's enemy only a hundred yards away.

Events on the remainder of the island had been going very badly however, and we were one of the few regiments not to have been forced to withdrawn from its allotted area. Singapore had no positions prepared for defence against an attack from the mainland of Malaya, and the story of the big guns is now familiar. For the previous few years our people had taught the necessity for all round defence in modern warfare, yet all Singapore's big guns were concreted in positions facing out to sea and incapable of swinging round to protect the rear. The main defensive weapons were therefore never used. This was at a time when nearly every army in the world was training paratroops, and our potential enemy had been advancing through the Chinese mainland for years. A few thousand pounds worth of concrete strategically placed, a few mobile guns or tanks and Singapore could well have proved, like Gibraltar, an impregnable fortress.

No plans seemed to have been worked out for deployment of troops should the Japs do the obvious in attacking from the dry land, instead of sailing into the muzzles of our big guns from seaward.

At the time of surrender the enemy had penetrated nearly everywhere. Singapore City was full of leaderless men making for the docks in the hope of getting on a ship away from this doomed place. We were told later that the order for surrender was given because the Japs had cut the water supply off from the mainland, and that we were giving in for the sake of the civilian population. Oriental people fully understand what face-saving is all about, and in the weeks that followed showed no gratitude to us for laying down our arms for their sakes. The Malays spat on the ground when they saw us during the first days after our surrender, but they were to learn that there are worse masters than the British.

We seemed to wait in our trenches after the cease-fire order for many hours. An hour and a half after we received our message, men dug in fifty yards away in the centre of a lawn decided to climb out of their trenches; a machine gun opened fire on them, and they all lay still around their position. I ran back to our RAP to try to borrow a Red Cross flag to take out over the lawn and fetch in any wounded. Dodging a hail of bullets from that same machine gun, I found our Medical Officer and explained my mission, but was told that since some of our men had fired on Japanese stretcher bearers, they had ceased to respect the Red Cross, and were firing indiscriminately at both stretcher bearers and ambulances. I was told to stay quietly with my men until further instructions were received.

Stepping out through the front door of the house wherein the RAP was situated, and seeing an ambulance standing there, I looked in over the tailboard. Within seconds I came under machine gun fire from an unexpected direction and tracer bullets whizzed past me like fireworks and into the ambulance. Although it seemed that I could have touched these bullets, again they all missed me. I jumped to cover into an alcove built in the wall of the house, and as I did so the ambulance burst into flames as a bullet penetrated the petrol tank. The fire spread and the ambulance became an inferno; the firing did not ease up, and I began to feel the intense heat. Soon I had to choose between roasting and stepping out again into the line of fire.

The house was built on a slope, and like most of the dwellings in that area it was built on piers, high off the ground. I leapt out of the alcove and fell flat on the ground in a spot where I could roll back under the house, and managed to accomplish this in one movement. I lay there for a few seconds, getting my breath back, and watching the tracers fly past, almost within reach of my hand. Then the heat increased, and I realized that the fire had spread to the house, so I crawled to the rear of the under-floor space.

Teams of men were carrying the wounded to safety out of the back door, and they were not being fired on. I met Capt Coppin at the rear of BHQ and stopped for a second to speak to him before carrying on behind the house. A steep bank arose a few yards from us, and I thought we were safe from fire for the moment. I continued on my way, but half-way along two Japs armed with a light machine gun suddenly appeared from behind a hedge, only four yards away. One yelled something that sounded like 'shoot', and the other released a burst of fire from point blank range. Before I could move, I felt a pain in the back of my neck, then I dived under the building and rolled out of range. I put my hand up to my neck; no blood, I had only been hit by chips of brick from the wall. Capt Coppin had quite a shock when we came face to face later on. He had watched my progress from the corner, and seeing what had occurred reported my death to HQ.

It later transpired that the Japs had brought up their veteran troops; as we had defended our ground so well they thought we were a crack regiment under the direct command of General Wavell. These enemy companies acted more or less independently and had few lines of communication; their leaders had therefore not been able to inform them of the cease-fire; this was our worst period, as without weapons, we were picked off one by one.

However, I continued to remain unscathed. Had I seen myself in a Western, being missed so many times at point blank range, I would probably have classed it as impossible fiction. Once again I reached my men unharmed, and as we awaited the next move our thoughts dwelt on what we had heard of the way that Japs dealt with prisoners. We had heard of soldiers' bodies found with their hands tied together with barbed wire and riddled with bullets; that they liked torturing their captives before disposing of them. We knew that the Chinese whom they had been fighting for several years did treat their prisoners this way. Our comrades out on the lawn had been shot down in cold blood. We did not discuss these things as we waited in silence; each kept his thoughts to himself.

Chapter 2

'O God, listen to me! Hear my prayer!
For wherever I am, though far away at the ends of the earth,
I will cry to you for help.'

At three o'clock in the afternoon under the hot humid Singapore sun, the Japs at last stepped out from among the trees surrounding us. One even descended from a palm tree growing beside our BHQ, where he must have been since the previous night. We now knew how we had incurred many of our hitherto inexplicable casualties. Approaching with finger on trigger, our adverseries were taking no chances; they halted a few yards from us, and what we presumed to be an officer stepped forward. He was wearing one of the traditional Japanese two-handed ceremonial swords, and with every step he seemed in danger of tripping over it. (We later became very familiar with the sight of these swords; they told us that they were handed down from father to son, but I saw a Jap blacksmith making them from old lorry springs, and fitting them with Woolworthsy tinsel bound handles.)

The ordinary Japanese soldiers were our biggest surprise, as they appeared like pieces of jungle, walking. Their uniforms, if such their shabby mud-coloured clothes could be called, were hung about completely with leaves and twigs. We had done nothing like that. Although we had of course heard that the Japanese are a short race, we had not dreamed that they were as small as this; as we saw that they hardly came up to our shoulders it was hard to take in the fact that it was to these mites that we were surrendering. Our amazement and shame were complete.

'Number One!' shouted the officer. Not knowing what he meant none of us moved. A moment or two's silence, then louder and angrily, 'Ingerissoo numbar one, speedo!' A few weeks later none of us would have failed to get the message which could be interpreted as 'Englishman in charge come here quickly!' We were however spared the pain of finding out what was meant the hard way, by the appearance at that moment of a party approaching from HQ, led by our Commanding Officer.

'You Wavellca?' asked the Jap as the party stopped a yard or two away. 'No, me Lt Col Carter' replied the Old Man. The officer chattered for a while with his henchmen, and then turning round, said firmly, 'You Wavell!' in a voice which brooked no argument. It was left at that.

Capt Stick sidled up to me as the officers were led away from us, and grabbed my hand in his firm grip. 'I don't know whether we'll ever meet again Sergent, but in case we don't I'd like you to know I think you did a good job.'

The boys who had been shot out on the lawn still lay where they had fallen as no-one had been able to approach to see whether there were any survivors. I walked up to what I thought was a Jap NCO and pointing to where the men were lying, made him understand that I wanted to go over and see whether there were any still alive. He impatiently shook his head. I decided to take a chance, and turning my back on him, walked out over the lawn. A hullabaloo broke out behind me and I had a job to resist the temptation to look back, but like Lot, resist it I did, and the next thing I knew was that a Jap soldier was trotting along behind me, his fixed bayonet held close to my back. Nevertheless, he did not interfere with me, and was evidently there to prevent me from pulling a fast one. There were no survivors around that trench. Sentiment played no part in my feelings while the fighting continued. As I now lowered the head of one of my young lads, lifeless on to the turf, I had difficulty in holding back my tears.

At this early stage, I had learned a lesson that was to stand me in good stead during the years of captivity that were to follow, namely that it was often possible to 'get away with murder' by presenting a bold front to the Japs, whereas humble pleading was usually ignored, and the pleader likely to be beaten.

We were now lined up and searched, anything found that took the Japs' fancy, together with any potential weapons were taken away. Our CO held a conference with our captors, and we were then herded together on the top of the bank behind BHQ where I had so narrowly escaped being shot. The CO was allowed to stand on some higher land, and he prepared to speak to us. (A voice behind me whispered 'They're letting him say goodbye before they polish us off'.)

Col Carter, in a breaking voice, tried to tell us that he was proud of us, and that a late despatch from Command HQ had informed him that he had been decorated for the regiment's performance. '. . . if you leave here alive, I want you all to remember your regiment, never let its name down.' As the Japs led him and the other officers away, we shouted our goodbyes.

After a few minutes, with much incomprehensible shouting of orders, we were herded off to a tennis court nearby. When we thought this was full, there were still about a couple of hundred of our men remaining outside. The Japs, swinging their rifle butts, soon convinced us that we had misjudged the court's capacity, and somehow we all got in. Machine gun posts were quickly established a few yards from each corner of our enclosure, and riflemen were spread along the sides, all with their weapons trained on us. Someone pointed out that they could not have found a better place to shoot us all if we were to be wiped out, as none could climb over the ten foot wire netting sides.

As I looked out towards the big house that had been our BHQ I thought for a moment that I was dreaming. A wide drive swept round the rear, and on it, in full view of both us and his own men, rode the officer in charge of this part of The Imperial Japanese Army. His charger? A captured child's fairy cycle! He pedalled round in circles, knees poking out sideways to miss the handlebars, his long sword dragging along in the dust behind him. Others were queueing behind in orderly fashion for their turn, and the game continued until nightfall. We knew now at least that the Japanese were human beings like ourselves.

We soon realized that for the time being, we were not going to be shot, and began to stake out our spot to spend the night; we all just about found ourselves room to lie down, albeit like sardines. However, reaction to what we had recently endured soon began to affect our internal workings, and with no toilet facilities, senior NCOs held a conference to decide upon what to do for the best. As no better idea prevailed, we decided to clear one corner of the court and to use this for a latrine. The top was asphalted so there was no chance of digging a hole. Darkness fell to the sound of protests as men were moved from their sleeping spaces and were trying in vain to squeeze in elsewhere. Many had to sit up with their backs to the wire, as there was just not enough room for all to lie down.

I still had a little water in my bottle, but those who had lost theirs had to go without a drink, and none of us had eaten for a long time, but that was the least of our worries. The nights in this area are cold at that time of the year, but although I was only wearing vest and thin tropical shirt, I was soon sleeping the sleep of exhaustion. I awoke shivering in the grey dawn, and picked my way over prone figures to find the toilet corner. Eventually I reached it, but one look convinced me that I would rather burst than go there, where six or seven hundred men, many of them with diarrhoea, had been going all night. About an hour later the Japs opened a gate, letting a few men out into the bushes at a time, and my turn came round in time to avoid me having to burst. We were allowed at the same time to fill our bottles from water in the anti-malarial ditch which ran nearby. Later we discovered that there were dead bodies in the ditch a few yards upstream, but even had we known, there was none other, and one cannot live for long without water in the tropics. Presently a few tins of army biscuits were pushed to us through the wire. We shared them out; they are as hard as stone, and those with dentures broke their share against the iron posts, and sucked them until soft enough to swallow.

There was no shade, and as the sun rose in the sky our position rapidly became untenable for Europeans; many became unconscious from heatstroke. At midday the Japs let us out under the trees and we moved out carrying those who had collapsed, flopping on the grass with relief. I am fair, and had not dared remove my shirt in the direct sun. Now, in the shade of the trees I stripped down to the waist to feel the air round my foetid torso. 'Whatever have you been up to Sarge?' Looking up I saw one of my neighbours pointing at my chest, and following his eyes I could hardly believe what I saw. The front of my body looked as though a tin of maroon paint had been poured over it, causing it to run down in tears and curtains. I rubbed my hand on my chest, but apart from a few places where the blood had burst through the skin, the stains were indelible. It was to be about a year before those stains finally faded.

Then one of our guards noticed my condition, and called me over, taking me to see the NCO in charge of his watch. He sent us both over to see our doctor, in the hut where our RAP had finally been established after the fire. The Japs evidently thought that I might have some contagious condition. The RAP was a very distressing place. As there was very little equipment, and only one or two beds left after the fire, severely wounded men were lying all over the hard floor, and our medical staff were only able to administer first aid. One of the orderlies told me that most of the patients would only have stood a fifty-fifty chance with proper drugs and equipment, but under these circumstances they were doomed to die.

The busy doctor had little time to spare for me. Before even noticing my condition, he asked for my field dressing, (every soldier carries one). He then took a look at my lurid skin, and told me that there was no disease, but that capillaries under my skin had burst during the fighting, during a time of 'severe nervous tension and physical strain'.

I returned to the sentry on guard duty (the guard who originally accompanied me had returned) and signalled that I was ready to return to the others. He refused to let me pass, and I had perforce to spend the night in the RAP. The heartbreaking sounds of the dying made me realize that we who were whole still had blessings to count. An hour after daybreak the sentry received orders that I was go go back with the others, and I entered the tennis court just in time to receive my ration of one biscuit.

We were again let out under the trees at midday, and this

time I noticed some hard-shelled fruit on one of the trees. I climbed up and picked one of these, and removing the shell found a jelly-like fruit inside. A voice from the ground called out, 'Don't eat those, they're poisonous!' I smelled it, and the smell was good. It tasted even better, and I gathered all I could reach, and ate them. They were, as I later discovered, mangosteens. Others saw me eating them, and the tree was quickly stripped. This principle of 'taste it and see' served me well all the days of my captivity, not without some narrow squeaks, however.

The Japs did not seem to be so trigger happy now; they were probably beginning to realize that, with thousands of miles of sea between us and our allies, there was nowhere for us to escape to.

Back in the court again, and with most of us having diarrhoea, conditions became bad, with many unable to reach the toilet corner in time. There was nowhere clean to sit, and we could scarcely see for the flies which had bred in the faeces. That night the stench hung over us like a vile blanket, and it was hopeless to think of sleep. When morning came we saw that our guards had migrated further afield during the night, no doubt unable to stand the smell. Probably because of the condition of our surroundings, we were moved out under the trees much earlier that morning. The Japs' attitude too began to change, and some of them tried to converse with the strange long-nosed creatures we must have seemed to them. Conversations did not develop very far, as their English vocabulary consisted of no more than 'OK, Numbar one, and No good!'

The day wore on and in the afternoon the sun became overcast. Within a few minutes the whole sky was clouded over and a gusty wind sprang up. As the rain began to fall the Japs let us crawl under the raised floor of the nearby house. This was the start of the wet season here, not continual rain as in monsoon climates, but rather sharp daily rainstorms, far heavier than we ever experience in Britain. The so-called anti-malarial drains had been dug to carry this storm-water away quickly, so that the flooded areas where mosquitoes could breed did not form. The malaria parasite spends an essential part of its life-cycle in the anopheles mosquito.

When the rain ceased we moved back into the tennis court. The rain, far from cleaning away the filth, had spread it from the toilet corner in an even layer over everything. We had thought conditions were intolerable before, but they were now indescribably worse. Our guards patrolled wearing improvised surgical masks. At long last another dawn raised me from the stupor into which I had descended. The Japs passed in a few tins of biscuits, and told us to be ready to move off at nine a.m. Without regret we moved from the court, and formed up outside the RAP. The wounded had already been moved out of the building and were lined up beside the road on stretchers. Although most of the worse cases had died by now, many of those we were to carry were very ill indeed, with broken limbs, burns, unstitched wounds and internal injuries. It is impossible to carry a man on a stretcher without some jolting, and they suffered greatly on the long journey which lay ahead. We paired ourselves off, all the fittest men, according to size. At first we carried the stretchers knee-high, the handles suspended at arms' length, as this is the most comfortable method for the patient. We soon found out that we were not strong enough to keep this up, and had to change to shoulder high. There were many wounded and our turns on the stretcher came round all too quickly. After five miles, many became too weak to take a turn, and our rest spells became shorter and shorter. I had just reached the point when I felt I could go no further, when what seemed like a miracle happened as a fleet of army lorries pulled up alongside us and we were allowed to load our wounded on them.

We were able to converse with the British drivers, and they told us that they had not been ill-treated, and that as far as they knew we were the only ones who had had such a rough time since the island fell. They themselves did not even have guards with them.

As we moved off again we began to obtain our first insight into the Japanese character; incredibly short temper, no patience, childlike emotions and lack of inhibitions; but no lack of intelligence, as we soon realized. I learned my first Japanese words on this journey, I also learned that some words were best avoided. During one of the short roadside rests a passing guard overheard the word 'Jap' being used by one of our boys, and running over he hit the man with his rifle butt. I was the nearest NCO and jumped up to ask the guard why he had done this. 'Dammeda', he shouted, 'Jap' dammi-dammi, 'Nippon' OK. Dammeda and dammi meant as far as we could make out, no-good, and we very quickly learned to stop saying 'Jap' altogether. Eventually we used the word 'Nips', as they did not seem to object to this abbreviation.

After travelling a dozen miles or so without water, and in our weak condition, we became stretched out in a long thin column, in spite of the continual shouting and prodding that the men behind received. It thus happened that when my part of the column was passing a Chinese biscuit factory (designated by a huge picture of biscuits hanging outside), there was not a guard in sight. The factory door was locked, but we soon broke it open and helped ourselves to a tin of biscuits each, which we shared out on the road, and threw the tins away before our captors saw us with them. We soon heard screams of rage coming from behind as the Japs caught some of our comrades in the act, but as they told us later, they only received a beating.

The guards told us they were taking us to Changi, area of the old civilian prison; this meant a journey of over twenty miles. As we approached one small town we saw trenches dug alongside the road, with our dead still lying in them where they fell. They looked as though they had been attacked with flame-throwers, and were badly burned. One lad was still gripping his rifle, and the butt was half burned away. These men had the guts to face flame-throwing tanks with only their rifles, but had held their positions to the end.

As we passed through several small towns and villages, we saw that practically every dwelling had a home-made rising-sun flag hanging out of the window. Although the Chinese hated the Japs because of the Sino-Japanese war, the orientals believe that the reed that bends with the wind does not break, so most of them kowtowed to the Japs. I believe that in those early days, the native Malays genuinely welcomed our conquerors, as they believed they were being freed from colonialism. The population of Singapore is mostly Chinese however, whose energy and business acumen was gradually ousting the more indolent natives.

The last lap of that journey was only accomplished by the stronger of us carrying the weaker ones; nevertheless at six o'clock that evening we did all arrive at a hutted encampment the far side of Changi gaol. Our cooks and other headquarters staff had not been captured with us, as cooking is not carried out in the front line; we now met them for the first time, and they told us they had been sent straight to Changi after being captured, and had been waiting for us for all this time. The sick whom we had put on the lorries had arrived before us, and forecast our arrival, so the cooks had prepared a good hot stew for us. Although it seemed like weeks since we had seen a square meal, most of us were too tired to eat; that was unfortunate as it was the last of the tinned food that the regiment had. We were allotted quarters in palm-leaf huts, originally built to house casual workers from the adjacent rubber estate, now unattended like all the rubber plantations.

Most of us ached too much to sleep, after the long march carrying our comrades. Next morning we began to take stock of our new surroundings, and found out that we were only a few hundred yards from the sea as the crow flies, but it was reached by a road which followed a tortuous route through a mangrove swamp. Mangrove are trees which grow on the shore at the water's edge. Their roots form grotesque legs at low tide as they stand close together high out of the water, looking like huge deformed spiders. Between us and the commencement of the mangroves was a coconut grove.

We were told that the Japs allowed us to visit the sea once a day, and had provided a flag of identification for bathing parties to carry. As the size of the party had to be limited, it would be a few days before our turn came round.

The camp covered many acres, so Sgt Atlas and I went off on a tour of exploration, my main object being to look for any object that 'might come in useful' during the days to come. We found a deserted shop the other side of our camp, and in it I found a bucket charcoal fire, a bag of charcoal and a teapot. These fires were the universal method of cooking out there, and consisted of a bucket lined with fire-clay, with a small aperture low in the side. Air is fanned into the aperture producing a fierce heat and a very effective cooking stove, but they are heavy; I carried my treasures back to our hut. We also found a stream during our reconnoitre, and later on that day I took my clothes over and washed them out 'dhobi fashion', that is without soap, dipping them in the water and bashing them on a rock. Cheap on soap but expensive on buttons. Drying was no problem, half an hour in the sun was quite enough.

Our kit-bags, containing spare clothes and personal possessions were handed in at the commencement of the fighting, and these were now handed back to us. Mine had been opened, and several items taken, the most important being my best open razor. In the years to come, when I was shaving twenty or thirty friends each day, it would have been invaluable; now I was left with the old first-world-war razor that I had taken into battle with me.

Our diet now consisted of little else besides boiled rice, and our cooks had not yet learned the right way to cook it. To those who have taken their rice only in the form of rice pudding, or tenderly boiled with curry, ours, just boiled in water and served with hard lumps in the middle of every grain was far from appetising. Yet before long men were squabbling over the remains in the dixie after all had been served. Thinking that sparrow stew would liven up this monotonous diet, I rigged up a trap from bricks, sticks and string. There were thousands of sparrows about, but although I baited my trap with precious grains of rice, in the crowded camp someone would always come by to disturb my prey before I could pull the string, so I had to give up.

On our fourth day in Changi camp, our turn came round for a visit to the sea, and we all enjoyed a swim from the beautiful sandy beach the other side of the mangroves, which only appeared at low tide. I found a towel floating in on the tide, and the name of one of the ships from our convoy was embroidered on it. I later heard that this ship had been sunk after leaving Singapore harbour, heavily laden with refugees, mostly women and children. My two towels had been among the items missing from my kit, so I was delighted to find this one.

Next day we were warned to get ready for a Japanese General to inspect us. By the time we had all spruced ourselves up we were told that the visit was off. The Japs were like that, and the mystery was how did they accomplish so much? Nothing seemed to be carried out to a schedule; an appointment kept to within twenty-four hours was good going. The phrase 'brute force and ignorance' seemed to suit them as they tackled what looked to us like an impossibly huge task without apparently any plan of action. When they seemed to be getting nowhere, everyone from the most senior officer downwards, shouted at, and perhaps bashed his junior, and somehow with frantic tearing about, the object would be achieved. Perhaps it demonstrated the Quantum Theory; with so many hopping up and down so quickly and all of the time, the pieces would eventually fall into place.

The Jap General turned up only one day late, though we were lined up in the blazing sun for hours before he finally appeared. Poor old Colour Sergeant Gold stood near me, sandy haired with milk-white skin and freckles. Although he was wearing a hat, as he stood there blisters appeared on his face and hands, and he was unable to stand by the time we were dismissed. He never became acclimatised, and within a short time lost his reason. He died a month or two later.

We had no salt, so a party was organized to carry up water from the sea and to boil it down. However, salt never became plentiful in Changi through shortage of fuel.

Rumours were now becoming a part of our daily life, and the general greeting was 'What's the griff?' or 'What's the latest borehole?' Our Pioneer Platoon excavated deep holes for latrines, and it was here that most of these tales started, hence a rumour became a 'borehole'. At that time we had not been disappointed so often, and the wish being father of the thought, we were disposed to give credence to the most optimistic stories that were passing round.

A few days later the Japs allocated some land outside the camp boundary to us, on which we were to grow vegetables for our own consumption. We felt quite excited as we lined up ready to go out on our first gardening fatigue; the chance to do something constructive was a welcome change. The area we were allocated was covered with stout rubber trees, and we spent all the first day felling these and grubbing out the roots. As we got each root out the hole filled with water, and it was evidence that this swampy ground would never grow vegetables.

During the lunch-break I climbed my first coconut palm. There are no branches to grip, and the task was very difficult as for forty feet of climbing there was no chance to relax the muscles of arms and legs. By the time I had dropped a few unripe coconuts and descended, I was completely licked, and it was weeks before the stiffness left my muscles.

As we recovered from the strain of battle, our Commanding Officer decided to tighten up discipline in the camp, and although it irked us to see the old 'bull' returning, looking back I can see that it was for the best; we would quickly have turned into a rabble without discipline, the strongest would have survived, and the weaker ones gone under. Later on we saw what happened to other troops who had not been subjected to discipline.

That evening we held a debate, the subject being 'Co-education is a good thing'. During the chat that followed I heard the latest griff. There was a fellow prisoner in the nearby Beds. and Herts. regiment who was a 'gifted' Spiritualist Medium, and his friend attended this debate. From him we heard that the medium had gone into a trance the previous day, and that his spirit guide told him that we would all be off the island by the twenty-eighth of March, which was only a month away; he had also seen a vision of the ships carrying us leaving Singapore harbour, and was convinced there was no chance of error. It is comforting to hope, and thousands believed. Although I had left camp by the designated day, I was told when I returned that the hill in the camp from which the sea could be seen was crowded with believers all day awaiting a sign of those Blighty-bound boats, which alas, never materialised. Our boats were well and truly burned and it was to be a long time before they could be rebuilt.

That Sunday I paraded for our first Christian service as

prisoners of war, and in the afternoon we had our turn for a sea visit again, but this was messed up by a tropical storm which caught us all unawares and we returned to camp soaked.

We were by now feeling the effects of consuming large quantities of rice, which is mostly water, and few of us were able to go through the night without visiting boreholes, and my bladder has never been quite the same since. Quizzes, impromptu concerts and sing-songs were being organized in the evenings and I was in the other-ranks team in an evening quiz when we beat the officers. The subject of soldierly conversation changed noticeably at this time. Wine and women were seldom mentioned, but we would vie with one another in conjuring up descriptions of super meals we supposedly ate before the war, and would doubtless indulge in again at the first opportunity. We would moan endlessly about our cooks and talk about shooting them. (A couple of years later we were to long for the 'good old days at Changi'.)

It was the third of March, and we had now spent twelve days in Changi camp. That evening I was warned to be on parade at eight o'clock the next morning as I was moving camp to Singapore with a working party. I had by now acquired quite a large heap of things that 'might come in useful', and when next morning I tried to pack it up into a form which I could march with, I found that I could hardly lift it off the ground; some things therefore had to be discarded, including my charcoal stove. We moved off on our twenty-mile march with the sun blazing down on us, and before the journey was accomplished, on empty stomachs, I was sorely tempted to shed some more of my heavy load. However, by assuring myself for the last eight miles or so that we must be nearly there, I finally made it, kit and all, at three o'clock in the afternoon. We were told that we were in Farrow Park, which although now surrounded by barbed wire had in peace-time been a polo ground. Before resting we dug latrines, made fireplaces for the cooks, and erected bell-tents the Japs provided.

Next morning before breakfast, we mustered for our first 'Tenko', which is Japanese for roll-call, and after eating our rice, we moved out to begin our task, which proved to consist of removing burnt-out cars from the highway, where they had lain since the capitulation. Our six guards seemed to behave quite reasonably, and we did a fair day's work. We had no food to eat, and midday suffered the mortification of seeing the Japs eat their beautiful white rice. (Our rice ration consisted of broken reject grains, and was off-white in colour.)

Back in the camp that night, we found that the guard duty had been taken over by big black-bearded Sikhs. These chaps had been serving in the British Army at the fall of Singapore, and now they had changed sides; it probably amused our captors to put these men in charge of us now. Some were vindictive and spat or lashed out with rifle butts if we approached them. Others said they were only serving their new masters because they had been told they would be shot if they refused. They told us they would desert when they had a chance. The Japs really despised them, and soon took their rifles away and made them carry staves. The following day our work changed to carrying sand, and as we still had no food with us at midday, the guards shared their meal with us. This comprised one wooden bucket of fish-flavoured rice, and one of sweet milky rice.

The fourth day was spent cleaning up an old Aussie camp, and I dug up two wide-brimmed Aussie hats out of the mud. They were both damaged, but I put them aside to take back to camp. We also dug up some tinned food, which the guards allowed us to take back to share with the others that evening. These guards were really quite good to us; one of them disappeared for half an hour, and when he returned he gave me two sergeants' shirts and a mess-tin. Again they shared their food with us, this time, rice and bacon, and it tasted like food for the gods.

Some of our men made it a point of honour to say nothing good of the Japs, and even went so far as to call anyone who said otherwise 'Jap Happy', which was our word for a quisling. Within my experience there were good men among our enemy. I never ceased to wonder that we were not treated worse than we were, considering the way the Japs and Chinese had been treating one another during the preceding years. Then again, the Japanese method of imposing military discipline was brutal in the extreme; any soldier may beat up anyone below him in rank, right down to the two-star private beating up his one-star comrade; it was mutiny and death to retaliate. Wounded in battle must try to get themselves killed and finally, rather than be taken prisoner, commit the 'Hara Kiri', literally, the belly cut. Those who were too ill to go on duty were put on half rations as they were of no use to their emperor; I think that after years of this treatment most of us would have found ourselves affected. We were told that living under the constant threat of earthquakes for centuries past had contributed to their hasty tempers and instability.

We also had some 'bad eggs' in our army. I well recall some of the regular soldiers with whom I had served in the commandos the year before. If half the tales they told of the way they treated the 'wogs' (as they called all other races) were true then our colonising troops between the wars were pretty well as bad as the Japs at their worst.

Back in camp that night I made a composite double crowned hat from the two I had found earlier in the day. This most probably saved my life on at least one occasion later on in the Thai jungle. I wore it for the remainder of my POW career.

Next day our guards, the best Japs I ever met, left us and were replaced by harder nuts, who marched us back to Changi through the hottest part of the day, almost without respite. On our return 'home', we were greeted with the news that we were to move out of the huts which had by now been made quite comfortable, and were to erect tents for ourselves in a sand-pit a quarter of a mile away. We spent the next day digging fresh latrines and levelling out spaces for the tents. The sergeants, however, were allocated an old native hut in the corner of the pit for their sleeping quarters.

Our CSM, Tommy Beatty, who had been so badly wounded in the battle, now returned to us from hospital, and I was delighted to see him recovered. Having a good look round our new area when we had finished our work for the day, I came across what was to me a new kind of tree. It was covered in nuts, which were not unlike 'conkers', but the kernal exposed on removing the shell was black with white spots. I tasted one, and it tasted good, so I gathered as many as my pockets would hold. On the way back to our hut I met Tommy, and told him of the nut-tree, advising him to help himself before everyone found out about them.

I munched about fifteen of these nuts during the half hour before our evening meal, which was always our main meal of the day. This evening we had rice and bully-beef gruel by way of a special treat. I was usually ravenously hungry, so was surprised to find that my appetite had complete disappeared before I was half-way through supper. As I stared forlornly at the contents of my mess-tin I suddenly felt very sick, and the truth dawned on me that I had probably poisoned myself with those nuts. I was rather a joke with my comrades for the 'rubbish' that I ate, so quietly, hoping not to attract attention I tried to make an unhurried exit. 'Ullo, ullo, ullo what's up with Snowy?' came an obnoxious voice from my left, 'surely 'es not leavin' 'is grub?' As my withdrawal became a rout I left my food to the rotter, and set full sail for the latrines.

Tommy Beatty sat on the pole beside me for the whole of the next four hours I spent over the latrine. He had only eaten six nuts, and had to sit there all night. They turned out to be castor-oil nuts, and not poisonous, but we were lucky not to have burst the newly healed wounds in Tommy's abdomen. These nuts were dried and threaded on a skewer to use as candles by the local population. The evenings are evenly dark throughout the year in Singapore, as the equator is not far away.

We had been back from Farrow Park for only four days when I was warned to be ready the next morning to move off to Singapore on another working party. As we paraded at dawn we hoped to do the worst of our marching before the heat of the day, but it was two hours before our guards came for us, and after another hour's wait in front of Changi gaol we began our journey in earnest. However, it poured with rain the whole way, and by the time we arrived at our destination, River Valley Road, we had nothing left that was dry. Before we left Changi, we had been told that we were an advance party to prepare for the rest of the group who were to follow, so we had to put down our wet kit and start work immediately.

Chapter 3

'Even when walking through the dark valley of death,
I will not be afraid,
For you are close beside me.'

My first impression of this camp was one of filth and disorder, after the comparative cleanliness and discipline of Changi. The huts we were to occupy still had the rubbish of the previous tenants strewn about, and the camp itself was a sea of mud. There flowed past one side of the camp, a sluggish, dirty and oily river. This was tidal, and our camp was very little above water-level at high tide. Consequently the water table was too high to dig deep boreholes, so that instead of our clean Changi latrines we had shallow trenches, which writhed with maggots. The edges were constantly disintegrating, and one of our number fell in during the first few hours, and another one within the first twenty-four hours. What better way of finding out who is a good Samaritan than by calling for help when lying in that mucky mess? There were no effective means of washing there, yet someone always came to the help of the victims, day or night. POW life brought out the best and the worst in us.

While our cooks prepared a meal, the rest of us did our best to clear the mud and refuse out of the huts, and by six-thirty p.m., when the main party arrived from Changi, the rice was ready, and the huts were at least habitable. These wooden huts had been built before the fall to house refugees arriving from Malaya. They were good huts with a gangway up the centre, and a platform each side well up off the ground, and another similar one about four feet above that. We had about three feet of floor-space each, some on the top and some on the bottom platform, I was on the top.

The rice we were now issued with was contaminated with lime, and we were only able to eat a few mouthfuls at a time. After the first day or so we learned to sift most of the lime out by shaking it in a mosquito net, but it never made good eating.

The next day the Japs called us all out on parade, and divided us into various trades, namely bricklayers (denga), carpenters (dicu), painters and labourers. Why I do not know, as we never did any work needing these trades. Our company, the bricklayers, was numbered 2B4, and we were instructed to forget our regiments, and in future always think of ourselves as 2B4 company. I was put in charge and told that I would be responsible for the behaviour of my company of bricklayers. A little Jap came up and told us that we should always parade under him. He would be kind to us if we were all good obedient boys etc. As he knew only three or four words of English, it took him half an hour to get this message across to us, mostly by signs. Then be produced a needle and thread together with a pile of numbered cloth tags, which he commenced with deftness and great speed to sew on the breasts of our shirts. As he sewed '101' on my shirt, I saw how to tie a knot with one hand, and never forgot the lesson.

With our new numbers, we were then lined up for a Jap officer to address us, and speaking in quite good English he said, 'You will all be well treated, in the warrior spirit, if you do as you are told. Do not try to get out of the camp, as any POWs found outside the wire will be shot.' Through it all it rained, and rained, and rained, and by nightfall there were over six inches of mud over the whole site. It rained throughout the night, and by morning the latrines overflowed.

There were several thousand of us in the camp, but only one tap for water; this was allocated to the cooks for two thirds of the day, and if anyone wanted a wash it meant queueing up for most of their spare time to get it. Therefore many remained dirty, or washed in second- or third-hand mess tins of water. I had already been without a shave for two days for the first time since leaving the tennis court, and seeing that most of the earlier residents in this camp were growing beards, I decided to grow one myself. At Changi we held inspection parades daily to ensure that we all kept ourselves clean and tidy, but there was nothing like that here. I now saw for the first time the results of too little discipline as opposed to the other extreme, too much 'bull'.

The earlier tenants of this camp were mostly Australians, and as individuals I found them to be the nicest fellows in the world, generous, loyal to their 'cobbers' and tough as nails. In a crowd, however, they often became an unreasoning, unruly mob, quite uncontrollable and sinking to the level of the lowest types among them. Our first two nights in the camp had been disturbed into the small hours by shouts and curses emanating from the Aussie huts, where they spent most of the night playing cards. Their NCOs were as bad as the rest, and made no attempt to quell the noisy ones, so the rest of us could get some sleep. As none of them would obey orders, their part of the camp was never tidied up, so after a few days our officers tried to improve matters. Duty officers were appointed each day, and parties of men organized to make an effort to clean up the whole camp. Fresh latrines were dug every other day so that the old ones could be filled in before they became too bad.

On a particular night during that our first week, a young British duty officer stepped into the din of the Aussie hut next to us at about midnight, and timidly attempted to persuade the men to quieten down, but he was completely ignored, so he went off to fetch his superior officer, Major Wilde, and he in turn was ignored. So in a loud voice he shouted, 'I am Major Wilde . . .'. He could get no further as fifty voices screamed abuse at him. I heard some of the phrases; 'Who made yer wild . . .', 'Get stuffed sonny . . .'? 'Go and chase yer b..... poms . . .'. He gave up, and this was the last attempt to bring them into line, and we paddled our own canoe after that.

All these days it had rained without ceasing, so the Japs had been unable to take us out on working parties. I spent all one night on the latrine out in the rain, as I had picked up a bug that was going round the camp. In the tropics under these conditions 'squitters' became part of our daily life. Next morning the Japs lined us up early and for the first time took us out to work. We found ourselves arriving at Alexandra

Hospital, where we spent the day clearing away rubble. There was a rubbish dump which our guards allowed us to look over; we found some rusty dixies, which we took back for our cookhouse, and trodden into the mud I found a mosquito net, which I carefully excavated, and when I got it back, cleaned and mended it. It was to prove the most useful part of my kit during the coming years. I had proved very susceptible to mosquitoes and already was suffering from an ulcer on my ankle where I had scratched a bite.

The next time we had a dry day we started clearing native huts to make room, our guards told us, for new warehouses. Our guards were friendly, and allowed those who had money to purchase food and tobacco from Chinese living a little way off. These had retained their faith in sterling, and exchanged our £1 notes at the rate of twenty Straits dollars to the £1. I had retained a few £1 notes when I was captured. Before I left Changi also, two senior NCOs had entrusted some of their money to me in the hope that I would be able to buy food here, and send it back to them. On this our first day, therefore, I exchanged my first £1 note, and was able to purchase two French loaves for thirty cents, six packets of 'London' cigarettes for a dollar, and a few tins of food to start building up a store in case I obtained an opportunity to send them back to Changi.

Back in camp I exchanged one loaf for a tin of milk, and dug a pit under my bed to bury the tins of food until the chance came to send them back. Until my squitters cleared up a week later I was unable to eat much of the food we were able to buy, myself. The second day out on this work, a party working close by had a vicious guard; something displeased him and he hit one of the men with a heavy stick and broke his arm. The next day the Japs decided that only the NCO in charge of each party was to be allowed to visit the Chinese, and he was to purchase food on behalf of his men. Accompanied by a guard, on that occasion I bought two tins of food per man, having first collected fifty cents from each one. We had soon discovered that tinned fish and tinned milk were the best buys when it came to having something to mix with our plain rice, which was all we were getting in camp at that time. I found that one of those oval tins if fish in tomato sauce could be pounded into a paste, two tablespoonsful of salt added, and then it would supplement my daily rice for four days. I had to eke my cash out, as unlike many of my comrades I did not have much when taken prisoner; I had arranged for most of my army pay to be sent home to my mother, who saved it for me.

Later, when my cash ran low and the price of tinned food escalated to astronomical figures. I went over to a native food the name of which sounded like 'Ballachang'. It was made from the small sea creatures left in the fishermen's nets which were otherwise unsaleable. It was pounded with plenty of salt, into a paste, then instead of cooking it they buried it in the sand for a few weeks to mature. The end product stank; it could be smelled from many yards away, and tasted something like rancid cod-liver-oil. Many were unable to face it, but since it was almost pure protein I managed to force it down, and eventually got used to it.

We now went to work daily, and the Camp Commandant allowed us to spend one day a week in camp to enable us to do our personal chores; this meant we could take a stand-up bath by queueing up at the only tap; as this was situated close to the wire and in full view of the houses across the water, our bathing was often accompanied by the giggles of Chinese girls.

On our eleventh day we were marching to work as usual; a young Chinese woman stood at the roadside, a large basket of bread on one hip, a young child on the other. As we passed she called her wares, 'One, fifteen cent.' Although we were not allowed to purchase in this way, the guard following up the rear could not see us. A few yards ahead of me two men left the column, one jumped on the woman's back rolling her and her child over on the ground, the other man grabbed the basket and tipped the loaves out; before I could act they had all disappeared into haversacks. The woman picked up her child and ran off weeping. I still feel the shame that I felt on that day. POW life certainly brought out the worst and the best in us.

We gradually began to see each other more and more as we really were as much of the veneer of civilisation fell away. All races seem to have a similar amount of good and bad, often lurking just under the skin, whether that be black, white or yellow. I was to see private soldiers, spirits unbroken after weeks of torture, refusing to give the names of those who had helped them in escape attempts. I saw one of our officers of field rank, in charge of one of our camps, who bowed to the ground every time a Jap called him, and they would shout his name just for the fun of seeing him tremble.

At work we finished clearing the huts away, and started levelling the site. Our guards were lax, and lunch-times I was able to explore the environment, including a rubbish dump a hundred yards away. I found two note-pads, upon which I was to write most of my diary, a British gas-cape which I wore to keep the rain off, and some dixie lids, which I took back to camp for the cooks to bake 'doofers' on. These were balls of cooked rice baked over the fire. Although only plain rice, they made a change and were much in demand. I never knew the etymology of the name. Visits to the dump became a daily event and I acquired no end of good junk. The most valuable among these things were a piece of Dunlopillo out of a lorry seat and an army blanket. These made my bed for the next two years or so. A set of webbing equipment with pouches and back-pack was also very useful in enabling me to carry my kit from camp to camp.

A day or so later we held a meeting to decide how to try to improve the camp food, which was atrocious. We decided to replace half the cooks, and to put Sgt Gross in charge as he was a Communist, and should stand for fair shares for all. In practice he proved even worse than his predecessor. Everyone believed that the cooks ate half the food themselves, but they actually had a thankless task.

In the evenings we would wander around the camp chatting until dark, then we would sit on the ends of our beds, and those who felt like it would usually sing old nostalgic songs. Sometimes during a quiet spell a patrolling guard, rifle and bayonet in hand, would poke his head in the doorway and call out 'More sing Soljah!' The Aussies did not sing like our boys, and some of them told me that our arrival had quite changed the atmosphere of the camp during the long evenings.

Out on the working party we finished levelling out the site, and on the twenty-ninth of March, the day the Spiritualist had predicted that we should be freed, the Japs brought along some of the little hand-carts which they had used to carry their equipment during the fighting, and told us that we were to make boxes to fit them in order to convert them to carry sand.

After eating our midday rice that day, one of the more aggressive of our guards stalked up to me. 'Gunzo (Sergeant), Nippon soldier numbar one bayonet fighter, yesu?' Never having been over gifted with tact, and since most of our guards were friendly, I retorted, 'English soldier number one, Japanese solder number ten!' For a few brief moments there was a silence of unbelief, then bedlam broke loose as all started to scream at once. Although arms waved all round me I remained calm and no blows were struck. They held a conference, and by the way heads kept turning in my direction I knew that my fate was being discussed. At first when we had heard the Japs talking we had thought them to be quarrelling, so vehemently did they carry on, but we soon discovered that they always talk like this. They have one set of words to use to a superior in rank or social standing, and these are quite different from those used to an inferior person. Thus to an inferior 'I' is 'Boko' and 'you' is 'kimi', but to a superior it had to be 'watukushi' and 'anatah', but to return to our story; the conference ended, and the senior guard came over to me, and sternly said 'Nippon numbar one soljah!' Discretion being the better part of valour, I had the sense to hold my tongue this time.

The atmosphere suddenly changed back to the relaxed mood of earlier on. Now these Japs were not front line soldiers, and carried captured .303 short Lee-Enfield rifles and bayonets. One of the guards (he had always been a friendly chap), now removed his bayonet and scabbard from his belt, fixed it on the rifle, and to our amazement he tossed it to me. The big-mouthed Jap who had originally challenged me was now being harangued by the others who, it transpired, were trying to persuade him to put his bayonet fighting skill where his mouth was, and at last, very reluctantly, he put his scabbarded bayonet on his riflt. (Bayonet scabbards are left on during hand fighting training to prevent serious injury.) 'Engerisso Gunzo bayonet fight!' called out the friendly Jap who had lent me his rifle, and he indicated that our arena was to be a six foot wide corridor between two huts.

I had always been useless at grenade throwing, map-reading and many other martial arts, but at bayonet fighting I excelled. And in my hand was my beloved Lee-Enfield. As my adversary approached I scowled, roared my war-cry and rushed him. I saw fear in his face as he held out his weapon at arms length more like a fencing foil; it fell to the ground as I purposely narrowly missed his throat with the point of my bayonet; turning quickly about I brought up my rifle butt to within an inch of his face, and again slashed down the bayonet to graze his shoulder. I had completely forgotten our circumstances as the pent-up feelings of the previous months found an outlet, but was quickly brought back to earth as I felt myself grabbed from behind by several pairs of Jap hands. 'Dammi-dammi!' murmured our friendly guard. 'No-good enah!' said his friend. They were relieved that no-one had been hurt, such behaviour would have taken a lot of explaining had their superiors found out about it.

The next day was an important one, as we were lined up for the first pay parade of our captivity. I drew five dollars forty cents, about five shillings and sixpence. From that time forward the Jap paid wages to those of us who worked, and although it was only a pittance it enabled us to buy the odd egg, sugar and cooking oil from time to time.

Since the woman who sold bread was attacked and robbed, there had been no breadseller on our route to work, but another one now made his appearance. This one was a young man, a cripple and his disability had to be seen to be believed. Both bones in one shin had been broken and he walked, one leg a foot shorter than the other, on the shin bone, the foot flopping about on the ground as he walked. He must have endured agony with every step. He was unable to run when the Japs saw him, and they kicked his legs from under him and continued kicking him on the ground. They helped themselves to as much of the bread as they wanted, and threw the remainder to us. This time I am glad to say, many of our chaps refused to touch it.

The Japs seemed to hate the Chinese with a psychological hatred whereas, although we were often ill-treated, I never had the impression that they really hated us. Later on, when the Koreans took over the task of guarding us, we did find out what it was like to be hated.

I have very fair hair and now that my beard was beginning to grow was told that I was acquiring the look of a Western 'Old Timer', and was given the nick-name of 'Zeke' by my men. Our first task in preparing for making sand-boxes was to be given a huge heap of second-hand timber, and told to pull out all the nails. There seemed to be no hurry in building these warehouses, and our guards knew no more about the way to set about the job than we did.

We had a very broad shouldered guard named Khano; he had gold teeth at the front and cavities at the back, a habit after meals of drawing back his lips in an ape-like grin, and sucking in air to dislodge food particles with a noise like a locomotive letting off steam. He loved to issue orders and to boast of his past exploits, but generally speaking we had found him to be pretty harmless. One day most of our guards had to attend a special duty, and to his delight, Khano found himself in sole charge of our work party. As we marched off, he condescendingly told me I might walk with him, sharing his glory in front of the column.

During our midday break, I was lying down resting, while a little way off Khano was showing off to a group of our lads. 'Me, Khano, numbar one Judo man!' he began. Khano invariably flew into a rage if anyone contradicted him, and someone usually did just for fun. He continued, 'Engerissoo soljah Judo no-goodenah. Engerissoo boxing OK, Judo no-goodo!'. Seeing me dormant on the ground, a wag replid 'Gunzo numbar one Judo man!' and he pointed to me. I heard the roar as Khano jumped up and came striding over to me. 'So-ca, Pinesu' (the nearest he could get to pronouncing my name) 'Gunzo numbar one Judo eh?'. Remembering my recent bayonet fighting escapade I said, 'Me no-good Judo man, Gunzo Judo dammi-dammi!'.

Khano was delighted to hear that I was no good at wrestling, and danced with excitement as he ordered me to stand up and take my stance. I was in fact an unarmed combat instructor, and also quite a good wrestler. He did not even bother to remove his belt and bayonet as he pulled me to my feet. We took up positions a couple of yards apart and I let Khano make the first move. With a bull-like roar he charged and he clearly knew nothing about wrestling, as after very brief contact I was able to convert his charge into flight through the air. The poor chap's bayonet touched the ground before he did, and the handle stuck into his ribs. It was a very long time before he could speak, and I think he had broken a rib or two. He was not able to walk unaided, so I had to let him lean on me all the way back to camp that evening. He never again came out with us, I hope his commandant did not find out the truth, or he would probably have had a few more bones broken.

A few days later we started reinforcing the floor of a hut, so that cement could be stored on it. For the first time our guards left us on our own while they went on a visit to some girls. While they were away a pig escaped from a nearby Chinese smallholding, and attempted to run through our working party. It disappeared under a heap of our men, and someone emerged from the melee with the pig in his arms. As we were not skilled butchers, someone produced a pocket knife and cut the animal's head off; the remainder was quickly cut into small pieces, and we carried these back to camp that night to toast for our supper. The Japs loved pork, and would have not let us keep it had they known of its existence. A Malay lorry driver passed our column on the way home, and he threw me a pineapple, which I hid before the guard noticed it. This was the first time I had seen a friendly Malay, perhaps they were beginning to change their opinions.

Our guards were all replaced at this time by new men, and they were at first very strict, and held themselves aloof from us. However within a few days they melted somewhat and became more friendly. The old guards had been with us from the start; they had seen my white beard grow, and it never puzzled them. These newcomers had never seen the young face underneath my whiskers, and to the Japanese white hair signifies old age. The first day we paraded under them, having arrived at the site, their leader came up to me and in a voice tinged with respect he said, 'You old man, no work, yasume (rest)!' I protested that I was only twenty-three, but he refused to believe me. As the days went by, seeing me do my share of the work they must eventually have realized that I was not as old as they thought.

The nineteenth of April was a red letter day for me, as I escaped the confines of our camp for the first time. I crawled through the barbed wire where the Jap lorries were parked at the far end of the camp. These hid the wire from the gaze of the camp patrols. As I made my way down the road, making for the Chinese shopping precinct a hundred yards off, I saw in huge letters over an ornamental gateway, 'THE GREAT WORLD'. This had been one of two permanent peace-time fairgrounds in Singapore. The other one was 'THE HAPPY WORLD', and both were now derelict.

The first open building I came to was a café, and I popped quickly inside. As I sat down at a table, not knowing whether the proprietor was a Jap collaborator, but knowing that any of us caught outside the wire would be shot, my heart was beating faster than usual. From the table I had chosen at the back of the room, I saw there there were two other customers, one a dark wavy-haired European, the other Chinese. Another Chinaman, evidently the owner, approached me from a room behind the café; winking at me he asked in English what I would like, so I asked for a cup of coffee, proffering a dollar bill. He quickly returned with this and my change, upon counting which, I found I had a dollar's worth; I looked up to tell him of his mistake, but he winked again and raised a warning finger. My coffee was on the house. Twenty minutes later I was safely back in camp. I had smelled the sweet smell of freedom, and could not wait for the chance to be out again.

Next day I repeated my adventure, and again went into the friendly café. The same European was there, and with trepidation I saw him get up from his seat and approach me; was he a German or other Japanese ally? To my relief he introduced himself in a friendly way. I was wearing a shirt carrying no sergeants' stripes on purpose, but he seemed to know that I was from the POW camp. I observed that he had a slight foreign accent as he asked me what things were like in the camp. After giving him a brief run down, I asked him for his story. He was born a Greek, he told me, and although Greece was at war with both Italy and Germany, Japan had never declared war on her. He had been working in Malaya but had joined the local equivalent of our territorials, the FMSVP at the beginning of the emergency. At the fall he went back into civilian clothes, and Greek passport in pocket, he was living a life of leisure until his money ran out. I asked him if there was a safe shop where I could purchase food, and he took me to an open stall off the main road where I obtained three small tins of cream and two packets of sugar. We called at the café again on the way back, and my new friend bought me a very tasty dish of a sort of Chinese spaghetti. I safely returned to camp again, feeling very elated.

We all at this time paid ten cents each pay day to a central fund established to supplement our rice ration. That evening we held one of our regular mess meetings, and it was decided to buy some cooking oil if possible. I volunteered to try to obtain some via my contact outside the wire, and I was given cash to purchase four gallons if I could. Out through the wire I went again, into my friendly café. I asked the proprietor where I could get the oil, and he told me that it was almost unobtainable. The plants which made oil had all closed down, and the Japs bought all they could lay their hands on for their own use. Nevertheless he said he would see what he could do for me and went off, leaving his wife in charge of the café. A few minutes later, to my profound dismay, two Jap soldiers walked into the café, and with sinking heart I saw them walk in my direction. They were not coming for me however, and sat down at the next table, one facing me and one with his back to me. The former caught my eye and nodded politely, so I nodded back. Although I was terribly nervous with my life hanging by a thread, my beard spared my blushes. They took no more notice of me; they could not have come from our camp as I was a well-known figure among our Japs.

By the time the proprietor returned with a well dressed young friend, the soldiers had left. Speaking in good English the young man told me that there was no good oil available, but offered a four gallon tin of coconut oil for six dollars. I ordered a tin and he promised to have it ready for me on the morrow. He told me how sorry he was for the plight of all the prisoners, and provided some cheering war news for me to pass on to my friends but this proved to be wishful thinking, probably made up on the spur of the moment to cheer me up. Still feeling on edge after the incident with the soldiers, I breathed a sigh of relief as I reached the safety of our camp.

Next day the young man was as good as his word, and I collected the oil without trouble. I gave him fifty cents for himself, and when he asked if I wanted any more I ordered another tin for the following day. Our cooks had also asked me to try to buy some 'Bisto' or other gravy salt, but the Chinese had never heard of this product.

As soon as the young man left, a Chinese lady, neatly dressed in the way of her race, came over and sat at my table, breathing a few words in her own tongue as she did so. She was birdlike in her movements, and very neat in appearance. With a sweet smile she pulled a parcel from under her garments and handed it to me. Thanking her, I made a movement to untie the tape but she raised a hand to stop me, and without a word moved out of the room, as unobtrusively as she had entered. Back in camp I dropped the oil at the cookhouse, and took my parcel to open it on my bed-space. It contained a vest, a Chinese dressing gown, a safety razor, a tin of pâté de foie gras, a tin of bamboo shoots and a tin of an unrecognized Chinese food. I kept the vest and one tin of food, and gave the rest away. Her little gift gave me more pleasure than double rations for a week would have done; it was satisfying to know that there was a reservoir of good will in the hearts of the Chinese all around us.

Next time out of the wire, I went further afield, and found an Indian café, where two Indians did their cooking on the pavement outside, tossing their chappaties up and down in the air and clapping them between their hands. A European in civilian clothes stopped to speak to me; he told me that he was a British soldier and that after capitulation a Chinese family had hidden him in their house. When he realized they were risking their lives in concealing him, he came out of hiding, and pretending to be Greek had got himself a job working for a Chinese firm, and was getting on very well there.

Hastily telling him that it was too risky for us to remain where we were I made a rendezvous for the next day, at the friendly café, but I never saw him again. I collected the cooking oil and returned to camp, where I heard that we were to make high-speed extensions to our hut as another party was expected to come in from Changi. They arrived in the pouring rain before we were half ready for them, and at their head were the two Colour Sergeants who had provided me with £3 cash to buy food for them to send back to Changi. No opportunity had yet arisen to send food back, and I had it buried under the floor, all purchased at half its present value.

I went up to greet the two men, and ignoring me one said to the other something like 'Well if it ain't the b . . . we trusted with our £3; scoffed the lot himself I suppose!' I was just about broke myself, and was tempted to justify their lack of trust. However, I dug up the sack of tins and dropping it beside them, handed over ten dollars change. I received no word of thanks or apology as they pawed over their loot while completely ignoring me. That night I walked round the hut extension which now housed the newcomers. A piece of sacking was draped across one corner, and I could see the glimmer of a home-made lamp shining out. The two Colour Sergeants had been behind there for the last hour I was told, stuffing themselves. None of their neighbours had been offered a bit.

The latest intake of men were not all from our regiment, but included fifty Royal Artillery gunners. Goodness knows why they had been brought to this grossly overcrowded camp, as there had clearly up to the present been insufficient work for us; and now we had to spend even longer queueing for water at our solitary camp tap. Among the fresh faces to arrive had been my old friend Len Dudley. When he heard that I made sorties outside the wire, he told me that as he still had cash he would like me to buy some tinned food for him, and on my next expedition I was able to get him what he asked for. While I was eating my plain rice that evening Len brought me half a tin of fish he had just opened. Since he was as thin as a rake I tried to refuse, but he insisted upon me having it. My faith in human nature was restored.

Up to the present our work had been easy, but from now on we noticed a gradual change in the tenor of our guards. In the early days the Japs had been so elated with the unhindered progress of their armies towards India that they behaved with comparative tolerance toward us most of the time, expecting The Imperial Japanese Army to continue through India, and to meet up with their allies in Europe. It now must have begun to dawn on them that it was not all going to be a walk-over, and that it could be years before they rejoined their families in Japan. As their advance slowed down, the worst types among our guards began to vent their spleen on us at the slightest opportunity. The first real sign of the change of tempo was when we were taken off the easy jobs and set the task of breaking up old concrete with sledge hammers in the direct sun all day, with rest periods halved. Any of us caught slacking, whether because of ill-health or laziness, was made to stand to attention with sledge hammer held overhead at arms' length, a severe punishment with the shade temperature in the hundreds. Notwithstanding the risk, I still found opportunities to sneak off to the dump, and at this time found myself a good sharpening stone. I kept it all my POW days, and it was the nucleus of a fine set of tools which I eventually made. It also kept my razor sharp later on.

We were paraded night and morning now for 'Tenko'. Japanese roll-calls were comic opera affairs. We had to fall in in fives instead of the usual twos or fours; our guards were so bad at arithmetic that they could not count us in any other way. Even so, great difficulties were encountered. Two or three of them would together pass along the line marking us off in tens, then when they came to a blank file at the end with perhaps one, two, three or four men in it they would argue and write out sums in the dust with their sticks. It was sometimes half an hour before the task was accomplished to their satisfaction. They would often agree among themselves that all was not well. 'More one man!' they would shout. Then I would have to go along the line with them counting all over again. At roll-call on the morning of the twenty-ninth of April, our senior guard reverently announced that as it was the birthday of His Imperial Majesty the Emperor of Japan, we were all to have a day's holiday. I did my washing and then went through the wire to drink to freedom in coffee in my Chinese friend's café. Dusk was falling as we paraded as usual for evening roll-call, and it soon became clear that the Japs had celebrated in stronger stuff than coffee. In the end our guard asked me to count our men myself, and I was able to report 'OK, koo-joo men to tenko'.

We all had to learn to count in their tongue. 'Nippon-go' as they called it; ichi, nee, san, see or yon, gou, rocou, sichi, hachi, koo joo; joo-ichi, joo-nee etc. Grammar seemed simple and to me seemed like not much more than stringing words together. 'I have cigarettes' was 'Watakushee tabacco aru' the opposite, 'Watakushee tabacco nay or armaseng'. To pose a question they added 'ca' to the statement, thus 'Have you a cigarette?' became 'Anatah Tabacco-ca?' As soon as they learned a few words of English, they added 'ca' to them to form a question. They used our words with their simple sentence construction, thus when one of them wanted to tell me that in future we must notify them each day what the morrow's requirements would be, he said, 'Gunzo, tomorrow want, today ask!'

They were always interested to hear how many children, especially boys, we had. Newcomers, seeing my venerable white hairs, would almost invariably ask me at the first opportunity, 'Gunzo, you children-ca?' When I explained that I was not even married, they would usually make sympathetic clucking noises.

The next major difficulty was that our cooks ran out of fuel. We used wood, and rice takes quite a lot to boil it, and we received the ultimatum 'No firewood brought back from working parties, no food!' From then on everyone had to try top pinch a piece of wood from somewhere each day; beams went out of our roof, bits of staging disappeared, and our lunch-breaks outside were spent looking for odd pieces of wood to bring back. Singapore is a densely populated island and had been short of firewood for many years, so I guess the Japs could not give us what they didn't have.

It was the seventh of May, and as the guards had a ceremonial parade before a visiting general, we were given another 'Yasume' day. I was busy in camp so did not have time to make my usual trip through the wire. That afternoon the camp patrol spotted footprints in the mud where I and others had been crossing to freedom. They lay in wait and caught three or four of our chaps trying to get back inside. They were taken away by the 'Kempi-Ti' military police, dreaded equally by both us and the ordinary Jap soldiers. We never saw or heard of them again, but the usual treatment was first torture to obtain the names of any contacts, followed by execution. I had drunk my last cup of Chinese coffee, as the Japs reinforced the wire, and removed the lorries so that all the boundary could be seen by the guards. From now on the Japs held 'Tenko's' at odd times, and were even more fussy in making sure that there were no absentees. Some of the guards let us count in English as the newcomers from Changi had not yet learned Nippon-go. We numbered down the ranks 'one, two, three four . . .' our guard knew no English, we still had a few wags '. . . nine, ten, Jack, Queen King'. There was a roar from behind as an English-speaking Jap officer heard the sequence. 'No-good enah, Bagero!' etc. A few cuffs, and it was all over; but from then counting had to be in Japanese, and anyone who did not know his number was clouted.

For a few weeks, we had a skip of reject fish issued on alternate days. These were creepy crawlies from the bottoms of the fishermen's nets, and varied from hideous devil-fish, to small octopus-like creatures. We boiled them all up together into a fish broth. There was never continuity of food, mainly I think due to lack of organization on the part of the Japs. We were told also that Camp Commandants received a fixed sum of money for each prisoner, and any savings they could retain counted as 'perks'. This probably accounted for the fact that in some camps food was so much better than in others.

I had now been two months in River Valley, and felt part of a community. Once we got this sense of 'belonging' in a camp, no matter how bad it was, we were always loth to leave, on the principle, I suppose of 'the devil we know'. Life was however wearisome in the mud and squalor, with disease now a major problem. Pellagra (an ugly and irritating skin disease caused by lack of vitamin 'B'), sores, ulcers, dengue and other tropical fevers were rife. Things would have seemed better had there been useful work to do, but our work now seemed to be more a punishment than anything else.

Marching home from work one day we passed a green space with three trees growing on it. To each tree was tied a Chinaman, three captions were over their heads reading 'Thief', 'Robber' and 'Pilfer'. They were covered in blood and bruised beyond recognition; the centre one appeared to be only about twelve years old. As they hung there they looked like a depiction of the Crucifixion. Our guards told us they had been there all day.

The dump was still getting my usual visits and at this time I brought home a bundle of hessian with which I made a bed, and partitioned my bed-space off to form a 'room' for a bit more privacy. I christened it 'The Nook', and a name-board over the door put the finishing touch. I could now work on my next project, away from prying eyes. Having found a pair of earphones and a load of wire on the dump, I was determined to make a wireless. Batteries were unheard of, so it would need to be a crystal set. During the next few weeks I made my coils and from the 'useful' items in my kit completed my set, right down to crystal-holder and cats-whisker. From then on although I tried hundreds of different kinds of rock, always on the look-out for likely pieces, I never found anything that produced the slightest 'Grerk'. In the end I had to dump my abortive effort.

We had our first air-raid warning the day after I commenced 'Operation Wireless'. We saw no planes, but our guards were shaken as they believed that all Burma and India were in their hands, so there should have been no airfields near enough to mount air-raids on Singapore.

A rumour began to circulate to the effect that we might soon be allowed to write home. We had worried ever since our capture that no list had been sent to the Red Cross to let our people at home know that we were alive. In the event it was to be three years before my parents received a year-old card telling them that I was safe and well. Up until then all that they had was their original notification from a government department that I was missing, believed captured. By that time my mother was about the only one left who still believed that I would return. She continued to write to me weekly for nearly four years, but only a few of her letters got through, and those that did were always over a year old.

I had by this time grown a fine curly beard but one day I felt sores coming along the hair-roots, so went to see our medical orderly. While awaiting my turn I saw a man being treated for impetigo; he was having the scabs pulled out with tweezers from among the stubble, and the stubs he was losing at the same time were causing him much pain, and tears were rolling down his cheeks. I left the queue, and went back to my hut. Early next morning before my comrades were awake, I fetched water, and with my razor hacked off my long hair and beard, and then shaved my face and scalp. I had no mirror and the blood flowed. When finished I looked like a jig-saw puzzle, but I was clean-shaven and bald.

After breakfast we paraded as usual for roll-call. I was the first thing the Japs saw. 'New-ca?' one of them asked. I pointed to the number on my shirt, and he peered at it in disbelief. Someone had exchanged the patriach for a lad in his early twenties. Half a dozen guards gathered jabbering around me, but I think that it was all my cuts that finally convinced them that it was really me.

That day I returned to the dump to remove a piece of ebonite that I had seen attached to some other equipment. This dump was about a hundred yards across, and as I started to emerge, ebonite in my haversack, a couple of the Kempi-ti who had been lying in wait some way off spotted me. I turned and ran as fast as I could in the opposite direction from our party. When I was out of their sight, I ran in a wide circle and finally dropped exhausted among our men while our guards still appeared to sleep. My rapid breathing had subsided by the time the Kempi-ti appeared and ordered a roll-call. Our guards were as relieved as we were to be able to report that we were all present. They did not search us; had they done so I would have found the piece of ebonite difficult to shrug off; my hut would have been searched, and my embryo wireless discovered. Had I not that morning shaved off my flowing hair and beard, the Kempi-ti could not have failed to have recognized me, the only Snow-White in the camp. I may not be able to convince the reader, but I know that it was more than a coincidence that I was preserved through all those years to come home whole. From that time on Japs patrolled the area, and spot checks were made during the day to ensure that no-one was missing. I did not visit the dump again. That night I completed the wireless, fixed the aerial along the ridge of the hut, and buried the earth wire under the floor. I only needed my crystal now, that was all; but the work and risk had been in vain. A few months later a group of our men in Thailand were caught using a home-made wireless. They were tortured for a week in a futile attempt to make them divulge the source of the components, and then thrown into the ditch outside the Kempi-ti's hut and left to die.

In running from the Kempi-ti I had torn the flesh on my big toe, and when this swelled up and festered I had to stay in camp for a few days. Having salvaged a conté pencil and some paper on one of my visits to the dump I now found time to do some drawing, and was in demand drawing wives and sweethearts from snapshots. Pte Birch across the gangway first put the idea into my head when he drew a sketch of me stalking up the road on a work-party, with flowing hair and beard and wearing the ridiculous long shorts which were army issue to protect the legs from mosquitoes and leeches.

The fifteenth of June saw clouds of smoke drifting up from the direction of Singapore harbour. Great excitement and rumours of Allied landings. Then the Japs told us that Chinese fifth-columnists had set fire to a ship in the harbour. Four days later we saw ack-ack fire, and thought that our planes must have arrived at last, but this time it transpired that the Japs were only trying out captured guns. That same evening Major E. W. Swanton spent the evening in our hut relating cricketing anecdotes. In civilian life he was a cricketing commentator and journalist. He was very interesting and much appreciated by us all. This was the last of a series of talks, debates, quizzes and impromptu concerts which we held to pass away the long dark evenings, and to keep our spirits up. On the eighteenth of June the Japs ordered that no more entertainment was to be held by the prisoners, and that we were not to gather together in large groups. They had been surprised to find our morale remained high, and the purpose of the latest imposition was probably to impair this. If so the result was the very opposite, as we thought they must be expecting an attack, and daily half expected parachutes to fall down from the sky.

Passing over that part of our hut where I slept ran an electric cable which fed the Jap quarters. Each night for some time, I had been climbing on to the roof to pull on this cable, so that every day it sagged closer and closer to the roof. At last came the night when it touched; I had a black-market bulb, wire and insulation tape ready, and now had to await the next power cut, and as these were not infrequent one came two nights later. Slitting the insulation in the dark and inserting my two wires was a tricky job, especially as I did not know when the juice would come on again. I had no bulb-holder, so I had to attach the wires with insulation tape. Neither did I have a switch, so an insulation tape arrangement had to be made for that too; thus switching the light on and off was a rather involved affair; but now we did have electric light, and we were I think the only prisoners ever to have this amenity. However it was a mixed blessing. To make our 'nook' light-proof and prevent our captors from discovering what I had done, it was also nearly air-tight, and in the tropical climate the heat became unbearable after a short while, so our electric light was not used very much.

Padding through the germ-laden mud every day, my injured toe was not progressing very well, and when our doctor saw it he said I would lose my foot if I did not return to Changi. I was mad to hear this, and did not want to leave all my friends behind; anyway, however bad the camp might be, River Valley was now 'home'. Prison camp atmosphere is impossible to describe. It took a long time to learn whom one could trust and rely upon. Which guards were friendly and the ones with whom no liberties could be taken. All the narrow squeaks one had in the camp made it seem like a friend when the time came to part. River Valley was a pretty bad camp, it seems strange therefore that even now I can look back upon it with nostalgia. It is probably that through the muck and pain there shines the glow of comrades I knew I could safely trust with my life.

At nine a.m. on the twenty-fourth of June I was ordered to parade with my kit ready to return to Changi. With regret and moist eye I said goodbye to all my friends. To my surprise one of the guards came up to shake my hand and to wish me speedy recovery; he hoped I would soon return to the camp. Together with other sick men I was put on a lorry, and made my first easy journey along the Changi Road, to finish up in ward U2 of Roberts Hospital. This had been handed over to our doctors after the fighting, and our wounded had been cared for there ever since. It had been damaged in the fighting, but much of it was still serviceable. The Japs had respected its Red Cross until Indian troops had withdrawn into it and fired through the windows at them, when they had advanced into the building and bayonetted everyone, soldiers, patients and medical orderlies.

Men at River Valley had given me the pleasant task of bringing messages and presents to friends left behind in Changi. First I called on dear old Sgt Clarry Pellet. Coming from a small Cambridgeshire village, he had worked with farm horses all his life, and called all his friends 'Me old beauty!' Len Dudley had given me a roll of tobacco to give to him, and Clarry could not have been more pleased had I told him he was free to go home. He was alas, never to see his beloved horses again. His name is now preserved for posterity with several others on a brass plaque in a tiny church, not far from my home.

My father had a silver 'Omega' watch which he carried all through the first world war, and it was still going strong. When I was mobilised in August 1939 he bought me a similar pocket watch. It was now the only thing from home I treasured; the first night in hospital I dropped it on the floor and irreparably damaged it. When I awoke next morning I found I had been bitten all over by bed-bugs, horrible things nearly a quarter of an inch long, and the ones I found were bloated by my blood. After biting they give off a horrible sickly smell and it soon became a familiar accompaniment to the remainder of our POW days.

Although food was no better here than in our last camp, conditions were clean and dry, so after five days my toe improved to the extent that I was allowed to walk on it for a short time each day. The first thing I did was my washing. Everything except my towel dried quickly, so I decided to return half an hour later for that. Alas, when I came back it had gone.

The fifth of July was a red letter day, as we were issued with the first cards to write home. They were printed thus:

> I am well/I am ill/I am in hospital.
> Please see that .... is taken care.

The interpreter had left the preposition out altogether rather than end a sentence with it. We were told to print our cards, and I printed mine in small letters. I was very upset when my card was returned to me with the message that I should have used capitals, and that I could not have another card so must miss my turn. I need not have worried as none of the cards got through. It was Sunday, and I was solaced by going to a church service conducted by the Australian padre.

While I had been away a first class concert party had been formed, and it was now able to present shows of a very high standard. Female clothing and make-up had been acquired or made, so the concerts were not without heroines, many of them indistinguishable from the real thing on the stage. The current production was called 'Camp Pie', and I thoroughly enjoyed it.

There was a fair orchestra comprising mostly home-made instruments, and many songs written in the camp were sung. These were either nostalgic pieces reminding us of home, optimistic songs foretelling rapid release or comic pieces, mainly about food. We never lost our sense of humour thank goodness, and it carried us through our darkest days. We were to share camps with other nationalities who had lost their sense of humour, and watched them die of complaints that we were able to shrug off.

There was something to do most evenings in Changi, church, quizzes, debates, competitions and lectures; there was never to be another camp like it. Had we been allowed to stay there many would have returned who now lie under far away soil.

The following Sunday, after going to see Clarry, who was far from well, I attended church again. The sermon was so effective that I went straight back and shared out two tins of fish I had brought back from River Valley, with the sick! I was discharged from hospital on the seventeenth of July, and returned to the Sergeants' hut in our regimental area, handing the remaining tinned food and sugar I had into the mess. I was pleasantly surprised later when Cyril Flatt handed me one dollar, thirty cents from passing the hat round.

I was put on light duty, which then consisted of making 'Attap' or palm thatch, for repairing our huts. Although very effective roofing, attap makes very good fodder for termites and other insects, so it constantly needed renewing. Also in the tropical storms pieces would often blow away. All the roofs in Changi were made of attap, so a lot of repairs were always needed. Some men collected palm leaves, some split bamboo, and others actually wove these materials into the 'tiles' which were fixed on the roof with ties which themselves were split from another cane called 'Rhotan'. The 'tiles' are made by taking a piece of split bamboo three feet long, bending the spear-shaped palm leaves over and along it, then weaving a thin sliver of green bamboo in and out every folded leaf to hold it in place.

As I recovered, so I became hungry, and our rations were very small. There was a clump of fruitless banana 'trees' behind the sergeants' hut, and there were dozens of huge pointed snails feeding on them. Pondering on the fact that we were getting no meat ration, I remembered that the French ate snails so I felt sure that these whelk-like creatures would be edible. I gathered a mess-tin half full, washed them and put them on to boil. As I tried to cook them so the water turned to very thick slime; in spite of changing the water several times I had to scrape each one in the end. A more unappetising dish would be hard to imagine; I tried to eat one and found it so tough that my teeth slipped off it. I swallowed some of them whole in rice until I retched, and then threw the remainder away.

Changi had now been a POW camp for four months. Becoming prisoner does not change a man's underlying nature, but rather accentuates it. By now the types who would have been layabouts or criminals had got together; gangs roamed the camp at night, stealing from their comrades, and they sold their swag to natives outside the camp perimeter. Therefore each regiment organized a guard to patrol the area at night to try to keep these vermin away. After serving my turn for the first time, and walking the camp all night without the protection of my mosquito net, I went down with a temperature of one-hundred and four degrees, and was told that I had dengue (pronounced 'dengi'), which is a mosquito carried disease. Although it can be severe, it usually only lasts for about ten days, and unlike most forms of malaria it is not recurrent.

As I recovered from the fever, I did some sketches of the camp. Unfortunately these were not easy to conceal from the Japs and I had to destroy them when we left Changi. I had only commenced writing my diary when we were captured, so I had no record of dates and events up to that time. Sgt Huey Moy had always kept a diary, and now let me borrow it. I was thus able to write up the course of events leading up to the fall of Singapore, adding my own comments while the events were still fresh in my mind. Huey later destroyed his diary, so I believe mine was the only one to survive.

In order to instil a competitive spirit, we again organized ourselves into platoons. We decided to run a platoon garden and our officers managed to obtain some vegetable seeds; I put Pte Naitin in charge and he took great pride in it. We grew what we called 'Singapore Spinach', a tasteless convolvulous-like plant, and sweet potato plants which never bore 'fruit' so we ate the leaves. None of the vegetables out there compared remotely with ours at home, such things as sprouts, cauliflowers and cabbages were unknown. I made a small garden outside our hut, transferring any pretty weeds I found into it. I also found a coconut by the sea which had commenced to grow, and this was given pride of place. It soon looked like a giant aspidistra.

Joe Viner was our Pioneer Sergeant and thus responsible for sanitary arrangements, together with any other job which came along from a collapsing cookhouse to a flooded hut. Weighing about twenty stone, he cruised through his duties like a battleship. He had been a stonemason in private life, and performed his duties well even though he ruled his domain with an iron rod. His command of language was rather limited, however, and much of his time as spent in giving serious replies to frivolous questions from mess-mates. Now and then Joe would 'tumble', and then woe betide the joker; although fat, Joe was as strong as a lion and had a very quick temper. He liked to talk ponderously, and to use long words; he also liked them to mean what he chose them to mean. Never admitting that he did not know a word's meaning it was very easy to pull his leg. 'Joe, have you decided the designation of the new latrine you're putting up for the officers?' 'They're plenty strong enough without that', and then with a roar 'Anyway, you look after your own qualifications and leave me to look after mine!' Joe's sayings were bywords throughout the regiment; 'Oose bin a-casting astertions about me?' 'They're a-dropping on em mates, they're them in-sanitary bombs'. Yet those who fought alongside Joe told us that he was steady as a rock and an inspiration to all those under him.

I found myself next to Joe in the mess, and he had developed bad ringworm, one of the curses of our existence during the coming years; being contagious I soon found that the complaint had spread to me. I saw Lionel our trusty medical sergeant, and he gave me a supply of sulphur and lime to rub in. Scraping the infected area with my open razor to allow the treatment to penetrate I applied the mixture, which although painful, soon cleared up the trouble. After that as soon as I found I had an attack, I always gave myself the same treatment, and thus remained clear until the end of our captivity. The lives of some of our boys were made a misery with this ringworm, as once it became well established it was very difficult to eradicate. In its advanced state huge red circles covered the body, overlapping one another. When one began to fade a fresh one would begin within the area, thus perpetuating the trouble. As they itched abominably it was usually not long before the constant scratching started the tropical ulcers which caused many amputations and deaths.

Since my boots were beginning to show signs of wear I

decided to make myself a pair of wooden sandals for about camp so that I could keep my boots for long marches. I was able to find some suitable wood, and carved the soles to fit the soles of my feet, nailing a piece of strap from my army equipment across to complete them. I soon became accustomed to wearing these and they served me well. It would of course have been easier to have gone barefoot, but our doctors had forbidden this owing to the scourge of hookworm. This parasite lurked in the dust until trodden on, when it bored through the sole of the foot and tunnelling through the leg it finally penetrated the intestines. Once there it was almost impossible to eradicate, and the disease was a major cause of debility and early death among the Malay and Tamil population.

A more pleasantly remembered member of the local fauna was the fire-fly. Although I did not see any from close up, I never tired of watching them on the trees during the dark evenings. In their myriads they would start to glow as darkness fell. Then as if by a word of command, they would all commence to flash in and out in unison. Neither were the nights quiet; although many of the noises were unidentifiable, crickets, lizards and frogs we knew. There were also great bats known as flying foxes. Luckily they did not suck blood but lived on fruit. Then we heard the cry of owls and other birds of prey but we seldom saw these. The most hateful sound of all was high pitched, the note of the accursed mosquito. Now many years later, I still cannot rest if I hear one in the room.

The Japs now decided to send all officers above the rank of colonel to Japan. Up until this time officers and men had all been in the same camps, although they slept and ate separately. According to the Geneva Convention they should have been in different camps. The Japs never signed the convention, but now evidently they had to go half-way by skimming off the Brigadiers and Generals whom they shipped off to Japan, where I believe they were well treated. On August the sixteenth therefore, we paraded to take farewell of all our top brass.

We were now allowed to organize an official canteen in the camp, and once or twice a week a party of officers went off to the local shops accompanied by a guard. A shopping party was at this time offered some ducklings by a Chinaman, so when they returned to camp a message was circulated to see whether any of us wished to take up the offer. I was the only one among our lot to take an interest, so ordered four, which was all that my meagre cash would run to. During the time which elapsed before the ducklings were to arrive I scoured the camp for materials with which to build my duck-run; wire netting trodden into the mud of the palm-grove, odd bits of attap and bamboo retrieved from a hut under repair before the cooks could get their hands on them; and with much pride I was able to survey my task, completed well in time. As there was usually little new to talk about, the news of my handywork soon passed from mouth to mouth around the camp, and a steady stream of visitors came along to see it.

The captain who had received a bullet wound in his neck when in my trench during the fighting now called to see my duck-run. 'That's far too big for your four' he said, 'I've ordered twenty-six and don't quite know what to do with them'. The offer he then made was so generous that I had a job to believe my ears. He said that if I would feed and look after all thirty ducklings, we would share equally the end products, eggs and fat ducks; needless to say I jumped at the opportunity. Shortly afterwards his batman arrived with a sack of poultry food which he had acquired. I had also gathered together a lot of potential fodder, including some limed rice which the cooks had found to be too bad for human consumption.

Our ducklings arrived on August the twenty-sixth, but when I went over to collect them I found that it was a part consignment of fifteen. I carried them back in a cardboard box and put them in their new home. That night I hardly slept, thinking about my dear little ducks, and planning their future! So exciting was it to have something constructive to do and some little lives dependent on me. The next day as I surveyed my small domain I saw that with fifteen more to come, my little flock would very quickly outgrow its accommodation; I had kept a few ducks back home and knew how quickly they grew, so I rebuilt the run, doubling the size of both it and the shed I had erected for their sleeping quarters. As I had not enough attap, this time I thatched it with grass. Four days later the other fifteen ducklings arrived and quickly settled in with the others. How different life now seemed with my little charges. I built my working day around them, and even dreamed about them at night. They were now my substitute family. To my friends and acquaintances I must have been behaving in a ridiculous way, and my leg was continuously being pulled. I had a job to hold back a tear on the third day when I found a little corpse in the run. One more disappeared during the 'Black Hole of Selarang' incident which is recorded later.

The captain who shared my ducks came round to look at them, and offered to purchase another twenty to share on the same basis; as those we had were doing so well, I naturally agreed. A few days later, while I was helping to rebuild some of the cookhouse fireplaces, my co-partner sent his batman down to collect six of the biggest ducks while my back was turned. I was very upset when someone came along to tell me of this flagrant breach of our fifty/fifty gentleman's agreement, but due to the difference in our ranks I was helpless as far as action was concerned.

Some of my ducks grew faster than others, and after a few more weeks twelve were twice as large as their brethren, and would soon be ready to eat if that were to be their destiny. I was, however, very fond of them, and began to worry over any plans my partner might have for their future. Then one evening when I had to leave our camp area, my run was robbed, the twelve were absent when I held roll-call. Very nearly broken-hearted I ran into the nearby sergeants' hut and asked if anyone had seen an intruder, and was told that my friend the captain had sent his batman round to take them while I was out of sight.

This time I stalked over to the officers' mess with 'murder' in my heart. The officers had more cash than they knew what to do with, as they received money from our captors, which in theory they were to repay when the war was over; so the arrangement whereby I did all the work and he provided most of the cash was really very fair. I found him sitting in his mess, and when I tackled him, staring up at the roof to avoid looking me in the eye, he blandly said he did not remember making any firm arrangement with me. Determined not to take this lying down, and knowing that in spite of his six feet odd that he was a coward, I told him in the loudest voice I could muster, of the kind of gentleman that I now considered him to be. To get rid of me before the other officers heard what was going on he said that he would return two of the ducks, and I had perforce to put up with that.

My remaining ducks grew and grew as I caught frogs and other creepy crawlies to chop up for them. As they became fledged they became too big for their run during the daytime, and I had to open it each morning before I went out to work, to let them forage for themselves, collecting them up again at nightfall. One night, after a busy day collecting firewood, I went straight into the sergeants' mess without first shutting my flock in their run, as a mess-meeting was being held. Suddenly a deluge dropped out of the sky, so heavy that I could only see a few yards from the window. I watched unheedingly for a minute or so before I remembered my ducks, and then I rushed out into the howling storm. There was already an inch or so of water covering the ground as I reached the run, but not one of my little charges was to be seen. A few yards away there ran an anti-malarial drain, and I remembered with horror that they had taken to swimming in this, so I made my way over to it as quickly as I could. No ducks were in sight, so I ran downstream until it disappeared underground into a culvert a hundred yards or so away. I arrived just in time to see the last of the little chaps vanish down the drain, and I never saw any of them again. I mourned my little flock, and even wished the captain had told his batman to take the lot; life seemed very empty for the next few days.

On the nineteenth of August all fit men were ordered to parade for a talk by a Jap General. It was our own adjutant who was in charge of us; his bullying tactics had endeared him to none of us, so it was with great pleasure that we heard him give the unheard of order to 'Right About Wheel' and spread ourselves unevenly over the parade ground until he was forced to call on our Warrant Officer to marshal us into order again. The General eventually arrived and having evidently learned the words by heart announced simply 'You are now under the rules of the Japanese Empire, and must obey all our rules'.

Ken Ireman was in charge of the cookhouse at this time, and being a friend of mine it was he who had given me the limey rice for the ducks. He had in private life been a carpet weaver, and during the evenings he took me through the long process of wool from the time it arrived at the factory in bales, to the beautiful end-product of either Axminster or Wilton. In after life I was therefore always to look at carpets with a more expert eye. We had really got to know one another when stationed in a small Scottish border town, during the year preceding our capture.

In the Commandos I had been taught the use of explosives, so when I returned to my regiment I had been appointed bomb disposal officer. Since we had no dummy two-inch mortar bombs with which to train my platoon at that time, I brought a 'dud' bomb back from the firing range where I had gone to blow up all the unexploded bombs. Sgt Ireman was the only other occupant of the sergeants' sleeping quarters that evening as I patiently and stupidly dug out the explosive and tried to ensure that the bomb was safe for my platoon to practise with. There was a blinding flash as I dropped the 'dud' on to the floor, and Ken who had been sitting on the next bed disappeared; the nearby toilet door was off its hinges and inside I saw Ken struggling to his feet. I tried to stand up but one leg was out of action, and as warm fluid poured down my leg I thought I had become incontinent; looking down I saw a pool of blood on the floor and realized for the first time that I had been hurt.

Hopping down that long first-floor room by holding on to the row of bed heads, I eventually reached the staircase, being passed on the way by Ken. I more or less slid down the stairs, and tried to hop across the parade ground to our medical room. Our medical sergeant Lionel and his assistant 'Skin' had heard the bang and seeing us struggling across had helped Ken and me over. Ken's main injury was a piece of shrapnel which had penetrated his knee joint. I had shrapnel in both legs, in my groin (that's still there), abdomen, nose and eyeball. The crotch had been completely torn out from my trousers as had also the under-arms of my tunic. In fact when they showed me my tattered clothes later it was incredible to think that no vital part of me had been hit; I had made a hole in the floor and one in the roof of the sergeants' hut, and one of the sergeants later gave me the tail of the bomb for a souvenir. He had picked it up where it fell after sailing skywards through the roof to over two hundred yards away.

We were both taken by ambulance to Peel House Hospital, Peebles, where we were operated on immediately. As it is necessary to grub up unexploded bombs carefully with the fingers, my nails were still full of mud. I remember so clearly coming out of the anaesthetic and finding a sweet little nurse cleaning my fingernails distastefully. Seeing that I had awakened, in her lovely singing Scottish Brogue she told me that she did not think much to boys who went around with dirty nails. I had never had a girlfriend and was too tongue-tied to tell her that my fingernails did not usually look like that. For the next few days my adoring eyes would follow her around the ward in silent devotion. The nurses were a lovely lot, and the ward sister came up to me and in a whisper asked me if I would like her to tell the sweet little nurse that I had fallen in love with her! Although I vehemently protested a 'no', the surreptitious glances I subsequently received let me know that I had been ignored.

Ken's bed was next to mine, and a picture of his beautiful wife was on the cupboard beside his bed. He would often talk of her, longing for the days to come when they could be together for ever. Those days never came. Ken died as a prisoner; be contracted diphtheria in Siam, and that was usually fatal there in those days. Together with Ken I was discharged within a few weeks, 'kept' through my first real danger, as I was to be through all that was to befall. When I returned home after the war ended I found out that my mother had prayed for me almost constantly, and that our little village church had prayed for me each week. I carried the New Testament which had been my church's parting, gift, right through until the end.

A few days after the Jap General's parade we heard that a Red Cross ship was discharging a cargo of supplies for us in Singapore, and for the next few days excitement ran high as we conjured up thoughts of 'lovely grub'. In the event at a grand share-out, we received nineteen sweeties apiece, and had to conclude that the Japs had helped themselves. It had been assumed that there would at least be plenty of cigarettes, so that it was perhaps the smokers who were most disappointed. I had given up smoking when I left River Valley.

By this time several hundred men had died from disease and malnutrition, also many had died from wounds received during battle. A cemetery had been made not far away from our regimental area, and a party of volunteers used to keep it tidy and planted with flowers. When one of our regiment died we would nearly all attend the funeral service. The cemetery was the one beautiful spot out there.

We had now been prisoners for six months, and we seemed to be getting more and more parades and general 'bull'. Far more indeed than were the other regiments who surrounded us, and our men were becoming restive and uncooperative. They sent a delegation to the sergeants' mess asking for a complaint to be passed on to our Commanding Officer. The mess held a meeting and we came to the conclusion that the complaint was justified, but how to bring it to the CO's attention? There were no volunteers, so lots were cast. (I subsequently discovered that the operation was rigged, as I was thought the only one naîve enough to undertake the 'impossible' mission.) I was apprehensive, and pointing out that I was one of the youngest there tried to pass the job on to one of the older ones, but without success. As a sergeant is not allowed to approach his CO directly, even as POW, I had first to see the duty officer, Capt Skinner. He asked me what I wanted to see the CO about and told me I was wasting my time. However, when I insisted, he did see the Old Man, who refused even to grant me an interview.

Life in Changi was at this time a long battle between the rank and file and our senior officers. The latter were determined not to let the men under them become undisciplined with all that that entailed. The men for their part, thought that now they were prisoners, if the Japs were prepared to leave them alone why could not our own officers? There was of course much to be said from both points of view, the difficulty was striking the happy medium. The CO contended that the slightest relaxation in discipline would produce a snowball effect. Once a hold over the men had been lost, it would be almost impossible to regain.

Now the CO decided that we must be prepared to help our army when they landed to release us. We organized ourselves into cadres for unarmed combat, and I was one of the instructors. Our unpopular adjutant originated from Canada and considered himself a tough guy. He decided to join my cadre and demonstrate on me what to do to the Japs. I had the very great satisfaction of demonstrating in front of the men how little he knew about unarmed combat. It was the only chance I was ever to have of throwing an officer into the crowd, and all quite legitimate! We made ourselves lances and bows and arrows, all from bamboo, to be ready when 'D'-Day arrived.

Then one of the officers ran a tactics cadre for senior NCOs and when he asked for a volunteer to climb a palm-tree and strap himself in (as we knew the Japs had done), I of course spoke up. Since my first palm climbing exploit, I had practised quite a bit, so now I was able to reach the top without too much trouble. As I tried to settle myself into a comfortable position, I suddenly found every square inch of my body covered with stinging ants. They were even in my eyes, and I almost fell the thirty feet as I tried to scramble down with my eyes nearly closed. When I eventually found my way down the tree and into the nearest water I was completely covered with stings and took several days to recover. I wondered afterwards, whether these ants walk all the way up those long branchless trunks, or if the nest is started while the tree is small, and leads a self sufficient existence as the tree grows.

Chapter 4

'And yet for a time, O lord,
You have tossed us aside in dishonour,
And not helped us in our battles.'

Changi was quite unlike any other camp in which we were to be kept. Firstly this was to be the only place where we were allowed to run our own affairs with little interference from our captors. Conditions were incomparably better than we ever again experienced. When Singapore fell the Japs could have had very few troops to spare to guard the forty or fifty thousand prisoners they had found themselves landed with, so the main body of them was put into this corner of the island and left more or less to fend for itself. The shoreward perimeter was thinly guarded by Sikhs and Japs, but seaward needed no guarding.

On the thirty-first of August, for some strange reason the Japs issued us with forms to sign, declaring upon our honour, that we would not attempt to escape. It is the duty of every member of the British armed forces, if taken prisoner, to attempt to escape at the first opportunity, so there was a hundred per cent refusal to sign. I was in the middle of making a swimming pool for my ducklings the next day when we were ordered at short notice to parade on the 'padang' as our sports field was called. Japs arrived, and spent all morning counting us, and we were dismissed none the wiser as to the point of the operation. We found out the next day, when we were ordered to parade with our kit, cooking utensils, tools, rations and all the battalion equipment. No exceptions were made in our lines, so sick men had to parade also. As the hospital was not to be evacuated, however, I managed to get a message to good old Dr Barber to ask him to feed my ducks while we were away.

The camp gear and sick in need of help were shared out among us, and for once we were marched off without the usual delay. The destination proved to be Selarang, a peace-time military barracks. Although only two miles off we had a job to make it without jettisoning some of our loads, as the Japs drove us at a fast rate with no rests.

When we arrived we found the buildings already occupied by Australian troops. Fifteen thousand of us were however, driven through the gates. The site was about two hundred by three hundred yards. The multiple storey barrack block was in the centre, and a hard road ran round the perimeter of the area. The Japs told us that any man setting foot on this road would be shot instantly, and the machine guns which they set up all round us reinforced their words. As our leaders tried to find enough room for us all another three thousand prisoners turned up from somewhere, and these had also to be accommodated. It was announced that we were here as punishment for not signing the non-escape document; we were to stay until we did sign it.

The officers cast lots for positions, and our brigade was lucky in getting the top floor of the barrack block; the majority were allocated space on the ground outside. The Japs told us that they would issue a pint of water per man per day, but no food. There was no water at all in the pipes, so no toilets could be used. Now the retention of discipline and organisation became manifest as work parties were formed and quickly started digging through the hard tarmac of the barrack square to make a row of latrine trenches. We worked like mad, knowing that if we did not get done quickly, dysentery would spread through the crowd like wildfire; within a few hours the first row was ready, and in continuous use. Our building was so full that even the stairs were occupied, and it took a quarter of an hour to reach the latrines from our floor. Our dysentery cases had therefore to remain down below.

As usual, I started to explore, and soon saw a trap-door in the ceiling, and by persuading a few comrades to form a human pyramid, I climbed up, opened the door and climbed out on to the roof. There were some old charpoys up there, so I took the string mattress off one and made a crude rope ladder out of it, and was soon joined by half a dozen friends. I rigged up a tent by fixing my gas cape up over one of the best of the charpoys, so was probably the best accommodated of us all. As it came on to rain I managed to squeeze a couple in beside me but the others sat around holding odd pieces of material over their heads to try to keep out the worst of the wet. The word of my discovery spread around, and there were soon a couple of hundred men up there with us, preferring the wet to the foetid conditions below.

The next day we were again given an opportunity to sign the form, but all refused once more. The Japs had decided to starve us out, but they did not know that our officers had retained a reserve of food for just such an occasion as this. We broke up doors and cupboards for firewood, and our cooks provided food. We were far from starving and for once appreciated what our officers had done for us. By nightfall of that second day however there were forty fresh cases of dysentery reported and two of diphtheria. We had no facilities for treating them whatsoever. Two men had died during the day, and when we asked the guards for permission to bury them outside the wire we were curtly refused. Delay would have caused those diseased bodies to decay very quickly, so we at once commenced to dig up the parade ground again to bury them before their germs spread any further.

From up on the roof next day we could see that the enemy were guarding us in their hundreds, Sikhs and Japs. It seemed pretty clear that they were regarding this operation very seriously, and intended keeping us there until we either signed or died. The Jap commander now sent round a message that the hospital, wounded and isolation cases included, would be evacuated on the morrow, and that we would have to find room for them in with us. The screw was to be tightened even further. Nearly a hundred new cases of dysentery developed as the day wore on, and several of suspected diphtheria. Many of the bad cases were unable to reach the toilet in time, and the barracks were beginning to become nearly as bad as the tennis court in those earlier days. That evening our top brass held an emergency meeting to decide whether they could be justified in holding out any longer. The consequences of bringing the wounded and infectious into our crowded camp were no doubt discussed, together with the moral implications of virtually condemning thousands of us to death to try to maintain our honour. They came to the only conclusion possible and issued the order to sign.

However, we found a way to sign and still to keep our options open; splitting up into pairs, each man signed his partner's name and thus the Japs were satisfied and we could still feel free to escape when the opportunity came alone.

Early next morning we paraded to return to Changi. The Japs allowed us to make several journeys this time, and as the resident Selarang Aussies lent us a handcart we had a very much easier trip. On our return it was announced that any of us on high ground from which the sea could be seen were to move into Selarang, and although this only affected third corps, we helped them with the move. Much speculation arose as to why this was found to be necessary, and some of us surmised that perhaps the Japs thought that submarines might surface at night and signal to us.

Our shopping party had by now purchased some sports equipment including a football. On the fifth day after our return from Selarang I watched our football team defeated three goals to two by the Suffolks.

A rugger ball had also appeared from somewhere, and I was invited to play for the regiment; after a few practice games we turned out for our first match. Then the CO asked me to take charge of the battalion rugger team, which I was very pleased to do. We had no ball of our own, so we had to hold scrum practice etc., with a bundle of rags. However, the CO promised to ask the shopping party to try to find us a ball, and a week later I received a message to the effect that I could collect one from the officers' mess. Unfortunately, there was a puncture in the bladder; having no puncture outfit I tried latex gathered from a local rubber tree, but this would not work as something is evidently added to it before it can be used. We never did get our ball repaired.

Then came a week's notice of another regimental move.

This time we were to go across the road beside an old railway crossing, not far from the cemetery. By now we had made our quarters fairly comfortable and were sorry to have to move again.

On the morning of the twentieth of September, we never heard why, the Japs paraded us to be weighed and measured. Some thought they were going to put us on a ship for Japan, and wanted to know how many the ship would hold! Two days later we moved into our new quarters. I spent the first morning paving the mess floor with some slabs we found in a derelict building. In the evening we went to the camp concert as our turn had come round, and we saw an excellent performance of 'I Killed the Count'.

Sport began to take an important part in our lives at this point, especially sports which did not need specialized equipment. Any with special skills were encouraged to lead the different groups. Someone persuaded me against my better judgement, to turn out for hurdling; however my short legs were not made for leaping, and I was not asked again as I caused too many repair jobs on the home-made bamboo hurdles.

Until now I had no close friend or 'mucker' in the mess, but on September the twenty-sixth it was announced on our battalion orders notice board that Cpl (Jimmy) Hame had been promoted to acting Lance Sergeant. Many of our Senior NCOs had been lost during the fighting, and it was felt that there were now insufficient to maintain the high standard of discipline that the Old Man required. Several other acting appointments were also made at this time. Jimmy was just about the best all-round sportsman in the regiment, a beautiful footballer, one of our best cricketers, and back home a good billiards player. I was neither good at nor interested in any of these games, yet he and I struck up a friendship, sharing all we had until separated by sickness in Siam, when Jimmy was sent off by ship to Japan.

We contracted many strange diseases as prisoners, and as we did not know the correct name for them they were all designated 'Changi' something or other. We had everything from 'Changi Ear' to 'Changi' unmentionables. I now contracted 'Changi Ear' which consisted of little boils right inside, and until they burst a week or so later they were very painful.

On the ninth of October as I was returning from the sea with salt water for our cooks, the news that there was another Red Cross ship in Singapore harbour was bruited abroad; it was said that we really were going to get a fair share of the loot this time. Two days later it materialized, sugar, ghee, lentils, jam, biscuits, bully beef, tinned meat and vegetable stew and condensed milk. We held a meeting in the mess to decide whether to issue out the tins individually or to give them to the cooks to improve our general rations. In the end we decided to issue all the tinned milk individually, together with half the sugar and biscuits. The remainder went to the cookhouse. Our sergeants' meals now became comparatively good, although I noticed that the men's food did not show much sign of improvement. Although we always drew the same rations as the men in Changi, the difference in the end product was often surprising. The cooks in the huge men's cookhouse seemed unable to take the same pride and trouble over the food as did ours, cooking for only a couple of dozen. Also much of the food often seemed to 'evaporate' before it reached the plate, and that was why there were so many calls for change of staff. Apart from a few weeks in Chunkai, Changi was the only camp where sergeants messed separately.

Up to the present I had written up my diary in pencil each day, as although I had a pen, I had no ink. Now I found an indelible pencil, thrown away because it had split in halves. Dissolving the core of this in water to make myself a bottle of ink, I re-wrote everything with my pen, and carried on with it until we reached Chunkai in Thailand.

Apart from lectures on my special subject of weapon-training, before capture I had never given talks on any subject. Now however I began to speak regularly to groups in the sick-bay, to help them pass away the time. I found, to my surprise, that I seemed to be able to find plenty to say about almost anything, whether familiar with the subject or not, filling the many gaps in my knowledge with conjecture. My audience did not seem to mind and I found myself much in demand. Among other subjects I remember lecturing on socialism, evolution, building, religion and my experiences in the Independent Companies, (which later became known as Commandos.) Things were so dull and monotonous for the sick, lying in their hut all day, that it did not take a great deal to entertain them.

I personally found life a bit more bearable now that I had a 'mucker', and it was also convenient while the Red Cross food lasted to open one tin between the two of us since food only kept a few hours once opened. Jimmy was of a quiet and steady temperament. I believe that I am rather of the 'scratch and claw' type, a bit impatient and sometimes prone to fly off the handle when things do not go quite as I think they should. Jimmy put up with me very well. Although our friendship really began with expediency we soon became firm friends. Ever since I found the Dunlopillo from inside the vehicle seat at River Valley, I had slept on this, far more comfortably than most of the other men. As it was thicker than I really needed, I split it into two thinner pieces and we slept on half each. Jimmy gave me half his blanket as I only had a sack up until then, and we pooled our cash, taking it in turns to hold the purse. He was to prove a great source of strength to me during the months to come.

Our guards now blithely informed us that they were going to cease feeding us and that we were to grow our own food. As I had more experience of working under the Japs than most of the other NCOs I was given a ten-man gardening party, and reported to the guardhouse with them. Moving off in the pouring rain, we were first taken into the vicinity of Changi gaol where Sikhs were guarding civilian prisoners, there to be issued with chunkels, axes, shovels and machetes. Chunkels were to become familiar tools; as the workers out there do not wear shoes they cannot use spades. The chunkel is a kind of heavy hoe with a blade the size of a spade; it is used in the manner of a pick-axe, for digging. The area where we were told to make our garden was behind the gaol. It comprised eighty acres of rubber plantation; the Japs told us to start work and sat down to watch us. Needless to say that by the time the end of the day came not much impression had been made. With the native tools it had taken all our time to fell three of the large rubber trees and to dig the roots out. Again we found that the water table was only just below the surface, and wondered how vegetables would grow in the mud even if we did eventually manage to remove all the trees.

Returning from our gardening party we found that fresh rumours were circulating; this time it was said that parties were about to be sent overseas. Although none did in fact go while I was there, it was not to be long before some left for Thailand never to return to Changi; and half of us were to remain, buried there. It was this night that my ducks, as mentioned earlier on, disappeared down into the culvert.

I had just about rigged up my new quarters satisfactorily when I was ordered out of them to make room for a Regimental Sergeant-Major (RSM) who was to join us from the Gordons. I had to move out to share a tent with two others. When he arrived he proved to be an old soldier of the spit and polish type, six feet three, and complete with waxed moustache; in fact a typical regular army 'Sarmajor'. I hoped he was uncomfortable on the bed I had only just completed from scraps gathered from the various rubbish heaps. It transpired that the Old Man had arranged for this chap to be transferred to us to try to tighten our discipline even further. In time I was able to see through the 'bull' to the very sound man underneath it all.

We were now told officially that a party of thirty men from our regiment together with all the remainder of the Recce battalion, were to leave Changi in a week's time for an unknown destination. I was to be one of the party, and we were to take a share of the cooks, pioneers and medics. Our new RSM called all the NCOs together for a pep talk. No-one could tell where we would finish up he said, but wherever it was, it was in the opinion of our officers likely to be very tough going. For this reason we would need to hold the men on a very tight rein, as without a very high standard of discipline, under adverse conditions they would quickly descend into a rabble, and the devil take the hindmost. We spent the next three days cleaning the camp we were shortly to vacate, lest any who came to fill our places should think us a dirty lot.

There was a general feeling of apprehension among us as we could not help worrying in anticipation over the devil we did not know. Bad though that 'devil' was to prove, I was always given the strength to face him. Now when I find a friend worried about the future I am able to say from experience that, when the terrible thing you fear comes about it can never prove quite as bad as you thought it would be. Just trust, and you will overcome. A month ago we had talked of how fed up with Changi we were. Now as we looked around, about to leave for the unknown, it was 'dear old Changi'!

I now had to prepare for leaving, first of all ensuring that my socks, shirts and underclothes were well darned. I had three shirts so I let Ken have one, since his only one was nearly worn out. Since being taken prisoner I had scarcely been out on a working party without gathering another item of junk, and I really had an enormous heap now, so I went through it carefully sorting out all the essential stuff, and making a separate pile of the remainder. I finished up with a very small heap of rejects and about threequarters of a hundredweight of 'musts'; and we had already been told that we were only to be allowed to take kit which we could carry on our own persons, and hands must be kept free to take our communal items.

Five days before we were to leave we practised packing up our kit, to make sure that no-one took so much of his own stuff that our cooking dixies etc. got left behind. Although I cannot remember all I had at that time, I certainly had the following: bucket, four gallon petrol tin, Dunlopillo seat, two shirts, two pairs of shorts, one pair long trousers, sheet, half blanket, three sacks, a bag of 'buckshee rice', water bottle, wire, rope, half a dozen books, New Testament, mosquito net, cooking tins, mug, mess tin, piece of canvas, ground sheet, gas cape, respirator haversack, full set of army equipment – complete with Bren gun ammo pouches, bundle of rags, bundle of paper, soap (which I had exchanged for Red Cross cigarettes), three enamel plates, and finally my bag of odds and ends, which included sharpening stone, old hacksaw blades and other items with which I hoped to form the nucleus of a tool kit.

I filled all my haversacks and pouches, and tied all the big things on to my belt. When I stood up I must have looked something like a Christmas tree, but I was able to walk with my hands free as specified. Each regiment has a 'President of the Regimental Institute's fund, known as the PRI. It is used for assisting needy cases and as a reserve for cash for special occasions. The CO allocated us with a proportion of the cash in this fund and I was sent off with an officer to spend the whole twenty-one dollars on smokes. These would be light to carry, and non-smokers would be able to exchange their share for other things.

Early in the morning, on the second of November, nineteen forty-two, we were called out on parade ready for our journey into the great unknown. Friends helped me to my feet; we had been issued with four or five tins of food each, company reserve to be handed in on reaching our destination, and they were to me the straws that nearly broke the camel's back. I stood on the parade ground (which had been a gun park), wearing my double-crowned Aussie hat, long shorts, and strung around with bucket, tins and all my other rubbish. I must have looked a strange sight and many were the cracks from the friends who gathered to bid us farewell.

Nine months earlier we had been captured, and we had reached the end of the first phase of our captivity. Up until now we had been able to live fairly civilized lives, running our own affairs, and with order and a degree of cleanliness prevailing at least most of the time. We were about to leave all these good things behind us. For the next three years they were to be exchanged for a world of chaos, filth, blows and disease. That was to be the general state of things under the direct rule of The Imperial Japanese Army. Farewell Changi; little had we thought to carry away a fond memory of you into the future.

Although we paraded with our kit early in the morning, it was five o'clock in the afternoon before we left for Singapore railway station. For a wonder, the Japs sent lorries for us this time, so that journey at least was painless.

Chapter 5

'Weeping we sat beside the waters of Babylon,
Thinking of Jerusalem.'

The railway, narrow gauge, had been built by the British of course; so also had the all-steel cattle trucks with no windows, and sliding doors that we found awaiting us in the station. What was to come would be our first insight into the way the Japs were to organize our lives in the future.

Those trucks had probably been made to carry at most half a dozen head of cattle, but not out in that climate. Cattle would have quickly died of heat-stroke if shut in them without ventilation in the tropical sun.

The Japs pushed thirty-two men into each truck together with all their belongings. I naturally received dirty looks from those who were crushed in with me. The walking Christmas tree took up room enough for two men. Before we finished our sojourn up country many were glad to have me with them, the only one with scissors and razor for haircuts and shaves, and tools to do the jobs about camp. Not only was there no room to lie in there, it was necessary to sit with knees under chin. I stacked my three-quarters of a hundredweight of kit in a corner and sat on top of it, so took up no more room than the others. My bucket and tin were to be the most useful articles in the truck before we completed that journey.

We heard the safety-valve on the locomotive blow, and knew she had steam up. Our guards came along and closed the doors, padlocking them from the outside. Our wildest fears had not included the possibility of travelling nearly airtight through the heat of Malaya; the temperature must have been about a hundred and twenty in there with the doors open, who would be able to survive now? But the Japs were taking no risks; with hundreds of miles of jungle to traverse, and many stops on the way in unscheduled places to build up steam, they were more concerned with avoiding escapes than deaths from heat-stroke.

The journey up country was to take three and a half days, but the hellish nightmare that it was seemed to last for weeks. I never went through a worse time during my whole captivity. The train always ran slowly, halting before climbing any gradient to get up steam. This was due to the fact that wood was being burnt instead of coal, and wood produces far less heat than coal in a furnace. The track had received no maintenance since the fall of Singapore, so in the hard-floored, springless trucks we were hurled from side to side like peas shaken in a box.

Sometimes, for no reason that we knew of, we would stop for hours on end, doors closed, gasping for breath in the fearful heat generated by the Malayan sun beating down on the galvanised roof and sides of the cattle truck.

Once a day we would pull into a station and the doors would open. One bucket of cold cooked rice and one bucket of water were placed against the door of each truck, and we were given only five minutes to fill our water bottles, share out the rice, go to the toilet and climb back into the high trucks. With the perspiration we were losing we needed a dozen times the water we got, and we had to use almost superhuman willpower and make our bottles last for twenty-four hours by taking tiny sips every half hour or so, just sufficient to keep our mouths moist. The only certain memory to remain was of one long continuous thirst. Those without the willpower to eke out their water, suffered even more.

Although we lost sense of time as our heads went round in the heat, one incident on the second day left an indelible mark on my mind. Dawn was breaking, and its first grey thews came in through cracks in the door. Otherwise all was quite black within our truck. As we negotiated a curve in the track I saw the light fall on one strained face after another; sleepless night was about to be followed by foetid day. The track straightened out once more, and the ray of light fell on the face of Private McGuire as he sat opposite me in the darkness. His eyes were open and unseen from my dark corner I saw tears running down his cheeks. I felt that I could read his thoughts as well as look into his face from my vantage point. He was about twenty, and a sincere and ardent communist. I imagined what he was thinking as he tried to relate his belief in the universal brotherhood of man and the dignity of the worker, with our present condition. He was never fully to recover in mind or body from our journey, and he did not have to work very long in Thailand before entering upon that last and greatest journey, when all is revealed, and we can discover that there can be no brotherhood of man without a Father.

Half of our number developed dysentery during that second day, and my bucket and tin came into their own. The other trucks held men in a very much worse state. I was in charge of our truck, and had great difficulty in restraining our boys from eating the tins of food which had been issued for us to carry on behalf of the whole party. Nevertheless, it says much for them that none were eaten in our group.

We caught glimpses through cracks, of the country through which we were travelling, and there seemed to be dense jungle most of the way. There were a few clearings occupied by a 'Kampong' or native hamlet, and at least one town, namely Kuala Lumpur. We also passed a few lakes, where prosperous tin companies had dredged for the richest deposits of alluvial tin in the world. The plant we saw all stood idle. As we moved through the territory we never knew when we actually crossed the border into Siam, or Thailand as the inhabitants call it. That word means 'Land of Freedom', but it was not to mean that for us.

No evil is allowed to last for ever; thus even that journey had to end, and at six-thirty on the morning of the sixth of November our train finally stopped at a small station, and we were allowed out of our dreadful trucks for good.

Two very scruffy Japs lined us up, counted us and then marched us off along a dirt track. One soldier brought up the rear, the other marched at the head of the column with me. He plied me with questions the whole route, wanting to know the names of every part of the female body in order that he might not be at a loss for words if he were lucky enough to be part of the army of occupation when England fell. He did not seem to think that time was far off either. Needless to say he got no straight answers.

We knew not where we were, but as the nameboard at the railway station was written in a script that was new to us, we knew at least that we must be in Thailand. Now, however, we arrived at a camp, comprised of rows of long attap and bamboo huts, an empty one of which was allocated to us, and I gratefully unloaded my kit on the floor and sank down on to the sleeping platform with much relief.

There were a lot of other prisoners in the camp, and they told us that it was called 'Banpong'. It was a staging camp, from which parties were constantly being sent to work on a railway, which we were told was gradually progressing further and further into the inhospitable hinterland. Forced native labour was being used in constructing some stretches of the track, the remainder was being built by POWs. The line would eventually run from Bangkok, through Thailand into Burma, to Moulmein.

Banpong initiated us into the state of things that prevailed in many places from now on. It had been for long occupied by men who had ceased to care. Our hut was absolutely filthy, littered by rubbish, scraps of food, and even excreta; all because no-one had enough authority to organize a party to clean things up. We were now in a different climate from Singapore, and in the monsoon season. It had been raining for weeks, almost without ceasing, and except for a few high spots, everywhere was ankle-deep in mud.

I was one of the youngest and 'greenest' of the senior NCOs, and often felt that I was given the worst jobs because I was less likely to complain than older soldiers, many of whom deeply resented the intrustion of our new RSM. When therefore he gave me the task of cleaning up our hut and its surroundings, without tools and with a gang of browned-off men who had only just emerged from those deadly cattle trucks, my heart sank within me. However, all bad things come to an end as I have said before, and although far from co-operative, none of my men actually refused to do what I asked, so at last our area was made fairly clean and I was allowed to take my men over to the camp well to draw water, to wash for the first time for four days. At the well it was a case of no bucket no water, so once again as the only one apart from our cooks with a bucket, our boys were pleased to have me with them.

There was a long queue of men waiting at the well as it had to supply the requirements of the whole camp, which was quite a big one. It was, incidentally, one of the few Thai camps that was not adjacent to the river. While awaiting my turn I heard someone swearing over losing his bucket down the well the previous day, and this set me thinking. Our cooks were very short of buckets and if this chap had not retrieved his, it was likely that there were others down there. Arriving at the well-head, I peered in; the water was about twenty feet down, but it would of course be deep as we were in the middle of the monsoon. Also there were no steps in the walls. However, I noticed that there were grooves every eighteen inches or so where the concrete rings, from which the well was constructed, met and did not fit very well. I whipped my clothes off, and telling my men to stand guard and let no-one drop anything down I started to descend. The well was about thirty inches in diameter, and by inserting fingers and toes in the grooves I finally reached the water. I could not feel anything with my feet, so I propelled myself downwards by pressing outwards and upwards with my hands. It must have been at least twenty feet deep, and by the time my feet encountered a heap of tinware I was seeing flashes of light and my chest was bursting. Hooking one foot under a pail handle, assisted by my hands I shot to the surface like a bubble, and gasped in the fresh air.

Thai wells are not equipped with rope and winch like those at home. Instead a long bamboo pole is suspended down to the water, the top end being hinged to the end of a see-saw like arrangement. The see-saw fulcrum was a long way out of centre, and it was the long end that was fixed to the pole. On the short end there was a heavy weight attached; by lifting the short end of the see-saw only a few feet, the pole descended the whole depth of the well, and the counterbalancing weight lifted the bucket full of water very quickly and easily to ground level. Although it took up a lot of room, it seemed much more efficient than our traditional way of doing the job. I therefore hooked my salvaged bucket to the suspended pole to be retrieved by my friends at the top. I was able to repeat my dive six times before lack of breath made me give up, and this provided a good heap of buckets for the quartermaster. I also found a canvas bucket, and as I thought that this would 'come in handy' I kept that, until it was stolen by a marauding thief during the night a few weeks later.

That night men came in from other huts, and told us more of the way things were going up there, and what they told us was not very encouraging. Banpong was the first real POW camp connected with the new stretch of the railway, work on which we were told had commenced some months previously. It followed more or less the course of the Menam river as it descended from the hills which separate Thailand from Burma. The embankments and cuttings were being cut through thick jungle, and all by hand without mechanical equipment of any kind. A camp was constructed every few kilometres along the proposed course; as a stretch of line was completed the gang from that camp would have to march off, leapfrogging other gangs, to arrive at a new camp site, and start work on a new task.

In peace time thousands of Tamils had been recruited from Southern India to work on the rubber plantations and tin excavations in Malaya. The Japs had conscripted these and some camps were manned by them. They were a poor undernourished people, and it was said that they did not live very long in Jap camps.

Other camps were manned by conscripted Chinese coolies, and as even the Japs could not make these men work without their opium, they received a weekly ration of it. Remaining camps were manned by POWs, including many from Java and Sumatra of Dutch nationality, and mostly of half native blood. We were told that news filtered through occasionally from up country, and it seemed that thousands had already died up there. The dirty conditions in Banpong camp itself were mainly due to the fact that the men consisted of odds and ends from different units, who therefore retained no regimental pride or discipline.

All the tinned rations entrusted to us were called in, and it was found that nearly a quarter of the men had eaten some or all of theirs on the train journey, and since the NCOs with them had eaten theirs also, there was very little that could be done about it other than give reprimands which were easily shrugged off. There was an air of righteous indignation among my men as they saw the baddies get away with their crime.

On our third day in Banpong we were told to pack our kit and parade for another move; at eight-fifteen a.m. we were all lined up ready to go, but not the Japs; we waited there until half past three in the afternoon before they turned up to march us to a row of trucks parked some way along the road. Some trucks! Each one seemed to be made out of two or three relics from the first world war; most surprising of all, they ran on wood, petrol being unobtainable. Beside the driver stood a huge vertical cylinder surmounted by a chimney, (or was it a funnel?). At the bottom was a fire-door behind which red-hot charcoal glowed. The main part of the cylinder was filled with firewood, and it was this that gave off the gas as it was being roasted. This gas was fed into the intake manifold, taking the place of petrol. The amazing thing about the Heath Robinson affair was that it worked!

The drivers were Thais, and this was our first experience of that hardy and independent race. As we moved off, engines coughing and spluttering, men had to crowd on every available ledge, even on the cab roof. Couldn't get another one on we thought, but quite wrongly. As our truck gathered speed four Thais appeared as if by magic, and leapt in among us, unseen by our guards; not unseen by our driver though, as with a skid he pulled up and hurled a stream of invective at the stowaways, who turned not a hair. At four-to-one our driver eventually gave up the struggle, and resignedly mounted his steed; with skill approaching that of the Mahouts we were later to see with their elephants, he coaxed it along in pursuit of the others, who we caught up at the start of the incline, where they were stoking up to provide extra gas for the climb.

After two hours of stopping and starting this strange journey came to an end at another camp which looked similar to Banpong. We were told not to unpack as we should only be staying one night, so we dropped off the truck and put our stuff in an empty hut before looking around. One of the 'locals' told us that we were at Kanburi, another transit camp with a permanent staff of cooks to provide rice for men passing through on their way up country. I could see the river from this camp for the first time, it was about as wide as the Thames at Hammersmith. We were provided with a meal of rice at nightfall and another one at daybreak, after which, at seven-fifty, we were paraded again, to embark on wooden native boats and cross the Mekong for the first time. For many it was to be the last time also.

These big boats were fuelled by paraffin, the engine having one big cylinder. To start them a blow lamp was played on the manifold and cylinder head, and the heavy flywheel was rocked to and fro until the engine fired. Once away the loud 'poof poof' could sometimes be heard miles away.

We assembled on the far bank, and our guards marched us off into jungle that came down nearly to the water's edge. The flora consisted of huge clumps of prickly bamboo, a kind of fruitless wild banana, great teak-type trees and endless creepers trailing from nearly everything; it was to become very familiar as we cleared thousands of acres to make way for our railroad track.

The land soon began to rise, and jungle gave way to paddy fields in about two miles. These are places where the rice is grown. Each field is only about thirty feet square and is surrounded by an earth wall to retain the water; from a distance they look like steps up the hill. In five miles or so the guards told us that we were nearing our destination, and in front of us we saw a big camp laid out beside the river which had meandered back to meet us. Our guards made us understand that we were to remain here and help to complete this section of the railway track.

They led us to our bamboo hut, and we saw that each one was about a hundred yards long and comprised raised floor covered with split bamboo, no walls, and overhanging attap roof. At intervals of sixteen feet bamboo poles rose out of the floor to support the roof, and these divided the huts into bays. The raised floors or stagings were divided by a pathway on the earth floor which ran the length of the hut. Each staging was about six feet wide. These huts became very familiar as they were standard accommodation in nearly every camp. Eight men were ordered into each bay, allowing two feet for housing both body and kit.

As we tried to settle in men from the next hut wandered in to see if we had brought any 'griff'. We learned that these chaps had already been there for several months, and that the camp was called 'Chunkai'. Working parties went out to the railroad each day they said, to build embankments. They were badly treated and beaten up if they did not work hard enough. We however were allowed to stay in camp for two days, building a cookhouse, latrine, and doing other camp jobs.

Then on the thirteenth of November, our third day in Chunkai, we paraded soon after dawn for our first day's work on the now infamous railway. An English officer in the camp warned us to work at a reasonable speed, without trying to hurry. If we completed our measured task too early, then the next day both ours and everyone else's would be increased. Should the Japs think we were deliberately on a 'go-slow' on the other hand, we would be punished. 'Try therefore to find a happy medium', he concluded.

Arriving at our appointed place along the line of the projected embankment, we found our gang was to build a thirty foot long stretch, averaging six feet high. The earth it was explained was to be excavated from between the trees each side of our task, and trod firmly down after being tipped in the right place. The tools were then issued out, and consisted of long-handled pointed spades-cum-shovels, with flat wicker baskets in which we were to carry the earth. We could see other gangs of prisoners working on the next strips. Our Jap could speak a few words of English, and benignly explained that our work for the day had been carefully calculated; he assured us that its cubic capacity was in correct relation to the number of men in our gang. 'Finish your task and you can return to camp, even if it is before midday', he continued, 'all men then have rest of day Yasumi'.

We surveyed the huge stretch of emptiness between the profiles and knowing smiles passed between us. He's surely potty, no-one could do all that work by hand in one day we thought.

Starting work, we decided to 'test the climate' and worked at a fairly steady pace. The heap of earth that was the embryo embankment began to grow, but painfully slowly. If anyone actually came to a full stop, the guard would yell 'Courra!' and run over and cuff the offender, otherwise we were getting away with our half-hearted effort, or so we thought. By midday, when we stopped for half an hour to eat the cold rice we had carried with us, we had perhaps completed a quarter of the day's work. After that the demeanour of our guards changed as they weighed up the situation and concluded that we were 'swinging the lead'. More and more blows began to fall from the heavy sticks they carried. 'Courra, Engerissoo soljah no-good!' they shouted. We thought that it was better to have a few blows today and to let the Japs see that we were not going to tear about in the hot sun, better for the future to suffer a little today. We felt sure that all this shouting and cuffing was just a try-on.

Come five o'clock, and we had completed about half the day's task. That meant that we had worked just about half as fast as the Japs wanted, and as it would be dark in an hour or so their bluff had been called. You can't beat the good old British Tommy into submission we thought. The Japs ate at about six o'clock, we'd soon be off back to camp now, so even less work was done for the next hour. A couple of fellows stopped work for a try-on; one of the guards walked over to find out why. 'No can see' said one, pointing first to his eye and then to the heap. 'No see' repeated the Jap, and turning to the rest of us.'Othar soljah no see-ca?' he asked innocently. 'No see' we chorused as with one voice. 'Oroo men yasume' he ordered. (Japanese are unable to pronounce our 'L' so they say 'Roo'). As we sat down it started to rain. With only half our task completed, we had won, but why were we sitting out here instead of going back to camp? Our only drink all day had been the water we had brought in our bottles from camp, and we were now thirsty as well as dirty and hungry. Two guards had left for camp already, but the remaining two put on their capes and seemed resigned to spending the rest of the night out there with us.

At about six-thirty we were surprised to see the two guards returning, struggling with some heavy equipment which they dumped on the ground. All four Japs started to erect some sort of tripod so I walked over to see what they were doing. Catching a whiff of acetylene as I approached I stopped in my tracks as the truth dawned. Lights! Within ten minutes two powerful flood-lights illuminated the whole site, and without any order from our enemy, despair in our hearts, we drifted back to work in the rain. The guards found themselves comfortable spots under the trees and settled down, clearly for the night if necessary. And so we started to *work*, with the fit ones among us moving at about four times the rate of our earlier efforts, and by half-past eight, working in the rain, we had finished our task.

Too tired almost to put one foot in front of the other, spirits broken, wet through, we stumbled along the track back to camp in the dark.

All was not well in the camp either. Fifty yards from our hut we started to paddle, and by the time we reached our hut we were wading through two feet of swirling water. The ground upon which our hut was built sloped, and the staging at my end of the hut was still clear of the water; but at the other end some of the men's belongings, including their bedding, had already floated away, and the staging was a foot under water. I crept on to my bed, trying to avoid letting my contaminated legs touch my bedding. Lighting my improvised lamp I saw faeces floating along the passage from the flooded latrines at the end of the hut. Men began to move up from the low end, and squeezed into our bed-spaces. We sat up all night watching the water rise; or were the legs supporting the staging sinking into the mud with the extra weight?

At four a.m. the filthy water began to overlap our staging; the time had come to move. Sliding off I felt the water come over my loins, so I was unable to avoid trailing much of my kit in it. Our thoughts, as we waded off, not knowing where we were in the dark, perhaps going uphill, perhaps down dale, are not difficult to imagine. Nothing was said, blank despair flooded our hearts as, staying together for safety, we realized we were going steadily deeper into the water; but no evil lasts for ever; with the water up nearly to our chests we met some more men passing through the waters, and they knew where they were. Follow us they said, and slowly but surely the waters receded as we climbed the only hill in the camp. The tropical rain continued to fall down in sheets, and we spent the remainder of the night under a tamarind tree. The older camp residents told us that a loop of the river meandered round this camp, and that it had overflowed because of the extra heavy monsoon this year.

When at last dawn broke, I saw an open-sided, bandstand-like building not far off, so we moved over under its shelter. To our amazement, we soon found out that this was a Thai junior school, and still in use; as the children together with their one master trooped in from somewhere in the vicinity, we had to move out and stand under the eaves. Ages of the pupils varied from six to about twelve years, but all sat together in one class, on a floor-mat. As they began their work there miles out in Thai jungle, they were having an English lesson! The master wrote an English word on the board and everyone intoned the nearly unintelligible Thai effort of pronunciation.

The rain ceased about midday, and I was able to explore this territory more fully. The rising ground became a small mountain a little further on, the sides were steep like a sugar-loaf. An avenue of beautiful trees led up to a Buddhist temple. The trees were unusual, the branches being formed like sausages joined together, without leaves, lily-like flowers growing out of the ends of smaller branches. There was a long dark cave at the foot of the mountain, and by shading the eyes from the sun a golden reclining figure, many times life-size, could be discerned.

It began to rain again, harder than ever. The Japs had left us alone since the flood; they had troubles of their own; and we still had nowhere to sleep the coming night. However our own officers now took control, and having closed the men up in the huts on the high part of the camp, we were allocated half a hut, sixteen men to a sixteen foot bay. However, lying on one side in the dry was better than standing out in the rain.

An old timer in the hut told me of a spot in the camp boundary where Thais came along at night to bargain for prisoners' valuables. I looked through my kit and sorted out a few items as I was out of funds, and putting on my gas-cape, made for the wire. After haggling for half an hour I received fifteen Tickel (or Baht) for the remains of my silver pocket watch, sixty Stang for the chain, and fifty Stang for my fountain pen, sold because I had now run out of my home-made ink (there are 100 Stang to 1 Tickel).

The next morning we went to work on the railroad, determined this time not to repeat our first performance. We were on our way back to camp by half past two in the afternoon, our daily task completed. That evening the British Lt-Colonel in charge of Chunkai camp came to give us a talking to. He stressed the importance of making our work last the whole day, if we did not he assured us, our tasks would most certainly be increased.

Later in the evening someone brought in a copy of a Japanese English language newspaper called 'The Nippon Times'. It was full of propaganda from cover to cover, with not one small bit of real news. Everything was so unrealistic that not even the dimmest prisoner's morale could have been affected by it. Someone came in with a bit of 'real news'. Anthony Eden had flown to Japan to discuss peace terms with Tòjo (the Jap Prime Minister). The Japanese soldiers had their own newspaper, full of optimistic and mainly untrue reports of the war's progress, and they often passed on their 'news' to us. Most of it was too ridiculous for words.

Many of us fell ill with dysentery the next day, due to the flooding of the latrines of course. I spent all night sitting on the latrine pole, and in the early hours nearly dropped off to sleep on it. That night our Quartermaster Sergeant, Bill Wilby, did drop off and dropped in; he was saved from drowning by his best friends, and during the next few days disproved the advert 'Your best friends never tell you!'

Those of us with dysentery were given a dose of Epsom Salts by our medics, but we still had to go out to work in order to fill the quota ordained by our captors. This was to be the last time I was to see any medicine of this kind, as stocks ran out shortly after and no more was ever obtainable. A large dose of salts, followed by twenty-four hours fasting, was the best cure for this type of dysentery. I later evolved my own remedy, burning twigs and quenching them, and eating the charcoal. Dysentery was a very enervating and wasting disease; luckily I recovered before losing much weight. I saw pityfully thin men creeping around, their legs hardly capable of carrying their weight, and they were dying daily in ever increasing numbers. Chunkai cemetery on the camp boundary, was already huge.

So that week we progressed from task to task, each day leapfrogging the work that others had done the previous day. It surprised us how fast the embankment was creeping on its way through the jungle.

On the seventh day we lined up for our first pay parade. I did not attend as I could not get off the latrine, but I was able to draw mine the following day, one Tickel, fifty Stang. This was not in genuine Thai money, but in paper, printed as required in Japan, without backing. Even at that stage of the war the Thais were loth to accept it, later on it was to become valueless. The face value of the Tickel was I suppose about the equivalent of a shilling, but the Thais would only treat the Jap issue as worth half this. Although 'Tickel' was the official name for the currency we noticed that the Thais always said 'Baht'. The Japs paid us twenty Stang a day, buying power of about a penny in nineteen forty-three. We were in future to be paid every ten days, to make it easier for them to work it all out.

We all had by this time made ourselves little lamps from old food tins. A hole was made in the lid and a piece of string threaded through for the wick. Coconut oil was our main fuel, a pint bottle bought from the Thais and shared between a dozen men. During the evenings it rained most of the time so we just sat on our bed spaces and talked in the feeble flickering light of our lamps. During the quiet spells we heard the constant noises of the jungle. Countless millions of frogs croaked and squeaked, those further away merging into loud background noise, which rose and fell in a continuous tremolo. My neighbour had put his lamp on the ground to avoid it being knocked over, and as I watched, hundreds of winged ants or termites flew around and into the flame. The shadow cast by the lamp was impenetrable. I dreamed of home as I watched the light, but suddenly as a draught caught the flame, I saw something strange going on in the shadow. Getting down with my lamp in hand, I saw a huge toad six inches across gobbling up the singed insects as fast as he could swallow them. For half an hour I watched, wondering where he was putting them all.

At midnight I was awakened by water soaking into my side; I was on one of the lowest spaces this time, and I called a warning to the others as I wearily packed up my wet gear again and slid down into the flood. The river had risen yet further, but having some idea of the geography by now, we trooped up the hill and spent the rest of the night in the Buddhist temple. Since everything I had was saturated I made no attempt to sleep, and sat there leaning against the wall awaiting the dawn. There were little shelves on the temple walls, and on them were many small carved figures. Some of the men helped themselves to these for souvenirs; Ken Ireman gathered up a couple of little goddesses.

The Japs turned us out for work at daybreak, and the rain stopped in time for us to start work. We returned at five o'clock to our wet beds in the temple, and found that the water had receded sufficiently for us to re-occupy our half-hut.

My foam rubber mattress was still soaked when I returned from work the next day, so I risked hanging it up outside our hut while I went to the river to wash. It had disappeared upon my return. This was my most precious possession, so I waited until the next day before combing every hut in the camp to try to find it. Sure enough, find it I did, cut up into smaller pieces to avoid recognition, in the kit of a man from the Recce battalion. I accused him of stealing it and placed him on report. I was disgusted when a couple of days later, coming up in front of the Major, he was only admonished.

The stretch of embankment on which we were working was now twenty feet high, owing to the fall of the land. As we were still given the same amount of earth to sift per man we really did have to work flat out to finish by dusk, and staggered back home in the evenings with trembling legs after climbing to the top with our loads all afternoon. The line was to climb from this point to a range of hills half a mile away, where a gang of our men were cutting a pass through very hard white rock. They cut deep holes with hammers and long chisels, and twice daily the Jap engineers filled the holes with explosives and blasted the rock away. Another gang was breaking the fallen rock into small pieces with hammers and carting it off to the completed parts of the track to use as ballast when the line was laid.

A few days later the camp buzzed with excitement as the news circulated that four men had escaped from a working party during that day. The Japs were furious and said that we were all going to be punished. Our camp commandant called us all together, and lectured us on the folly of trying to escape at the moment. We could be of no help to the Allied effort as our nearest forces were separated from us by over a thousand miles of disease-ridden, foodless jungle, and in addition tigers roamed therein. If that were not enough the Japs had offered the natives high rewards for reporting or returning escaped prisoners, dead or alive. 'Please make no attempt, you can do no good, and others will suffer.'

That evening our ears were alerted by the new sound of aircraft passing high overhead, and the Japs sounded their air-raid alarm. They came round ordering us all to stay in our huts, so we had to be content with peering out under the eaves into the clear starlit sky. Someone said he counted five planes, but I saw none. The thrill of the realization that up there in the sky were our free comrades kept us awake with excitement for most of the night. Perhaps the Jap soldiers were having a re-think too bearing in mind the ridiculous stories they had believed of their victorious advance through India and into Europe.

I slept beside my friend Jimmy Hame, and the other side of Jimmy was the bed space of Sergeant Charlie Stever our elderly cook who was then on night duty; his bedding and belongings were in a neat bundle at the head of his space. At about one o'clock in the morning I awoke as Jimmy leapt out of bed with a yell and disappeared under the eaves into the (by now) bright moonlight. Jumping out after him, I saw Jimmy chasing someone across the adjacent open space so I joined in. Seeing the two of us after him the fugitive dropped what transpired to be Charlie's kit, in the hope of getting away. However we caught him and took his name and number. Jimmy went back to collect the kit from the ground where it had fallen, but I followed the miscreant to his hut. Once in the shadow of the hut he took to his heels again, and only by luck I saw him dive into a bed and draw the clothes over him. I snatched the clothes off and asked him what he was up to, but he professed indignation at being awakened from his 'sleep'. He could not however help blowing like a grampus from his exertion, so I yelled for the NCO in charge of the hut, and in spite of epithets from those all round, I kept yelling until he reluctantly came forward. The man had of course given us the wrong name which proved to be Jackson.

There was unfortunately a lot of thieving from comrades going on in Chunkai camp. Wasters in civilian life are still the same men when they become prisoners of war. 'Can the leopard change his spots, or the evil man forsake his way?' Blankets, most valuable of all the captive's possessions, were stolen and sold to the Thais. With no protection from the malaria-carrying mosquito many must have died solely because of these camp thieves. Even the medical hut was broken into, and our scanty supply of medicines robbed for private gain. Some became so wealthy that they were able to bribe those in charge to let them stay in camp as sick men, while the really sick were forced out to work. Jackson was court-martialled a few weeks later, but I did not hear the result.

The Japs now told us that if we finished the task in nine days we were to have the tenth day off. On the ninth day of our first task under this scheme, although we worked flat out all day, and right up until it became too dark, we did not finish. I was very despondent as I had much to do, most important of all, my washing. However, the Japs, realizing that we had done our best, showed that they *were* human and obtained permission from the officer in charge for us to have our free day after all. Or did they want to do their own washing?

I was sharpening my razor the next day when shouts brought me quickly outside the hut, just in time to take part in a snake hunt. I managed to kill it, so I skinned, cut up and cooked it for my midday meal. As it had been about three feet long there was just enough for one, which was as well since no-one else fancied trying it. The flavour of the white flesh was like rather fishy chicken, not at all unpleasant. It was very full of thin bones, and therefore took a long time to eat. I was to have quite a few before we left Thailand. In the afternoon I decided to sell my newly-washed sheet as I was unable to keep it clean now that we were working such long hours. I sold it through the wire to a Thai woman, and after long bargaining settled for three Tickel, fifty Stang, and two bars of 'nutty-nutty' as we used to call the Thai peanut confection. The Thais would squat on their haunches at secluded points along the long camp boundary, with their wares on display. Some men offered their cash and then at the last minute snatched it back together with the goods. One boasted that he had polished up some farthings, and sold them as gold coins. The Thais soon became fed up with us and would only let their wares into our hands after receiving and examining our cash. Some even got their own back by keeping the cash without parting with the goods.

The vendors were however mostly transparently honest and full of goodwill to us. They were nearly all old ladies, and they would sit behind their baskets until the last of their produce was sold. Besides 'nutty-nutty' there was a sweet jellified concoction (made from unripe coconuts), dried fish, fruit and both raw and hard-boiled eggs. The egg sellers had their eggs in separate heaps, and sung their continuous cry of 'cook-cook' and 'no-cook' pointing the while first to one heap and then the other. All bargaining and pricing was accompanied by finger-arithmetic.

Thais sing their language in several tones, although it is quite unlike Chinese. I soon learned a few simple words, such as 'di', good, and 'my-di' or no-good. Any positive could be negatived by the prefix 'my'. I became fond of the Thais, although some of them were obviously rogues. The men stalked along the jungle paths, some in sarongs, others in shirts and shorts with shirt-tails flying loose. They were a brave race, and always carried a big knife or 'parang' in their belts as a defence from tigers and robbers, or to cut a path through the undergrowth. They did not appear over-keen on steady work, as most of the hard jobs and cultivations seemed to be executed by the Chinese. There was inter-marrying between the races, and the local population varied in colour from mid-brown to nearly white. First thing in the morning many of the Thai women looked quite beautiful, but they all seemed to chew betel-nut, and by midday their teeth gleamed like pieces of anthracite through their smiling lips. Ugh!

Out on the railway the embankment had by now reached a height of thirty feet, and as we were allowed to organize the work ourselves as long as we finished by the tenth day, our guards slept under the trees, or moved along to chat and play games with guards from other groups. As soon as we were unobserved we rolled the huge bamboo and other roots we had dug up to the bottom of the heap and covered them up with dirt as quickly as we could. The Japs never seemed to remark on the fact that they were missing, so we continued to do this all along the line. Occasionally someone would be caught red-handed, and then he would be beaten up. A year or so later, after the white ants had eaten the stumps away, huge holes appeared all along the embankment, and many gangs of men were employed in filling them up.

It was now the beginning of December 1942. The rains had stopped but the nights became cold, some nights it almost felt like a frost. Those who had had their bedding stolen suffered a lot as they tried to keep warm under odd bits of rag and sacking. Other parties of men occasionally passed us as we worked. They were on their way up country from Singapore and the route of the railway was the only road up. Among these parties was one from River Valley, and this included our old pals Skin Barker, Len Dudley and Ron Kitton, sergeants from our regiment.

Life in camp had by now settled down to a monotonous routine. Breakfast at dawn, on the railway at eight o'clock; break to eat our plain cold rice at midday, and back most evenings just in time to wash in the river; but as there was only time to disinfest our bedding once every ten days, and sometimes not even then, we became as lousy as coots, and the split bamboo from which our bed-stagings were made was filled in every crack with the repulsive bed-bugs. With mosquitoes during the day, life was one long itch, and we dare not scratch for fear of producing the ghastly tropical ulcers which were by now killing many of our men. The one saving grace was that we could at least get in the river to cool off and remove the grime most evenings.

The day after Skin and Co. went through I was unable to eat all day and felt so bad that on our return from work I called at the medical hut where I was told that my temperature was one-hundred and five point nine, so I was excused work for a week. The next day I was seized by the uncontrollable fits of shivering known as 'rigors' which are typical of malaria. At this point we still had supplies of quinine, so after a week I was pronounced fit to return to the railroad; it was the eighteenth of December.

Theft had by now become so rife that our officers decided to try to take measures against it. The criminals had organized themselves so well that there were receivers who would take anything, no questions asked, out of the camp each night to sell in the nearby village. The measures resulted in orders that the NCO in charge of each hut was to mount a guard each night, every man taking a turn once a week. Many of the men deeply resented this and insinuated that we were worse than the Japs, who did at least let them spend the night in peace. It was not much fun trying to see these men did as they were told, but I did my best.

As long as the quota of men was available for work each day the Japs did not at this time make the really sick men go out to work, and our medics were allowed to decide who was fit enough. Up to now no officers had to go out on the work parties; they were provided with what seemed to us a substantial cash allowance by our captors, and they amused themselves in camp all day as best they could. Whereas they no doubt felt themselves to be hard up, to us on our penny a day they seemed to live like millionaires.

Life changed for the officers on the twenty-first of the month, when the Jap Commandant ordered them out on parade. They were told that their days of leisure were over, and that they would in future be required to work on the railway like the other ranks. In accordance with the Geneva Convention which states that officers may not be put to work if taken prisoner, they refused to go. The Jap said that his race appreciated the principle of death before dishonour, and invited those who would like to be shot in preference to working to stay behind. After a hurried conference it was decided to submit under protest, and from then on the officers had to work.

We were struggling to finish our task by the twenty-fourth of December; the Japs had given us a twelve day task, saying that if we completed it in ten days we could have both Christmas and New Year's Day free. On the night of the twenty-third I broke out of Chunkai for the first time to do the Christmas shopping for my men. Although there was an official canteen in the camp where most things could be bought at a price, outside they could be bought for half that. I bought among other things a bottle of native rice spirit, thirty eggs, and a load of biscuits.

Christmas Eve saw us finish our twelve-day stretch with a late night ending, but we felt the effort worthwhile. That night Jimmy and I drank to freedom in a cocktail we made up of rice-spirit, lime juice and rice-water. We thought it was lovely. The cooks, having been putting rations to one side for weeks, excelled themselves with that our first Christmas dinner, and in the evening there was a concert accompanied by a band of home-made instruments. It was a very good effort. I remember finding it hard to believe that it really was Christmas, and wondered if my folk had heard that I was alive and a prisoner, since I had heard nothing from home. The Japs wandered through the camp during the day, and seeing us trying to enjoy ourselves, told us that news had come through that the Allies were retreating fast on every front. Of course no-one believed a word of it. Where did those aircraft we heard take off from we wondered?

Diphtheria was a killer disease in our camps. Although tracheotomies were performed, very few were successful owing to the impossibility of keeping germs out of the wounds in our filthy conditions. One of our officers contracted it in this camp, a Mr Bradley, and I used to visit him. He was one of the few to recover. Ken Ireman now also contracted the disease and went into the sick bay.

On New Year's Day we were issued with one pig to about a thousand men. I went to the spot where they were being killed, and collected two sets of entrails, which the cooks were not going to use. Cleaning them out in the river, I fried the lights for my tea, salted the chitterlings for eating later, and produced a pint of pig oil from the belly fat. (There is no lard out there as pig fat does not set in that heat.)

After our New Year's Day break we started on our next ten-day task. As usual I made my rule of thumb check to ensure that we were not being given more than our designated one cubic metre per man per day. On this occasion I calculated that we had half as much more than we should have had, and protested to our guards accordingly, but to no avail. Each succeeding day it became more obvious that an error had been made, and every day I tried to make the guards see reason. At last the Jap measuring team came along to check the task, and after much arguing among themselves they announced that we could have three extra days to complete the work. Before the extra work was completed I was to be put on a charge myself.

On the seventh of January, after returning from work I heard that my old pal Sgt Ken Ireman was very ill with malaria in addition to the diphtheria. The next evening I found out that he had died during that day and that his funeral party was to leave shortly for a service at the cemetery. When we returned, his kit was shared out among his fellow sergeants as was our custom. I was given his puttees, and as no-one else would accept them I took the two small goddess figurines Ken had taken from the temple at the time of the flood. This was the first Chunkai death among our sergeants, and there were those who murmured that it might not have been a coincidence that Ken had been the one with the 'idols'. However I shunned superstition and put them under my pillow for safety that night. I awoke the next morning feeling very ill, and decided that discretion was the better part of valour. The temple was now out of bounds to us, so that evening I managed to pass the offending objects through the wire to a Thai, and hoped he would put them back where they belonged.

By now I had a good deal of experience of working under the Japs; I had learned enough of the tongue to understand their orders, and was becoming familiar with both their mentality and way of working. In addition I had one of the best gangs of men, and we understood one another; they also trusted me to get the best possible deal out of our captors.

On the last day of our task then, our 'beloved' adjutant came out to work with us, the Japs having said that one officer could accompany each working party of other ranks; the remainder were to form a separate working party which would go up country. Our adjutant had chosen to place himself in charge of 'my' gang. I was not very pleased, and neither were the men. As we started work, he sat down on a log beside the track and watched us for ten minutes.

Up to the present we had nearly always managed to finish our tasks fairly well on time, not too early and not too late. I attributed this partly to the fact that I always worked with the men myself, and could then tell when they had had enough; and I was never afraid to tell our guards.

I had split our working party into four, friends together wherever possible. We made stretchers with bamboo poles and rice bags to carry the earth on, as we found the baskets the Japs provided useless. Two men dug the earth and put it on the stretcher, two carried the stretcher to the embankment and emptied it, and as that was the most tiring job the 'stretcher bearers' obtained a short rest while their next load was dug. Every half-dozen loads diggers and carriers changed round. This way every man could work with his 'mucker', and considering the circumstances we were a pretty good crowd. We were as democratic as we could be and when awkward jobs or trouble arose everyone had his say.

After that first ten minutes, our officer called me over in his usual lordly way and told me that he was not satisfied with the way I was running things. I was on no account to work myself; I was to put one quarter of our gang on rest, while the other three-quarters worked extra hard. He would lend me his watch and my sole job would be to call 'change' every ten minutes! He had been a commercial traveller in peace time whereas I had been a builder, yet after seeing us at work for only a few minutes, and having never worked under the Japs before, he was about to change our system of working that we had evolved over months of experience. It also meant that I could no longer work with Jimmy; I was not pleased.

I called the men over to where we were instead of going over to the men, so that our adjutant would hear what the men felt about it all. After the initial uproar which broke out when the new rules were announced, one after another, first the NCOs and then the men each said his piece, unanimously predicting that the new idea would entail everyone working less efficiently and therefore later. Not one word in favour. I turned my head interrogatively in the direction of the Major who deliberately turned his head away. I waited for a few seconds for him to speak, and when nothing came took it to mean that rather than admit he was wrong he chose to carry on as though he had never mooted the scheme. So I told the men to go back to work and to continue as before. Our officer continued sitting on his log for a while, then called me over out of earshot of the men. In his lordliest manner and speaking so 'posh' that the words were loth to come out, he looked up into the sky and said 'You will consider yourself on report sergeant, and the charge will be "disobeying the order of a superior officer".' He made no attempt to tell the men to change their working himself. I spent the remainder of that day seething with indignation, and although I was not feeling well, I probably did twice my usual stint, as there was nothing but the embankment on which to vent my spleen.

My diarrhoea had gradually worsened during that day, and I went to the medical hut in the evening. The MO told me that I had returned to work too soon after the malaria, and that I must rest for a couple of days. In fact for five days I had chronic 'squitters' and ate little but ground charcoal; I felt very weak when on the sixth day I went back to work on the embankment. I was relieved to find that when the adjutant found out that I was not to be on the work party he had managed to find himself a camp job. He had not attempted to run the work his way himself. We now had a decent young officer in his place, and I was very grateful for this. It had been bad enough working under our main enemy, the Japs. I never heard what happened to my 'charge' as I was never called up in front of the CO as I should have been.

Our part of the railroad now transversed an area of paddy, some of which was still flooded. The lowest of the fields were wet nearly all the year round as the higher ones were gradually drained into them. Fish lived in these lower fields, and the Thai women fished for them. They used a funnel-shaped wicker affair, the narrow part the diameter of an arm. The anglers paddled through the mud, at intervals stabbing the open end of the 'funnel' down between their feet. Their hand was then thrust through the neck of the apparatus and waved around in the mud trapped inside, often retrieving a small mud-gudgeon type fish which they put in a basket slung over their backs.

I had only been back at work a day when, on January the fifteenth we paraded with our kit to move up country. I had narrowly missed being left behind sick; quite a tragedy then to be separated from one's mates when friendship was all there was to live for.

Chapter 6

'God is our refuge and strength, a tested help in times of trouble,
So we need not fear, even if the world blows up,
And the mountains crumble into the sea.'

We moved out of Chunkai along the mostly completed embankment, and presently arrived at the next camp, Wun Lung where we were to spend the night. It had only been a few kilometres, which was just as well as I was still weak from my 'squitters'. There was a yell from a crowd of the 'Wun Lungers', and as we got closer I recognized them as the River Valley boys. We had some rice and I then sat down for a chat with Len Dudley, Skin Barker and a few others. Skin had been Lionel's assistant in the medical room. Lionel had been on the plump side; Skin was one of the lean kind. He was one of those chaps who could raise a laugh by an expressive glance alone. He had the habit of talking out of the side of his Joe E. Brown mouth, and with his lop-sided grin he could make a joke of the most morbid subject. After hearing the latest 'griff' and telling all we knew of life and death, Jimmy and I went for a walk round the camp.

Wun Lung had no perimeter fence as the other camps we knew had. One side was bounded by the river, one by the railway, one by jungle, and the other by a clearing which was being created by two very hard-working Chinamen, who were trying to make a small farm. We were told that they worked from dawn to dusk cutting the great trees down, burning the trunks, then digging round the root and burning that out with the branches. Their only tools were axes and chunkels. The ground they had already cleared was planted, partly with a kind of lettuce, the remainder with peanuts. (These look much like garden peas while they are growing.)

Next morning we moved off on the next stage of our journey, this time along ten miles of jungle paths to 'Wun-tu-Kin'. I still had all my kit, and was still weak from my sickness, it was therefore only with Jimmy's help that I made the last stretch to the new camp. Fortunately the Japs allowed us to spend the first day in camp getting the cookhouse and latrines ready, and we were also able to clean the place up and do our washing.

Our first job on the railway was cutting down trees and debarking them for use in building culverts to allow streams to pass under the embankment. We wondered how long these would withstand attacks from the ever-present termites.

The nights were very cold and I could not even keep warm with my blanket and rice-sack. Many of us had to get up in the middle of the night and run round the camp to keep warm. Sometimes we built a fire between the huts and warmed up round that.

Wun-tu-Kin provided me with one of my few fond memories of a Japanese soldier. His name was Yoshio Suzuki, and he was an engineer. The Koreans had taken over the task of guarding us now, the Japs were reasponsible only for the engineering and surveying work. These Koreans were vile to us, many times worse than the Japs had been, and we quickly learnt to loathe them. When Suzuki saw the Koreans being beastly he would stride over and shout at them. I never heard him raise his voice at any other time. He could not speak any English but the first day out on the railway he made me understand that he regretted having to order us about and that he would do his best to make things easy for us. That evening he came over to our hut; this was most unusual as the Japs seldom wandered from their quarters after returning from work. Sitting beside me he produced a large piece of cake and a handful of cigarettes. Shyly he handed them to me, and waved his hand round in a gesture for me to share what he had brought.

Practically every evening after that he would wander over to our hut with some tit-bit or other from his own rations. Sometimes a bit of 'banjo fish' as we called the lyre-shaped dried fish the Japs ate, sometimes a few sweets. When I attempted to thank him Suzuki cleverly attempted to change the subject by trying to teach me to say the Japanese word for 'thank you' properly, 'Arrigato'. I tried; 'Ah-rding-gah-to-ooo' he tried to get me to pronounce. I never learned to say it properly. I would like to know if my friend survived the war, it would be good to write to him after all this time with some little token of affection and gratitude.

Our stretch of the railway was four miles from camp, so it took quite a long time to get to work. During our meal breaks I often explored in the jungle, and once or twice I got lost. Once out of sight of the embankment, and with the trees overhead hiding the sun it was very easy to lose sense of direction without a compass. Being lost could be quite frightening under those circumstances with trees all round and no idea in which direction one's comrades were to be found. Usually by sitting quietly one would hear a chink of a tool or a voice eventually, but on one occasion I waited for a long while without hearing a sound. I wandered off through the trees hoping I was going in the right direction, and after about twenty minutes came to a cleared area where obviously the railway was to run. Unfortunately I had no way of knowing whether I had circled to the right or to the left so I sat down while trying to make up my mind which way to turn to find the working party. After a few minutes a Thai came along and I asked him to tell me the way to Wun-tu-kin. He looked quite blankly at me as I tried over and over to make him understand. Just as I was about to give up a gleam of understanding came into his eyes, and he sang 'Wun-tu-ki-en' and directed me with a forefinger.

I hurried back along the track, and within a few minutes came in sight of our gang. Not wanting our guards to see me coming I entered the jungle skirting the track and proceeded out of sight until I was close enough to approach from the trees. Our guards spotted me before I could merge with the other men; that was the trouble with being so fair. I was easily missed. There was the usual roar of 'Courra!' I saw that I was seen, so I walked over to the guards, and looking as ill as I could I said 'Speedo Benjo, taksan taksan', which in pidgeon Japanese meant that I had 'been taken short'. Luckily they did not query this, and waved me back to work.

On another sortie I followed a track into the jungle, and after a few minutes came to a Thai house or 'Kampong' in a small isolated clearing. Standing on six foot legs to keep out beast and flood they were not houses in the western sense but bamboo and attap huts. Floors were of split bamboo and the walls simply hanging mats which were rolled up during the day. Even the larger ones were usually not more than about ten feet square, and many I saw were only about seven feet by four feet. The larger ones were split into two rooms. There was also a small verandah on a level with the floor, and this was approached from the ground by a retrievable ladder. The householder and his wife would spend their leisure moments sitting on the verandah, usually chewing betel nut and smoking their pipes.

Many Thais kept a wad of black tobacco in the corner of their mouths when chewing the nut. As this left a thick deposit on the teeth, every now and then they would spit and take the wad from their lips and polish their teeth with it. Unfortunately only the high spots were whitened and when they smiled the thick black lines between their teeth looked singularly unattractive. Betel nut seemed to preserve their teeth as even elderly Thais seemed to have gleaming full sets when they cleaned the black off.

This Kampong appeared to be occupied only by one old man (and his dog) and he had hardly any possessions. Normally the Thais (who are a very hospitable race) would keep a ripe paw-paw hanging on the wall, and the visitor would be offered a slice. This old man was only able to offer me a piece of tamarind together with a piece of rock salt to suck with it. Tamarinds grow on huge trees, and when unripe look not unlike broad beans. As they ripen the skin hardens into a shell, and the inside shrinks round the hard seeds into a reddish sticky toffee. It is just about the sourest thing I have ever tasted, and I have a sweet tooth. I was unable to avoid the risk of upsetting the old chap, as in vain I tried to maintain a smile of appreciation with the stuff in my mouth. However, he grinned at my wry face.

A sweet little girl of about five came hurrying down the ladder to greet me from one Kampong on another occasion. As she looked up at me with a smile I saw the red stain of betel nut in her mouth. Brown skinned Thai children seem to be able to climb up the ladders almost as soon as they can crawl, and the young mothers nearly always had a new baby or were expecting one shortly. They were quite clearly devoted parents even if they did give their children betel nut.

It was a week or so later that I found a path leading from our railroad to the river during one of our midday breaks. Tethered to the river bank was a raft of bamboo on which was erected a hut, so small that from a few yards off it might have been a dog kennel. Legs dangling in the water, a young man sat on the edge as I approached, and he beckoned me to come nearer with a friendly smile. The hut walls were rolled up and I could see a young woman sitting inside on some bedding, which appeared to be all they possessed beside the cooking pots and charcoal fire bucket on the raft. As I sat down on the bank the woman came out to sit beside her husband, and I saw that she was pregnant. After some initial shyness they allowed themselves to be drawn into a sign-language 'chat'. (The Thais are very good at this and by now I was fairly proficient also.) I asked if they had any other children, and the husband told me that there had been three but that all had died in childbirth. The telling made them both very sad as they explained that they now spent much time in prayer for the little one who was now on the way.

There were no doctors or nurses there, and I was told that only one child in five reached maturity. We often saw men and women in remote Kampongs dying of terrible complaints without any medical attention; and yet the Thais as I remember them seemed to be a very contented race, a happy smile on nearly every face. We in the West, with all our possessions seem a miserable lot by comparison. I asked this couple why they had built their house on a raft, and such a small one too. They explained that young couples with no money could not buy land, so they had to build on water; as for the size it was big enough for their present needs. When their family arrived safe and sound, then they would build themselves a bigger home. After working for someone else for a few years they would be able to buy land and build a proper Kampong.

At one stage in the embankment's progress we passed an abandoned native vegetable garden, and we soon stripped it of everything edible. There were several sizes of chilli, which we gathered both red and green. The smaller the chilli the hotter it is, and the green unripe ones have a different flavour from the red ones. I used the chillies to make 'sambals', a Malay side dish to eat with rice. My favourite was 'Sambal Katchang' made by frying ground chillies and peanuts and then cooking them with a little water and sugar. There was also a vegetable with a hard bristly skin, a cross between a cucumber and marrow. The fine bristles come off and stick in the flesh if not rubbed off first. There were also a few brinjaws or egg-fruit but these soon went.

The river at the camp was full of fish, but we never found a satisfactory way of catching them. Our quartermaster sergeant Cyril managed to get hold of a set of pig's 'innards', and as he did not know what to do with them he offered to go fifty/fifty with me if I would prepare them. No sooner did I enter the river with them than I was surrounded by hundreds of fish, all sorts from six-pounders to tiddlers, and I lost nearly a quarter before I could retrieve them from the water. These fish had very sharp teeth and would bite at any sores we had on our body. In one camp a prisoner had a very private part bitten off by a fish, which were often as long as three feet.

Thais used to catch the lizards which were plentiful in the jungle, and were often seen running across the paths. They were about eighteen inches long from tip to tail, the latter being carried high in the air as they ran. They were skinned, dried in the sun, and sold in the shops in bundles of a dozen. The method of capture was to follow a lizard until it ran to its hole in the ground and then to insert a bamboo trap into the hole. The trapper would carry on until he had used all his traps up, and then go round collecting up the lizards which had been caught when they tried to emerge. The traps were ingenious, consisting of a nine inch length of two inch diameter bamboo, one end of which was cut down to form a ring, a strip left up the side to form a spring, and a noose of string suspended in the ring was released when a lizard put its head through; the spring then straightened and the lizard was held tight pending the return of the trapper.

There were also wildfowl in the jungle, and we would often hear them crowing. They looked not unlike the Indian game cocks which are bred in this country. The Thais trapped these by staking out a tame cock by his leg, and surrounding him with wire snares. When he started to crow the local birds came in, heads down for the attack and finished up with a snare round their neck. The tame birds were carried around head first in a wicker funnel.

It was now the fifth of February, I would be twenty-four on the morrow. The embankment at this point was low, so we were spread out a long way to provide the same cubic capacity for our task. We had a decent young British officer with us named Gates, I was working at one end of our task and he was keeping an eye on the other end for me. Suddenly there was a cry from Mr Gates' end and looking up I saw one of the Koreans beating Pte McNab over the head with a heavy stick. Mr Gates ran over protesting but the other Korean started to beat him also. Snatching up my spade I rushed over yelling at the top of my voice, taking care to shout 'Suzuki' as I joined them. The Koreans were so taken aback that they stopped their beating and for a second just stared. I kept remonstrating including threats to tell 'Nippon Number One'. Recovering from their initial surprise they rushed screaming at me. I think the Koreans must have the worst tempers in the world. However, I knew what to do and stood my ground without batting an eyelid. They threw down their sticks and snatched up their rifles and swung their butts at my head. Over and over again they deliberately missed me, trying I knew to make me flinch or lower my eyes as they got as close to my face as they dared; any sign of fear and I knew that I'd 'had it'. They soon calmed down and returned to the shade of the trees. Poor McNab was far from well, and although he'd done nothing wrong as far as I could gather, I suppose the guards picked on him because he was not working hard enough for them.

Yoshio Suzuki had by this time learnt a few words of English. We would sometimes only see him once or twice a day as he knew that he could trust our gang to get on with the work, and he was responsible for a long stretch with many gangs working under him. When next he came along I took him over to those guards and explained what had occurred, and he saw the bruises on the two victims. It was only then that we saw for the first time that our friendly Jap had another facet to his character. He stood the Koreans to attention in the sun, and in front of us all shouted at them for five minutes. They hid their faces from us the rest of that day, and we were never troubled again by that particular pair.

On the ninth day of February, nineteen forty three I succumbed to another attack of malaria, and initially this was worse than before, but I received quinine and recovered quicker this time; I was back on the railway within a week. However while lying in the sick hut I made a new friend. My diary entry on the twelfth reads, 'I don't think I shall be staying here much longer as I have seen Cpl Rivven and joined his EC . . .' My new friend had formed an Escape Club, and they were concealing maps and weapons about the camp ready for a break-out. Since we knew now that our aircraft had a base near enough to launch the attack we had heard, we thought there must be a possibility of reaching them. For the next few days I thought of little other than the glorious prospect of freedom. I had to swear a solemn oath of secrecy and undertook that I would be prepared to leave if asked at a few seconds notice, or to help someone else to do so. I could not even tell my 'mucker', Jimmy. I was unable ever to take advantage of the 'EC' as we moved further up country within a few days. Before we left I developed my first tropical ulcer, luckily only a small one, on my ankle. There were whole huts full of ulcer cases in the camp, some of them a terrible sight, and the victims suffered agony as the infection ate through flesh, sinew, nerve and bone. Thousands of limbs were amputated, sometimes several times over as another ulcer formed on the stump.

We paraded on the twenty-first of February, another stretch

of embankment completed, ready to march further up country to our next task.

First impressions of our new camp, Bancow, were far from favourable. There were no huts for us and we were told to sleep on the ground. As I unrolled my bedding to rest after the long march carrying all my kit, what I thought was a wag from among the older residents called out 'Watch out for scorpions, they're killers in this camp!' Jimmy said that we'd better look, and rolling my bed up again I saw a huge black scorpion advancing, stinging tail high in the air at the 'ready'. Needless to say I had little sleep, especially as at about midnight I had the cold prickly feeling of an eight inch long centipede crawling over my forehead. I stayed still until it had crawled clear before I killed it. These hideous creatures scratch and sting if they are knocked or brushed off, and as they live on filth the scratches produce the dreaded ulcers. Next day the guards took us into the jungle to gather materials for hut-building. I found out for the first time where the 'ties' came from that we used to tie the bamboo poles together. An oblong of bark was cut from a particular kind of tree, and from the inner side it was possible to peel off fifty to a hundred of the tough stringy tape-like pieces. They had to be soaked in water for a few days before becoming flexible enough to use.

On our second day the Japs told us that we were to be given a special treat that evening, and sure enough when we returned from work there was a cinema van parked in a clearing. It was the only one I ever saw, and must have been brought up by boat, as there was no roadway to Bancow. About a hundred of our guards were sitting cross-legged on the ground waiting for the show to start and we were told we could sit behind them.

It was a 'talkie' and the scene opened with a clash of cymbals and captions in Japanese. It was all about the Jap war effort, and soon became exceedingly boring. There were long scenes depicting the factory floor. A 'conductor' stood on a raised dais while hundreds of blacksmiths beat their hammers in unison on similar pieces of steel in an impossible way. That particular episode lasted quite ten minutes, and during that time I saw no change in the shape of the steel or any article finished. Every scene took place at breakneck speed, and had so obviously been speeded up that I could not see that it could have had much propaganda effect as it was all too ridiculous.

Those of our men who became incurably ill on the railway were at intervals sent down to base camps. We who were left became tougher and more used to working on rice. Up until this time we had been allowed to excavate the soil for the embankment from wherever we chose, so we always looked around for soft spots. Our task was now made very much harder to perform as the Japs made us dig symmetrical ditches extending along both sides of the track. Each ditch had to be one metre deep, one and a half metres wide at the top and half a metre wide at the bottom. Any rocks, tree-stumps or ant-hills in the way had to be removed, and now that the dry season was upon us, the ground was flint hard. The trench sides had to be geometrically sloped and the whole neat and tidy. We could no longer dig the earth with our spades, but had to use the inadequate picks with which we were issued. Yet we still had to move the same volume of earth on to the embankment, so we were forced to work from dawn to dark in order to get our rest day and de-louse and wash our kit.

When digging the trenches we sometimes found spherical holes a couple of feet down in the rock-hard earth. In the hole would be a frog, blown out with water and looking like a balloon, dimples showing where the legs were buried. If they were knocked they would pass all the water and resume their more usual frog shape. At the end of the wet season they had tunnelled down in the mud, filled up with water, and then gone off to sleep to await the return of the rains.

The gigantic termite (or white ant) hills were also a source of wonder to me. As we cut through them no two were alike inside, and they often contained other creatures besides termites; I once found a black scorpion eight inches long with a row of white babies clinging to its underside like baby pigs. I hadn't the heart to kill it and hoped no-one would get stung as I let it run off. The Queen termite consisted of a big soft bag of eggs with a little hard headpiece. There were also several kinds of specialized termites that went to make up a colony. The workers were small and white; they could sting, and their job was to forage for wood, chew little bits off and take them back to the nest. They were unable to withstand sunlight, so wherever they went they built clay tunnels; when they reached a piece of wood, they first covered it with clay and then nibbled the wood out from inside. To protect the tunnels, large black fighter termites marched back and forth. They were armed with huge pincers on their heads and could endure being in the sun all day. If your foot came within reach they would bury their pincers in the nearest part, and the pain this caused was considerable. The only way to remove them was to pull the body off, split the head in two and extract one half of the pincers at a time. Unlike the workers which had two little black eyes, the soldiers appeared to be blind, and must have used smell and touch to sense danger. I hated the centipedes most of all. Their bodies were about an inch thick and their legs spanned about two and a half inches and were barbed. There seemed to be something obscene about them and I would prefer to sleep with a poisonous snake.

On this stretch of the line we built our first 'station' consisting solely of a platform built up with turf walls, and filled in with rammed earth. We were to see that these washed away during the next wet season.

Soon after the platform was built a party of Japs worked their way past our camp laying sleepers and lines on the embankment we had recently completed. The lines had been brought up from Malaya and were British made. They were not of the kind that is fixed in 'chairs' but they had a wide bottom flange which lay directly on the sleepers, and was held in place with steel dogs driven in.

Now that this stretch was completed our next task was to return along that part of the line where no ditches had been dug, and to dig them. We spent most of the time travelling, so we were not surprised when they told us that we were to move out of Bancow on the ninth of March. They gave us two days rest so I boiled up everything I had to kill the vermin and their eggs, and at eight forty-five we marched out. We were to go to Wun Lung which was two camps down the line, nineteen kilometres distant. We arrived at six o'clock in the evening.

We were not found much work to do during those first days, and the river at Wun Lung had a very long boundary with the camp as it was built in one of the river's meanders; thus we spent many hours bathing. On our third day I was sitting by the river when I saw a hand waving out of the water as it floated off downstream. I was able to run down the bank and swim out to carry out the one and only rescue in my life. One of our lads, a non-swimmer, had stepped off the underwater shelf and lost his footing in the quick-flowing water.

I set up a barber's shop in our hut, and by the time a few days had elapsed I was shaving about thirty men a day. Our task here, we were told, was to maintain the track, and we started going out daily to hammer shingle under loose sleepers, and to replace the ones that had split. As they had been cut from the jungle and laid green many of them had dropped in halves. There was a little Kampong in one corner of the camp, and here the Thais sat cross-legged and sold their wares. We had not been in the camp many days when a bunch of us were caught red-handed buying food. We were lined up, smacked across the face and had our shins kicked.

A sudden storm arose on our eighth day in the camp, and when we returned from work we found that the entire cookhouse had blown away, and our hut roofs were full of big holes; however, we were allowed to spend the next day in camp to carry out repairs.

Looking back I suppose that the river here was about fifty yards wide; I figured that with practice I might be able to swim across under water coming up once in the middle for air. With the curve in the river and the long length of bank, it was not easy for the guards to see it all at once. I started swimming a little further under water each day, ready for the time when I might decide to swim across to escape.

Now that the railway track was laid the Japs began to make good use of the railway, running their dual-purpose vehicles past our camp. Before the war Japanese goods had been thought of as shoddy imitations of European goods. However, we had already seen beautifully made Jap rifles, machine-guns and other goods. The brilliant engineering of their air-cooled diesel powered Locomotive/Lorries, finally convinced us of their manufacturing proficiency. As lorries they could travel over roads loaded with portable rail-trucks in the back. When they came to the railway the rubber-tyred wheels were taken off and the six brake-drums were locomotive wheels. The portable trucks were assembled on the line, and they had a train. One drawback was the apparent lack of adequate starting arrangements, and prisoners were called out at all hours to give a push start.

At this camp we had to unload rice from barges and carry it across an open space to the rice store, from where it was loaded on to trains for up country. Those of us who still had boots were keeping them for when we escaped or were set free. Sandals would not keep on our feet carrying the heavy rice; the ground was so hot that we had to run half-way across then drop our load and stand on it for a while to avoid our feet blistering. One day while standing on my rice-sack I heard a furious tooting from a passing train. Looking up I saw our old friend Suzuki waving frantically out of the cab to catch my attention. When I waved back some of the men who did not know me made jibes about me being 'Jap Happy', a term used to denote anyone who collaborated in the Jap war effort. Some of the lazy ones also used this term to describe those who were prepared to do their best at anything while we were prisoners.

It was by the river at Wun Lung that I saw my first giant lizard; it measured five or six feet and was running through the scrub at the water's edge. I was naked at the time, but with visions of lizard joints I chased it for twenty yards or so before it slid into the water; I was told later that these creatures had formidable teeth, so I was lucky in not having managed to corner it.

I never ceased to wonder at the marvellous way in which nature seemed to provide everything for the local population, without need of office or factory. Here I found out how the Thais illuminated their Kampongs, and made the torches which they carried when they traversed the jungle tracks at night, keeping off wild beasts and showing the way. There is a certain tree in the jungle in the side of which the Thais cut a hole about a foot into the trunk and just about large enough to lay a baby in. The floor of this is dished so that it will hold about half a gallon of fluid. Once the hole has been cut a constant supply of an oily resin flows in, and I think this was gathered about once a week. The torches were made by soaking palm leaves in the fluid and tying them in bundles a foot or so long with dry leaves on the outside so their hands did not get sticky. They would burn for about half an hour, giving quite a good light.

Far and away the most versatile and useful of the flora was of course bamboo. Although only a giant grass its uses were so many that I can only mention a few. It grew in the course of a few months from the ground to a hundred feet high, some said they could see it growing. At the end of the season it gradually died and eventually fell back to the ground. The fresh new shoots were cut and used as a vegetable. As they grew up to a foot thick, sections were cut from the thickest to make buckets. A longer piece of the bamboo, including two of the dividing joints, made a barrel, and three or four inch thick sections made all the bottles the locals needed. When the Thai went to a party he carried, slung over his shoulder with a leather thong, his bottle of home-made liquor.

No saw-mill was needed to cut up planks. Thick bamboo was cut into the length required, the joints smashed with a heavy maul, and when the bamboo was split down one side and opened out, lo and behold, a plank! All our bed stagings were made in this way, the only drawback being that the thousands of cracks harboured unlimited numbers of the repulsive bed-bugs that made nights so miserable. Bed-bugs cannot stand the sun, so on our rest days we would take the stagings up and leave them outside in the heat of the day, then bash them with a stick and watch the bugs roll over and die in the sun.

Further up country we found that the bamboo leaves and thin twigs were used for the elephants. As we passed Kampongs I often saw women weaving beautiful mats and panniers from thin slivers split from the outside of different shades of bamboo, making most attractive patterns. The mats, used to form walls of their dwellings, were so cleverly woven that they were wind-proof. A coarser matting was made in the same way, but sewn up to make into rice-sacks. Sharp knives could be made by slicing a segment from a fairly thick plant, and I was told that in Malaya the ceremonial knife used in circumcision by the Moslems was of bamboo. Bundles of bamboo were tied together to form huge rafts, and these were coupled one behind the other to form trains which were poled down the river with heavy teak logs slung underneath. Teak is so heavy that it will not float. The 'trains' had a crew of two, and as they floated down the fast flowing stream the crew jumped frantically from raft to raft staving off from the bank round the continuous bends.

If a rat were trapped in the end of a long bamboo and made to tunnel its way through the sections and come out the other end, a good water-pipe was produced, and these were used in many places to carry water down from mountain streams to the Kampongs. Several kinds of musical instruments were made from bamboo, drums, xylophones and woodwind instruments.

The most ingenious and interesting of all the things I ever saw made from bamboo was far up country in a very remote and isolated community. It worked on the same principle as the diesel engine, believe it or not, and was probably invented hundreds of years earlier. The instrument was made from just two pieces of bamboo, each about four inches long. One was about an inch diameter inside, and the other was sufficiently thicker to slide over the smaller one; one of the dividing joints was left at the end of each piece, so that when one was slid inside the other, air was compressed in the chamber. The purpose of the artifact was to provide a means of ignition. To operate it a pinch of charred kapok fibre was put inside the chamber, the two parts slid sharply together with a blow from the hand, and when they were drawn apart the kapok was glowing red. This was quickly tipped out on to tinder and blown into a flame.

Thus it could continue. I believe that life would have come to a standstill out there without the ubiquitous bamboo.

After a month in Wun Lung I had made sufficient progress with my underwater swimming to be able to travel half-way across the river without coming up for air.

On April the fourteenth the first steam locomotive came puffing into the nearby station. A plate on its side indicated that it had been made in England in the year 1900.

The embankment began to sink in many places, and we

worked late now trying to keep up with the task of ramming in extra ballast under the sleepers to compensate for the shrinking earth.

In action our Capt 'Dare-Devil' Danton, had fearlessly roamed in no-man's land, Tommy-gun in hand and batman at heel. Many times we saw him slink past our positions and wondered how he escaped being hit. He was now senior British officer in the camp and seemed to get on extremely well with our captors. The night following the locomotive's arrival, we heard noisy celebrations in the Japs' quarters, and at about ten o'clock Danton came staggering out well and truly 'plastered'. This did not help the reputation he was acquiring of being 'Jap happy'. He later said that he was simply trying to put himself in the position of being able to influence our captors on our behalf. I suppose he found it difficult to know where to draw the line, but apart from a repetition a few days later, that was the only occasion I ever saw anything like this happen.

We had quite a lot of men of Dutch nationality with us in this camp. They had been captured on Java, Sumatra, Celebes, Ambon and other islands that go to make up what was then called the Dutch East Indies. They told us that they weren't soldiers at all really, and that after the capitulation they had donned military uniform in the hope that they would be treated better as prisoners of war. However, I understood later that as there was much resentment and even hatred from the native Indonesian population, those hitherto regarded as masters were afraid of vengeance. When loads of conscripted Javanese came through the railway later on, they spat and shook their fists when they saw the Dutch.

Holland is of course a small country, and before the war it had a comparatively big empire, the climate of which was mostly hostile to Europeans. The Dutch soldiers posted there were generally speaking unable to find white wives, so the government had adopted a policy of encouraging the men to marry natives, and the offspring of such unions were granted the status of full Dutch nationality. Somewhat different from their brethren, the South Afrikaaners. Provided that one had Dutch nationality there had been no colour bar in the Dutch

Empire. Citizenship was also granted to any native who performed an outstanding service. Thus there was one fellow in the camp, pitch black, and unable to understand any Dutch or English. He was a native of Ambon and had saved the life of a Dutchman. No one could speak Ambonese, a completely different tongue from the Malay dialect spoken by most inhabitants of Indonesia, so he led a very lonely life. The Ambonese, unlike the indolent and retiring Javanese, were a tough and warlike race not unlike the Ghurkas.

Of course had the Dutch been really progressive they would not have made the critical distinction between the 'natives' and those with Dutch citizenship. It had been that which caused the bitter hostility, and made the local population welcome the Japs with open arms. That hostility continued after the war, and succeeding governments refused to co-operate with the Dutch.

Many of our men however were prejudiced over the colour of a man's skin; they did not take too kindly to sharing huts with 'natives', especially as they had such different habits from us. For instance, instead of using toilet paper, they used a bottle of water to wash their bottoms, pouring with one hand and washing with the other. I personally thought this at least as hygienic as what we did. Again their relationship with the Japs was quite different from ours. They would bow low to every guard and cringe when spoken to. This was of course just the way of the East. Then, in spite of being brought up in that climate, (or was it because of it?) these men with Indonesian blood had nothing like the stamina of our men, and on work parties we often had to do much of their work. Their constitutions were not as robust as ours, and a condition that would perhaps only have laid one of us low for a few days would produce an inertia which sapped their will to live. They were soon dying three times as fast as the British. I learnt to speak Dutch later on and made many friends among them. They were pitifully helpless when laid low by anything and would creep round from one man to the next vainly pleading 'Can you "helup" me?'

On the twenty-fifth of April a party of Chinese coolies came into the camp, and were billeted in our hut, separated from us only by a thin bamboo screen. They indicated to us that they had been press-ganged. They took over the railway job that we had been doing; we were put on the job of carrying rice from the river barges, and loading it on to trains. That evening I peeped through the partition separating us from the Chinese and saw that most of them were smoking opium. They smoked in pairs, one pipe loading only lasting for a few seconds. There was quite a rigmarole involved with specialised equipment. The pipe itself was of earthenware, shaped more like an electric light bulb with a small hole in one side, and a long stem of bamboo fixed in the narrow end. There was also a candle, a thin sliver of bamboo, and a bamboo pillow. The opium was like a lump of sticky toffee. The smoker lay down on his side, head on pillow, candle a foot away from his face. The server rolled a piece of opium as big as a small dried pea into a ball and stuck the sliver of bamboo through it; the pellet of opium was then pressed into the hole in the side of the pipe, and the sliver twisted and removed carefully in order to ensure that a hole was left through it. All was now ready for the great event, and the server put the pipe into the smoker's mouth, holding the bowl over the candle in such a position that the opium started to bubble. Then the smoker sucked on the pipe with one long breath, and it was all over. A minute or so and then rôles were exchanged. To my surprise no-one went into a trance or even dropped off to sleep, so I don't know where the phrase 'pipe dreams' comes from.

On the third of May we were told that we were to pack our kits ready to move up country again the following day. Now that I was proficient enough to swim the river underwater (coming up only once for air), I realized that this evening would be my last chance. The other side had always been a mystery to me as I often obtained glimpses of movement among the trees, but never quite knew what went on over there. As I swam across that evening for the first time, I was only intending to escape if a very favourable circumstance presented itself, especially as I had only the clothes and possessions on me with which I came into the world.

Unseen by either the Japs or our own people I reached the comparative security of the trees on the opposite bank, and lay still for a minute getting my breath back. These long swims were a strain on my malaria-affected spleen, and I always felt uncomfortable for a few minutes after making them. Then I arose and followed a jungle path running for a hundred yards downstream, parallel to the river. Abruptly this entered a clearing, and before I could dive back out of sight, I saw that I had been observed by a Thai sitting on the verandah of a Kampong in the middle. He beckoned to me to come over, and remembering the small fortunes the Japs were offering for live or dead escapees it was not without some apprehension that I approached him. I climbed his ladder feeling somewhat conspicuous also, because I was naked! It was quite a large Kampong, and mine host arose and beckoned me through into the first room, where to my consternation two Thai ladies were sitting cross-legged on the floor. I followed their example with alacrity, hands in lap, trying to make my person as inconspicuous as possible. One woman was young, attractive, and as was the custom before the Japs arrived, bare-bosomed. I assumed that she was the wife; the other was elderly so I assumed that she was mother or mother-in-law. Although they both giggled self-consciously when they first saw me, they soon started chattering away to each other, clearly wanting me to feel at home, and I was surprised to realize how little embarrassment I was feeling, naked in the presence of two strange women. It would have been a different kettle of fish back home among 'civilized' folk.

The man offered me a slice of paw-paw hanging on the wall. It was cut with the same huge knife from his side that would be used for fighting wild beasts. Once given the status of 'guest' I knew that I was safe from the Japs. We conversed for a while in the usual sign language aided by the few Thai words that I now knew. A half hour passed before I realized it, and told my host that I must return across the water before dark. I was given a farewell glass of rice-spirit, and departed to a chorus of farewells from those delightful people, returning uneventfully across the river after my first slice of freedom since River Valley.

On parade at eight fifteen the next morning; waiting all day ready to move off; loaded on to a steam train at ten o'lock that night; moved off at three o'clock in the morning. We travelled in the open trucks for the rest of the night, at ten miles an hour much of the way as we climbed the gradients, fuelled by wood. This wood was stacked by the embankment, cut and put there in heaps of one cubic metre by parties of prisoners. We stopped every ten miles or so to take on a few more of these 'cords' of firewood. At six o'clock in the morning we arrived at Arrow Hill station having been without sleep all night. After a dollop of cold rice apiece, we stepped out once more into the unknown.

For twenty miles we marched. I had felt strangely tired as we started out; before we were half-way I felt as though I was carrying twice the half-hundredweight it really was. Many times I fell down and Jimmy pulled me to my feet. The last few miles I moved as in a trance, not able to think of anything except the fact that I must keep going and not get separated from my friends. Reaching Tarso I dropped down into my allotted space, lying there in my clothes and unable to rise and take my rice. I remember vaguely that we were under canvas, and that as the rain started to teem down during the night the tent wall above me leaked. By the time dawn broke both I and my kit were soaked through. All my stuff was still wet as I staggered out on parade again the next day ready for another long march. We moved out of camp at three p.m. but for the first mile or so I hardly knew what I was doing. Jimmy was carrying the four heaviest of my books, and I had his half-blanket.

I had been at the head during all our other marches; as this column gradually strung itself out, the fact suddenly penetrated through to my befogged consciousness that I was at the back with the stragglers for the first time, and with dismay I frantically looked round for Jimmy. We had heard of the men who fell by the wayside on marches up country being shot out of hand by the guards to save the bother of having to send them back. Despairingly I tried to summon the strength to hurry and catch my 'mucker' up, and staggering like a drunken man finally collapsed on the track, semi-conscious. I do not remember being picked up and put on a truck for the four kilometre trip back to Tarso. As I began to be able to think again I was filled with the strange terror of utter loneliness. Jimmy and I had supported one another through trouble and sickness ever since we arrived in Thailand, now I was to be dropped among strangers; and penniless too for the first time, as Jimmy was carrying the purse. Never had I allowed myself to be without money before, always keeping back a few Tickel for emergencies, and since mucking in with Jimmy I had insisted on holding back most of our cash for the inevitable rainy day.

In Tarso I was put in a hut full of Dutchmen, and later was able to attend a sick parade, together with hundreds of other prisoners. When I eventually reached the poor overworked doctor he diagnosed a relapse of malaria. Tarso proved to be a filthy place mostly populated by the sick who, like myself, had fallen by the wayside. They were preyed upon by a large group of lead-swingers and racketeeers. When I was able, on the seventh of May, I wrote in my diary, 'Hope I can soon get out of here and back with our own boys . . .'

Had I known what our boys were advancing into it is doubtful whether I would have been so keen to join them. However bad Tarso might have then seemed to me in my depressed state, it would have been like a haven to those lucky enough to return to it from those terrible camps up near the Burma border. I heard afterwards that after many days of gruelling marches the survivors of our party from Wun Lung arrived at their destination in very bad condition. The Japs had difficulty in getting rations through to them, and they lived on nothing but an inadequate supply of plain rice. As they pushed on through malaria infested primeval jungle, men died daily. Then, when all were at their lowest ebb, that most dread disease of all, cholera, appeared among them.

Cholera, untreated, will dissolve away half a strong man's body in less than a day; it is so contagious that contacts are almost sure to contract it; the virus can survive even boiling water. During the weeks that the disease raged through the camp hundreds of our friends died, until there were hardly sufficient men left to perform the essential task of burning the bodies of the victims. The Japs left them unguarded in the custody of the germs, and retired a few miles upwind to wait while the disease burnt itself out.

Thus, on the only occasion of my POW life when I fell out on a march, it was to save me from making the acquaintance of arch-enemy Cholera, whose touch meant death. I had been 'kept' once more.

I spent only two days in Tarso, and then paraded to return to Kanburi. We waited on the station until seven o'clock that night, and then boarded a train which moved off three hours later. Japs do not bother about feeding sick men, so we received no food for thirty hours. The train stopped for a long spell in Wun Lung station, and I began to feel a little like my old self again. In my kit was my pair of long drill trousers, clean and pressed, held in readiness for the day we were freed. I unpacked these, and awaiting my chance, when no guards were in sight made a dash to the Chinese cookhouse. I sold my slacks to the Chinese cook for two Tickel, and he also gave me some rice and Chinese pickles. With food inside me, and funds to keep the wolf from the door, I now felt decidedly better as I regained the train undetected.

Passing Chunkai, we waved to our fellows there; I was not looking forward to Kanburi, which I remembered as a dirty camp, undisciplined and with a passing population. To our surprise we stopped at the first station after Chunkai, and were told to get out of the train. This was not Kanburi.

The guards marched us to a camp a few hundred yards away, and handed us over to the British Camp Commandant, a Lt-Col Toosey.

Chapter 7

'Now I will relieve your shoulder of its burden;
I will free your hand from its heavy task.'

Col Toosey told us to sit on our kits while he spoke to us. 'This is Tamarkan camp,' he told us, 'and it's about the cleanest in Thailand; I'm going to rely on you to help me to keep it this way.' This was the first and only time that I was welcomed to a camp, but then Toosey was a quite exceptional officer. He introduced us to his second in command, Capt Boyle, who he told us spoke Japanese. He was the only Britisher I met with this ability, and it made a very considerable difference to the way we worked with the Japs. After our pep talk we were allocated a space each in a nice clean hut, and at five o'clock given our first meal. As soon as we had eaten we were called out again, and taken down the river to wash. The Colonel had no intention of letting us remain in our dirt any longer than was necessary.

When I got the chance to look around, I had to admit that it really was clean and tidy. Col Toosey proved to be the best officer I was to find running a camp. The river was about two hundred yards from the nearest huts, and was shallow at this point; unlike other camps, here there was a gently sloping shingle beach instead of the usual steep bank or cliff. Nearby I saw the railway crossing the river via a bridge consisting of steel spans resting on concrete piers. I heard later that the spans were British and had been brought up from Malaya. A little way further upstream I could see a wooden bridge. This we discovered had been built first, and was now being kept in reserve.

The next day we were allowed to have as our rest day, so I made a tour of all the huts, and was delighted to find several men from our regiment. I heard that a rumour was circulating to the effect that a batch of letters from home had arrived in the camp. This materialized into what was a rara avis those days, a rumour that proved correct. Few working parties were sent out from Tamarkan, which was officially a hospital camp. The Japs worked closely with our Colonel and interfered little with the camp administration.

A high hill overlooked the camp, one of the few in this otherwise flat part of Thailand. The river was much wider, and more sluggish than we had been used to higher up country. Col Toosey had stamped out all the rackets, and the atmosphere was very pleasant when compared to most other camps. I got out my razor the second day and was soon doing a roaring trade at five Stang a time. However I was soon told that I was not allowed to charge for this spare-time service. Looking back I find it difficult to believe that I could have been mean enough to discontinue my barbering just because I was not being paid for it, but I fear that this is what happened.

Although this was designated a 'hospital' camp, we had only one doctor; he was Australian, a Major Moon; not only was he a doctor, a good surgeon, but also a very fine man, and he was well loved as he carried out his duties with very little respite. Most days limbs had to be amputated, and cutting the proud flesh from ulcers was a constant task.

After a few days of better food in better surroundings, the doctor pronounced me fit enough to return up country with the next party to be called for. For a strange wonder, none were called for a week or two.

Quite a high proportion of the sick here were Dutch with Indonesian blood. Most of the sick Europeans recovered quickly under the better conditions. Most of these Dutch however seemed to give up and lie on their 'tampacha' all day as soon as they became ill. Most of them died and the funeral parties that left each day were about four to one Dutch to British. I have not said very much about the killer diseases in these camps, so a resumé might not be out of place at this point, as vitamin deficiency, undernourishment and unhealthy climate were by now combining to cause deaths daily in all camps.

The first disease to strike was usually malaria; as Europeans have no resistance to it, the results could be devastating, and lower the victims' resistance to other diseases. Malaria is caused by a parasite which multiplies in the blood by dividing each into three or four at specific time intervals, thus causing the uncontrollable shivering fits or 'rigors'. After the rigor there is usually vomiting for several hours, followed by lack of appetite for a couple of days. The parasites live and multiply by destroying blood cells, and this in turn causes anaemia and damage to the spleen. There are several varieties of the parasite, some also cause the dreaded 'black water fever' when the kidneys break down, and destroyed blood cells are passed out with the urine. Yellow fever, often fatal also, results from the liver being unable to cope with the huge number of damaged red blood cells. Lastly I will mention the virtually always fatal cerebral malaria. Here the patient would suddenly begin to act strangely, perhaps accuse a neighbour of some impossible treachery. Many cases were not unlike delirium tremens, with the sufferer becoming violent, and perhaps being held down screaming in terror by his mates.

The three main types of malaria we contracted were: BT or 'benign tertian'. The last word denotes that the parasite splits every third day. Benign, because with this variety it is usually necessary to be re-bitten by the carrier mosquito to have a recurrence. ST stands for 'sub-tertian', indicating that the parasite splits or multiplies in less than three days. Therefore the fever is almost constant, and the patient does not get the two days clear of rigors as with BT. ST was more serious, and two men died next to me with ST induced black water fever. MT or 'malign tertian' followed the same pattern as BT but remained dormant in the blood after quinine had apparently cured it. Recurring every few weeks, it caused the patient to become more and more debilitated and therefore prone to other diseases.

The first result of debilitation was usually the vitamin 'B' deficiency disease, beri-beri, and this could manifest itself in two forms, so-called 'dry' or 'wet'. With the latter, a man would today be so undernourished that he was not much more than a bag of bones. Then as the disease began to take hold, he would start to drink more and his body would start to fill with water. Fingers pressed into his flesh produced the typical indentations of oedema. Scrotum, ear lobes, cheeks, any piece of loose flesh blew out like a balloon, and the body would double and treble in weight until the patient could not rise from his bed. The side of his body underneath him would become as flat as his bed-boards, so that he could not even turn over without help. Finally he would become unable to see as his eyelids ballooned out over his eyes. Yet even at this stage, if bran, rice polishings, yeast, Marmite or any other form of vitamin 'B' were administered, the patient could literally begin to pass water by the bucketful, and within a day or so he would resume his former skeleton-like shape.

Dry beri-beri menifested itself in a very different way, the first symptoms usually being pins and needles in the feet, which gradually became numb. This effect gradually spread upwards through the body as the nervous system deteriorated, and when it reached the region of the chest the heart generally became affected, causing the commonly fatal 'cardiac beri-beri'. Without the administration of vitamin 'B' death followed quickly, and quite a high percentage of deaths were due to this.

Dysentery was another important taker of life, and it also came in more than one form. Bacilliary dysentery was very violent while it lasted, and it could prove fatal to those already debilitated by malaria. However, once overcome it left no resident bugs to reopen the offensive at a later date. Amoebic dysentery was quite the opposite, the first attack often being quite mild and even unobserved. However without the drug 'immetin' the infection remained present, and the affected person was a carrier. Amoebic dysentery gradually advanced, and as the weeks and months passed the system became unable to digest food, which would pass through the alimentary canal almost unchanged in a few minutes. This stage reached, death was inevitable.

The most terrifying and hideous of all our diseases in those days were the ghastly tropical ulcers. When resistance became reduced to a low ebb, the flesh would often commence to rot away. Sometimes the commencement could be attributed to a scratch or other wound, but often the ulcer would start spontaneously with a spot or blemish on the skin. Once started they would sometimes enlarge at an amazing speed, and the foul stench of putrifying flesh kept away all but the good samaritans and our ever-faithful medical orderlies. An active ulcer looked much like a lunar crater, and our only medicine was brine. The screams coming from the ulcer hut each day told us that the orderlies were trying to squeeze out the pus that advanced between muscle and sinew; once in the bloodstream that caused rapid death. I have seen daylight under a man's shinbone, and yet saw that man recover. Once the critical stage of the ulcer passed it would sometimes start to heal faster than one would have believed possible, muscle, sinew and bone tissue being re-generated in an incredible way. Skin could not advance quickly enough from the edges of the wound, so at this stage Major Moon would perform a skin-graft operation. These were performed with home-made instruments such as needles stuck in corks, but a surprising number were successful. If the ulcer would not pass the critical state, as a last resort to avoid amputation the wound would be scraped out with a sharpened table-spoon, the patient held down the while by three or four orderlies. Finally the last option; I watched Major Moon through the unglazed window of his operating hut cut through a man's thighbone with a carpenters' saw. The small amount of anaesthetic left in the camp was retained for these cases. Bamboo 'peg legs' were made in the camp for the legless, and eventually we had dozens of men strolling about very effectively on these legs.

(Now each time we hear of refugees starving on the other side of the world, we may safely assume that they will be enduring the same diseases, pain and misery that we knew so well).

The dry season now began to break, and there were showers every evening. My working shorts disintegrated, and as I was saving my other pair to wear on our faithfully anticipated 'victory parade', I decided to make myself a 'Jap Happy' or 'G' string. This was simply a loin cloth made from a piece of string and a strip of cloth about nine inches wide by two feet long. Once made, I found it was much more pleasant to work in than my shorts in the tropical heat, and much easier to wash.

After two weeks in Tamarkan I began to feel really fit again, and recommenced giving haircuts and shaves in my spare time, and this time with the emphasis on 'give'. Then on the thirty-first of May Col Toosey asked me if I would care to take on the responsibility for burials, quite a big job in this hospital camp. Needless to say I was delighted to accept this opportunity of working for our own people instead of the Japs. He explained that until now no one person had been in charge of this operation and that consequently the cemetery had not been laid out to any pre-conceived plan. Three or four men were dying every day, so it was becoming important to work in a more orderly fashion, in order to facilitate the work of the War Graves Commission after the war ended. Another trouble was that with different people doing the job every day, many of the graves had not been dug deeply enough, and wild animals were getting at the bodies. Because of these things, after much persuasion the Japs had at last agreed to allocate a full-time NCO to the job.

I soon discovered that the cemetery fatigue was very unpopular among the men as the Jap in charge was a bullying devil known as 'Pig's Eyes'. He beat up any who did not appeal to him, often without any apparent reason.

The ritual of gravedigging, ropes, un-boxed bodies and the service soon became all too familiar to me, as three or more times a day, seven days a week, we marched with our load the half-mile or so from camp to cemetery. The only minister of religion in the camp was the Dutch 'Padre', and he is one of my fondest memories of the otherwise depressing job of burying our dead. He was I believe a Lutheran, a little man in stature, but great of heart. He was one of the most lovable and tolerant men I have known. His English was quite good and he conducted every service, whatever the denomination. Many of the Dutch were Roman Catholics, and 'Dominee' as he was called, had acquired a Catholic service book, and meticulously carried out every jot and tittle of their ritual, although some of it was against the teaching of his own church. He told me that he was not really allowed to bury them, but that as it seemed to make the other surviving Catholics happy he hoped the Pope would forgive him if he ever found out. I soon got to know the burial service off by heart.

The camp authorities now issued the instruction that no-one was to wash or bathe in the river; there was a cholera epidemic up country, and bodies had come floating downstream. It was most probable that the water was carrying the germ, so all drinking water must be boiled.

Every day my work-party of about ten men went out to clear more jungle and to dig more graves; our route lay through the village of Tamarkan, the first real village I had come across. There were about twenty dwellings, an earth road running through, and a village shop. This was run by a buxom Thai lady, one of the few I had seen without teeth blackened by betel-nut. I only met her husband twice, so I assumed that he worked in the surrounding fields. Often our guard would absent himself, and I would slip back and spend a few minutes in this shop. The lady was sweet and kind, always greeting me with a motherly smile and some little tit-bit or other. The naked baby boy sitting on the floor became used to my visits, and seemed to look forward to seeing me. I would purchase tinned food and other goods for both myself and for those left behind in camp. This shop, unlike the Kampongs, was not built on stilts, but had an earth floor. The Thai mum did not use nappies, but when the little boy performed on the floor she skilfully flicked the result out of the door with her bare big toe. Thai children seem only to need feeding. It is true that the little girls did wear one garment of modesty; a little chain-mail apron about three inches square. Girls' heads were shaven, but boys retained a pigtail growing from the crown. Boys with two crowns and therefore with two pigtails were regarded as lucky. As crowns do not usually grow in the centre of the head, their asymmetrical pigtails gave them the appearance of what an old countryman friend of mine would have called 'A pig wi' one ear!' Thai elder sisters look after their baby brothers and sisters, and it was quite common to see little girls of five or six years old playing together while carrying a baby on their hip.

Although the Thai housewife may not have had much

washing or housework, besides working in the fields there was much food preparation to carry out. Every day the home-grown rice grains had to be husked by passing them through a pair of bamboo 'mill-stones', or by pounding them for a long while in a large mortar. Then the winnowing was carried out by putting the grist on a large wicker tray, and skilfully throwing it up in the air and catching the grains again, letting the air movement carry off the husks. Rice needed much hand cultivation; the seed was broadcast in the small flooded nursery paddies towards the end of the dry season. When the rains came and the higher paddies flooded, the women and girls, working ankle-deep in the mud that had been stirred up by oxen drawing under-water ploughs, pricked out the rice plants one at a time. I tried to imagine what English farmers' wives and daughters would have to say if they were called upon to plant out fields of corn, one plant at a time, twice a year.

The rice crop is heavy compared with wheat, and the straw is over four feet long. It is hand cut, a handful at a time, and tied into sheaves weighing about twenty-eight pounds each. These are tied on each end of a bamboo pole, and carried on the shoulder back to the kampong, where they are tied, head inwards, to a large bamboo pole standing upright in the ground. This eventually makes a stack about nine feet in diameter, and the cattle are allowed to eat the straw on the outside, but as soon as they get near the rice this is removed, allowing another lot to drop down. I never saw any draught horses, carts were pulled and ploughing done by hump-backed oxen, and the long horned grey water-buffalo.

The Japs now started building an Ack/Ack post on the hill overlooking the camp. Our men were required to carry sand and cement up from the river to make concrete, and water every day for the guards. A party of men was also detailed to dig slit-trenches for the gun-crew to shelter in. (These were to be needed before the end came.) The Japs emplaced a Bofors gun, captured earlier from the British, and now pointed skywards, awaiting our planes.

After five weeks sojourn in Tamarkan Col Toosey one day accompanied my work party to the cemetery, and he showed me exactly how he would like me to lay the graves out in future. We were by now burying on average six men a day, and planning had become very necessary.

On June the twenty-third a large party of sick men arrived in the camp from up country, and searching their ranks for friends, I found three of our regiment, Cpl Scales, and Ptes Dusty Miller and Whitby; they told me that they came from Tak-a-Nun camp, where nineteen of our boys, including Sgt Jolly had died from cholera; they looked in poor shape themselves, and it was clear they had been through a rough time since I saw them last.

I received no wages while working on the cemetery, so apart from what I was keeping for a rainy day, I now ran out of cash. On the night of the twenty-sixth of June therefore, I broke into the Jap store and helped myself to six tins of food and a bar of soap. All had been made in England, and filched from Red Cross shipments intended for us. However, I felt very guilty about what I had done as should the theft have been discovered the whole camp might have suffered. I shared the proceeds with my neighbours, and never again did anything like that.

A few days later I was to get beaten up for the first time in that camp. 'Pig's Eyes' was in charge of my grave-digging party, and was shouting his usual stream of incomprehensible orders. I started my men off digging the first batch of graves in the spot where Col Toosey had directed; the Jap ordered me to start in a totally different place. I tried to explain that I was digging to an agreed plan, but he pretended not to understand. For my part I refused to move the men, and as Pig's Eyes got madder and madder, I finally turned my back on him and told the men to dig where I had told them. The next thing I saw was the stars generated by a rifle butt hitting me over the head; but my faithful double-crowned hat saved me from being knocked unconscious, and I turned before the next blow landed to face my attacker. He threw his rifle to the ground and punched me about the head in blind rage, but as I found no difficulty in standing my ground and looking him in the face he soon calmed down. I fell my men in, ignoring the Jap, and marched them back to camp without digging one grave. I had no more trouble from 'Pig's Eyes', and was in future allowed to run the work party without interference.

On the first of July another hundred sick men arrived in the camp, from Kinsio this time, including six-feet-seven 'Tiny' Lee from our regiment. (As he was too tall to parade in the ranks he had been put in Joe's Pioneer Platoon back in England. Another man who was well under five feet had also been sent there for a similar reason. We were stationed at Weeting Hall, near Brandon at the time, where our toilets were of the bucket type. Tiny and his short colleague had the job of emptying these toilets, and the sight of the two of them trying to carry one of these buckets without spilling the contents should have been filmed and preserved for future generations.)

Out at the cemetery one of my men was caught by a guard trying to sell his shoes to a Thai. It was Pig's Eyes day off and we had another guard in charge of us; I heard the yell of rage and looking across saw our boy about to be belted. I called to the guard and ran over as quickly as I could, and then joined in shouting and gesticulating at the terrified man. I made the Jap understand that if he would leave it all to me I would ensure that the villain received adequate punishment for his crime. This was of course done in order to avoid the usual beating up that was the punishment for such offences.

Returning to camp I was surprised to discover that our guard was far from satisfied with leaving the punishment to unsupervised British justice; he asked our officer to let him know when the 'trial' was to be held, as he proposed to attend it himself. Thus we had to go through the motions of charging the man with 'Conduct prejudicial to good order and military discipline', and he was awarded four days on rice and water, and fourteen days detention. We were all getting little else than rice and water, and we were all being detained, so his sentence made little difference to him. A beating however could have left him on the road to despondency and the Jap cooler could lead to death.

One day an officer thought he would like to come out on our cemetery party with me, and he was therefore nominally in charge. During our lunch break one of the men saw a Thai signalling from the bushes that he would like to buy his wristwatch, so he slipped out of sight and spent a few minutes bargaining in the bushes as was the custom. Price agreed, our lad unwisely let go of the watch before getting a firm grip on the cash, and the Thai disappeared with both into the jungle. The poor victim ran over and told his tale to our officer, though goodness knows what he thought could be done about his lost watch then. To add insult to injury however, the officer put him on a charge, and I was called upon to give evidence against him the next day. The crime with which the man was charged was 'Communicating with Natives!' This charge was not, I am sure, in what was then known as King's Rules and Regulations.

Since being taken prisoner I had not heard one genuine piece of news. We listened to the endless rumours with much interest but little credence. In Tamarkan however, I was told that the 'pukka griff' was being communicated to one of the working parties by a 'well dressed Thai'. In truth officers in a camp down the line had rigged up a radio receiver, and when they passed news items from camp to camp the recipient was always told to say that a 'well dressed Thai' had told him. This was of course in case the Japs heard what was being said. The first news I heard was at this time, and it was to the effect that a big naval battle had been fought off the coast of New Guinea, and that twenty-four enemy ships had been sunk. A big battle had taken place in a place called 'Orel' or something like it, and the Russians had knocked out fourteen hundred Jerry tanks. That of course was in the European theatre. Lastly we heard that General McArthur had at last launched a campaign in the Far East theatre, believed to be in the chain of islands which runs from Australia to Singapore. The 'well dressed Thai' subterfuge did not work for long, and when the source of our news was traced the culprits were tortured and left to die in a ditch.

In Tamarkan I was the senior NCO in my regiment, and was therefore responsible for the welfare of our lads. A few days after hearing our first news I was crossing the open space where we paraded for work on my way to the hospital huts, where I was going to visit Pte Buckle and a few other sick men. It was evening but not yet quite dark; too late I saw that I must pass one of the most sadistic of our guards, and he was clearly the worse for drink. All prisoners had to bow when a Jap passed by and this always stuck in my gullet. 'Courra!' screamed the drunken Jap as he took in my apology for a bow. 'Engerisso soljah no bruddy good!' Lifting his thick stick he proceeded to beat me about the head and shoulders. No bones were broken however, and although I was sore for a few days no real harm was done. This Jap was not liked by his own mates, so none of them came to his assistance, which was just as well since when there was more than one they vied with one another in inflicting punishment.

Shortly after this, having got several graves in hand, I was sent with my party by truck to Banpong to fetch a load of bamboo poles for hut building. On the way we stopped in a large Thai village, and were left to our own devices while our guards regaled themselves in a café. Seeing that we were unguarded I went for a stroll around the 'shops'. These were in fact more like market stalls, and the shopkeepers sat or stood behind them. Not knowing that we were to walk round in public I had only donned my loin-cloth, and to the Thais I must have looked immodest; one of the stalls was hung with garments of all kinds, and an elderly Chinese lady was sitting to the rear of the platform working a sewing machine. A few yards past this stall I was halted by hearing the clip-clop of wooden shoes hurrying to catch me up; turning, I found the little lady tailoress, black eyes smiling, holding out a strange pair of black Chinese pattern shorts for me. Seeing me hesitate (I felt that I was parading under false colours as I had a pair of shorts back at the camp), she made signs that I was to put them on right away. I opened my mouth to explain, but then seeing her sweet smile I said thank you instead, and put the shorts on. She stood back and surveyed me with pride, but then suddenly ran off; looking in the direction of her startled glance I saw the guards leaving their café, so I hurried back to the lorry.

Col Toosey gave a lecture on 'Dunkirk' on the evening of the thirteenth of July, but I was called out half-way through as a hundred sick had just arrived from Tarso. Two of them had died during the journey, and needed burying in a hurry. We now always kept a few graves dug ready, so led by our dear

Dominee our little burial party went forth in the dark. Next day two medical orderlies who had been serving the sick up country, and had come down with the Tarso crowd, died of typhoid. This caused much concern lest an epidemic occur, and the order went out that all drinking water must be boiled and all eating utensils and mess-tins sterilized. There was, thankfully, no spread of the disease.

Throughout our days as prisoners the medical orderlies stuck to their task with faithful devotion, and tended the sick when often nearly as ill as their patients. They had a truly thankless task with night shifts in the foul ulcer huts, pain and suffering all around them and no relief to offer; perhaps spending months trying to clean up an ulcer without dressings, inflicting pain each day, only in the end to see the limb amputated. I would not have exchanged jobs with them even when railway work was at its worst. From this time on there was a continual stream of sick men arriving in the camp from even further up country and in progressively worse condition. They came down in open barges, and the direct sun killed many before they arrived, so the number of funerals held each day soon doubled.

A permanent concert party was now formed in the camp, and performances reached a high standard, with a character named Bobbie Spong performing the female rôles so well that we could forget his true sex. The Jap guards attended the shows, and they would applaud vociferously, especially Bobbie's turns. The first performance I attended included an invitation to members of the audience to mount the stage and give a 'turn'. Plucking up the courage to give my first ever public appearance, I ran out at full speed lest my nerve fail me. There was a bamboo root protruding from the ground just in front of the stage and I did not notice it in my haste. My bare toes felt as though they had been pushed back into my heel as I rolled on the ground in agony. The crowd roared their appreciation, thinking it to be all part of the show. My song, when I recovered enough to sing it, received only polite applause.

For some time I had been having trouble getting work out of some of the half-blood Dutch workers who were now daily on my cemetery party. When I told them what to do they would gesticulate and say 'No spik Inglis, no understand'. On one occasion when I had mostly these chaps, and I was left with only a few British who would work, I even tried clouting one of them who I knew did understand what I was saying; however the fellow screamed out at the top of his voice in pretended agony so that I had to desist before the guard came over and beat the man up in real earnest.

That night back in camp, I decided to try to learn to speak Dutch instead of reading the novels which were circulating in the camp. Then I would be able to speak to the lead-swingers in their own language. Walking into one of the Dutchman's huts I asked if there was anyone who would teach me to speak Dutch, and a schoolteacher volunteered to take me on. He proved a clever and patient tutor. We had no grammar or other text books; however I had a New Testament, given to me by our village Free Church when I went into the forces, and my teacher lent me his Dutch New Testament. First of all I had to learn by heart the pronunciation of the alphabet, and the rules concerning vowel sounds in open and closed syllables. Unlike English, Dutch spelling and pronunciation are quite regular, so that once the rules have been mastered, to see a word is to know how to pronounce it. Not having much else to do in the evenings I had mastered this part of the exercise within a week or two. Now all I needed to do was, phrase by phrase, compare my English New Testament with the Dutch one, since our Authorised Version and the Dutch are translated from the Greek almost sentence for sentence. I was surprised how easy it was to begin to get the feel of the language by this method, and how much more pleasant it was than learning dreary lists of words from a vocabulary. By the time I had read through the four Gospels I found myself beginning to think in Dutch. Of course my neighbours got a bit fed up with my gutteral mutterings every night, as part of the exercise was always to read aloud.

After only a month or so I tried out my learning on a group of Dutchmen, and could not understand why I was laughed at. However, I soon found out that, like my version, the Dutch New Testament I was learning from was couched in an archaic form of the tongue, and that I was in fact saying something like 'Yea verily, the guard hath said unto me . . .' and so on. From now on I joined groups of the Dutch whenever I got the opportunity, and gradually acquired the modern idiom. Within two months there was not much that I could not communicate in my new language, and 'No spik Inglis' was no longer heard on my cemetery work party.

A football appeared in the camp with a party from up country, and although I am a rugger man without a clue concerning soccer, due to shortage of fit men I was roped in to play in a British versus Dutch match which one of our officers organised. To my surprise, we won, two goals to nil. The Japs watched the game with considerable interest, and afterwards gave each member of the winning team a packet of cigarettes and a bar of soap as prizes.

The rainy season now set in, and our bed supports sank down through the mud so that we had to drive in longer ones. During my captivity I had gradually been making myself a kit of tools, starting from the day in River Valley when I found the sharpening stone, one or two old hacksaw blades, a file and a small hammer in the dump. For instance, I had annealed one of the blades, cut coarser teeth in it and made a bamboo frame to convert it to a wood-cutting saw. I could exchange the blades so this also served as a hacksaw. Up country I had found a small native meat cleaver, and I had cut this into strips to make chisels and a plane blade. Therefore I was now able to tackle many jobs, including tin-smithing; often in the evening someone would bring round worn-out or broken items of equipment to see if I could do anything with them, and very often I was able to help.

To celebrate the anniversary of their entry into Thailand, the Japs called us on parade, and the head one made a speech in Japanese, translated for us by Capt Boyle. Those who had performed good service in the camp were awarded small prizes. I was called and given a small hand-towel for my work in the cemetery. I had been without a towel since having mine stolen when at Roberts Hospital.

The Japs now gave us authority to make crosses for all the graves, so all the carpenters in camp were called together and given the job of making these, and carving the names on them. On the twenty-fifth of August we took all the crosses out to the graves, and after we had put them in their places it began to look more like a cemetery. The next day I heard that L/Cpl 'Peanut' Runham, and also Pte Seamark, both from our mob, were ill in the sick bay, so I went over to see them. Peanut had TB and was coughing blood, Seamark beri-beri and general malnutrition. When Seamark and Pte Cornwall (also one of our boys) died five days later the doctor entered 'starvation' on their death certificates. There were twenty-two men from our regiment at the funeral. The sense of unity and regimental pride among our men lasted until the end.

Out grave digging the next day 'Pig's Eyes' insisted that he had heard one of the men use a bad word and he kept us all standing to attention in the sun for a long time waiting for the guilty man to own up. When this failed to obtain results he selected six men whose faces he did not like and smacked them all round the face. I am sure that he had heard nothing wrong, but just felt like 'kicking the cat' as the Australians would say. A Thai man had been watching all this, concealed in the bushes. When the guard was not looking he sidled up to me and gave me a parcel of tobacco and cigarette papers to share among the men.

Tamarkan was the only Thailand camp where the Japs allowed us to have Sundays free. The next day was Sunday and it coincided with the birthday of the Dutch sovereign, Queen Juliana. The Dutch spent the day in sports and competitive games, and in the evening they held a very good concert, much of which I was able to understand.

Two days later 'Pig's Eyes' was put in charge of another working party, and accompanied by a British officer. On their return to camp we heard that for no apparent reason the Jap had bashed our officer up, and that he had been brought back to camp in quite a bad way. The next day, to everyone's intense delight 'Pig's Eyes' was himself bashed up by his own NCO for what he had done, and transferred to the less honourable job of working in the Jap cookhouse.

In order to engender a competitive spirit in the camp our CO announced that in three days time, that was on the ninth of

September, an exhibition of Arts and Crafts would be held. I had done quite a few drawings since our capture, so I stuck some of my better efforts on to a piece of cardboard, in preparation for taking first prize. On the appointed day I entered the hut where the Exhibition was to be held, and my breath was taken away by what I saw. Incredibly good works of art had been produced from somewhere among the men's kits; I could not have guessed that such talent existed in a cross-section of ordinary people such as we had here. Everything made from improvised materials, there were both oil and water colour paintings, engravings, woodcuts, statues, ornamental boxes, models of engines and aeroplanes and many other things, all executed from memory. My own poor effort was quite insignificant. Although the Dutch were in numerical minority I noticed that three out of four exhibits were from them. Our Colonel awarded the many prizes that afternoon at a special ceremony, and all but four went, deservedly, to the Dutch. Needless to say I won nothing. The only things I had which might have stood a chance were my tools, and as the Japs did not allow us to have these I had been unable to enter them.

Among the full-blooded Dutchmen in the camp was a short and slight old fellow who I only knew by his nickname, 'Outje', which literally was I suppose 'Oldlet' or 'little old one' in English. He had spent much of his life working among the natives of Java, and learning the healing properties of local herbs. In Tamarkan he was our unofficial herbalist, and was not sent out on working parties, but instead spent his time ministering to the sick. The main trouble he explained to me, was that he could not get hold of the right herbs in camp, and that most of the disease could be cured if only what he wanted could be obtained. One of his main remedies was turmeric, or as the Dutch called it, 'Kunier'. It grows in that part of the world, and the plant is very similar to ginger. The root, shaped like root ginger, is one of the ingredients of curry, and its bright yellow juice was what Outje used to massage into the limbs of sufferers from dry beri-beri; from the grated root he made poultices for ulcers, and he also produced a concoction for the treatment of dysentery from it. Outje's arms and clothes were always stained saffron. At this time he ran out of the herb, and knowing that I went through Tamarkan village daily on my way to the cemetery he asked me to try to purchase some for him. He had a Thai dictionary, and told me to ask for 'Kah-min'. I was also to try to purchase some betel-nut as he could, he said, make a pain-relieving drug from that.

I managed to slip away unseen from our working party a few days later, but the Thai lady shopkeeper looked in blank incomprehension at my effort to pronounce 'Kah-min'. She even fetched some cronies from next door. I drew a picture of the root on the floor, but they brought me ginger. I made faces to indicate that it was hot and pointed to some yellow material, and one of them recognized my requirement and with an 'Oooh!' of understanding she sang 'Kah-min'. I had no more trouble after that, but the shopkeeper explained that as she had none on the premises I was to give her one Tickel and collect the goods next day. True to her promise I was able to take a big parcel of the right stuff back to Outje the following day, much to his delight. I concealed all the things I purchased from the Thai shop in the blankets and ropes we used for lowering bodies into the graves, as we were occasionally searched by the guards. We did not have coffins of course, and the dead were sewn up in their own blanket or rice-sack. Once or twice we found bodies had been dug up during the night, and their blanket stripped off. I never knew whether this had been done by local people or by our own boys.

On the twelfth of the month poor old Peanut died. There was neither cure nor hope out there for anyone unfortunate enough to contract TB. That same afternoon we buried a Scot. We had a piper in the camp, and marched to the cemetery following him as he piped a sad lament. Even the Japs seemed moved by it as we passed their guardroom, and in the village all the Thais turned out to see us when they heard the strange sound approaching along the jungle track.

We were now issued with another of the printed Jap letter cards, my second to date. I was careful this time to complete mine in capital letters; on the fifteenth of September a party of prisoners called at the camp to collect them, and a member of this letter party told me that there were four letters addressed to me lying at Kanburi camp. So near and yet so far, as we had no means of communication unless the Jap willed. Men in the letter party also told us that they had heard that there had been landings on the continent of Europe, and that we were pushing the Jerries back in Italy.

Three days later, during the night, the Japs caught five prisoners outside the camp selling chunkel-heads to the Thais; they had been purloined from the Jap tool-store. These men were taken to the Jap office and beaten without ceasing until four o'clock in the morning, by which time they were only semi-conscious. During the following day they were again beaten by different Japs every few minutes. By evening, when the Japs took their victims to Kanburi, none was recognizable, their features having by then been kicked out of shape. Two days later they were again brought back into the camp, and tortured for another whole day. This may have made one or more of the men divulge the names of others involved in the escapade as the Japs now took another five men from the huts, and tortured all ten of them for eleven days. Three of the latter five were then set free, and the remainder taken away from the camp, never to be heard of again. While the men were under interrogation, a man from my hut was caught picking up a note one of the captives had poked through a crack in the Jap office wall. He was beaten black and blue and was very lucky in not being taken in with the victims.

A party of two hundred men was now called to leave for Non-Produck, a camp the other side of Banpong. I made a list in duplicate of all men of our regiment in Tamarkan together with a letter to our CO who was in Chunkai. I gave these to one of our boys in the party, asking him to drop one copy and the letter off as the train went through Chunkai, and to give the other copy to any of our officers he could find in Banpong when he passed through there. This was done in order that whoever had our letters might know where to send them.

I now noticed that the wooden crosses were beginning to be eaten by termites, so I pointed out to the Colonel that there was not much chance of the names of the dead remaining legible until we were freed. He asked me if I had any better idea, and I offered to punch the names on strips of tin, and to bury them in bottles in each grave; he told me to go ahead. Within a week I had prepared enough name tags for all the graves, and then I asked our quartermaster to obtain the empty bottles for me. However, he said there were not enough bottles in the camp for my purpose and refused to help. That evening, sack over shoulder, I walked up and down every hut in the camp calling for empty bottles, and obtained enough and to spare. 'Are you a Pelmanist?' asked L/Cpl Keyes, the quartermaster's clerk, when he saw the result of my efforts.

The CO now told me that all fit men were shortly to leave for up country, but that as he needed me for the cemetery work he would try to keep me back. A day or two later about three hundred men left on the first stage of their journey. On the second of October it rained so hard that our hut was flooded. With the rest of my kit, my diary was soaked, and I went to our cook-house to dry it out. That part which I had written in ink had run, and in later years I was to find it very difficult to decipher. The next day we heard very strong rumours that the war in Europe had been won.

Among the other sick men from our regiment was a Pte Grace. He was exceedingly ill, and as I went to see him each day I knew it was miraculous that he survived at all; I have never seen a man lose so much weight and live; chronic dysentery had literally reduced him to skin and bone and he weighed little more than two stone. Yet he was always cheerful throughout his suffering, and although the doctor told me that there was no hope for him now, I still hoped that his terrific willpower would pull him through. There was no flesh to absorb the shock of lying on bare boards, and when we buried him a few days later his bones protruded through the torn skin.

I made friends with a Dutchman named Willem Poel, in the ulcer ward with a bad leg ulcer. I noticed that he never had visitors, and in a hut with most Englishmen he had no-one to talk to. So I got in the habit of stopping for a few words with him when I visited one of our mob in the next bed. He was well over six feet, slow of thought and speech and I liked him. He never uttered a sound when he had his ulcer squeezed, although many of the bravest could not help crying out when this job had to be carried out. His infection had started six months earlier, and he was rapidly becoming worse. Major Moon had now to amputate through the knee joint, to prevent the ulcer encroaching on his thigh. During the next two weeks Willem had two more amputations before an amputation through the hip finally halted the advance of the disease. There were no anaesthetics to relieve post operative pain, and lying on the bare boards the patient often suffered such intense pain that he was affected mentally. Willem was to become so affected, and he took such a dislike to me that he refused to speak after he recovered from his last operation.

On the twenty-fifth of October the Japs told us that the railway was completed up to the Burma terminal, and they gave us a day off in celebration of the event. A sick man arriving brought me news that my 'mucker' Jimmy was also back from up country, safe and well in Chunkai. I wrote him a note and gave it to a member of the next party to leave for up country, and asked him to throw it out at Chunkai station as he passed through.

The following day was a great milestone in the days of my captivity; I received six letters from home. There was one from my father, one from my brother Reg and four from my mother. One of the letters told me that my sister Marjorie had given birth to a daughter and that they had called her Jennifer Jane; now I was an uncle! The letters were all over a year old, as must my niece now also be. I was one of the few to receive letters at this time, and I spent every spare moment I had reading them over and over again. Difficult to understand now perhaps, but that first evening all my friends, and even a dozen strangers came to me with a whispered request to read my precious letters. Many of our men, some with wife and children, received no mail during the whole of their captivity.

My mail changed my whole outlook for the next few weeks; they were the first communication from the outside world; we were not forgotten men after all. I slept with the letters under my pillow, and felt them now and again during sleepless hours of the night. During the day I read them over and over again, and when going through moments of depression I was comforted by the thought of them.

One of the Dutchmen gave me a small ball of home-made (or

home-grown) dried yeast. He said I should crumble it into cooked rice, leave it for a few days, and remove a ball of it for future use. Sugar and water was to be added to the remainder, and I would then, after a few days have the Malayan dish known as 'Tappy'. He let me taste some of his finished product, and I found it quite pleasant although rather acid, and it smelled quite fruity. My effort was a failure, my rice just became sour and I had to throw the precious stuff away, so I went to see the expert, my friend Outje (whose real name I had by now discovered to be von Braam). He gave me another ball of yeast, and he told me to multiply it first before making tappy. This I did, and from one of my six balls produced my first successful dish of tappy. However the next time I tried, it went wrong again, but this time I had produced a very strong flavoured rice vinegar; this failure was a great success, and I found that a spoonful helped plain rice down very well; as I had made rather a lot, I found a ready sale for some of it among my friends.

Men stopped returning sick from up country at this time, so the number of funerals soon halved. I went to see Col Toosey and asked if I could do the cemetery job half-time only, and do a paid job under the Japs for the rest of the day. He seemed quite shocked, he did not know that I had been working for all that time without pay. He gave me some cash to be going on with and promised that I would in future receive fifty Stang every ten days. He did keep his word, but I was only to remain there for another eighteen days. For the remainder of my Tamarkan days I spent about half my time working on jobs about the camp, including the task of building a pigsty, the Japs having promised our CO a pig for Christmas.

The enemy had completed the Ack/Ack gun emplacement, and they now fired a few practice rounds. It was only then that the truth dawned on us that in the event of a low-level air attack, any shells missing the aircraft would hit the camp; Col Toosey asked for permission to make a Red Cross flag to lay out during air-raids, but this was refused. Many of our men were later to die because of that refusal.

On the seventeenth of November I saw my first Allied plane since the time of our capture. It flew right over our camp, so high as to be barely visible, certainly at more than three times the effective range of the Japs' Bofors gun. However they let fly at it, effectively admitting to us that it was 'one of ours', and of course giving their position away. As the plane was so high we realized that it must be on a reconnaissance flight, and we hoped that the pilot saw that this was a POW camp. The adjacent bridges were of course prime targets for air attack, and the camp was only a few hundred yards away.

Now we were all ordered to stay in our huts out of sight during any future air-raids; any men seen outside would be shot on sight. Out on the cemetery party I also noticed a change in the attitude of our guards; I was watched more closely and was finding it increasingly difficult to contact my Thai friends in Tamarkan village. Outje ran out of turmeric again and asked me to get another lot; I ordered it by signs for collection the following day as I passed the village shop.

Next day I was so closely supervised that I found it impossible to get away to collect the goods. At this time we were short of firewood in the camp, so an extra duty for my grave-diggers was to carry back to camp any tree trunks from the jungle we had cleared during the day. On this occasion I asked the strongest of my men to assist me in carrying back a heavy log about eight feet long, and perhaps ten inches thick. I was at the rear end of the log as we passed back through the village that evening; the shopkeeper's husband was leaning against a tree with my parcel in his hand, and with a furtive glance around me I proffered the cash and was handed the turmeric. However the heavy log on my shoulder had prevented me from observing one of our guards lying in wait in the jungle opposite. As the Thai handed me the parcel I saw a look of apprehension appear in his eyes and he tried to draw back at the last moment, but too late; a scream of rage filled the air as the Jap came rushing over. A teak two-handled practice sword was raised high over his head, and in his fury he sounded like a madman. The heavy log on my shoulder made it impossible to dodge as the weapon came crashing down on my skull. Again and again it landed, half the blows missing my head and cutting pieces of bark off our log. I felt little pain, but as each blow landed I felt as though my brain were soft, and was gently being pressed in while everything became momentarily dark. After about the third blow blood came squirting out of my Aussie hat, which remained jammed on my head throughout. The Jap's anger spent, he stopped hitting me and stepped back, dazed with the shock of not seeing me fall though looking as though my head were bashed in. Blood by this time was everywhere, over my mate at the other end of the log, over the Jap and dripping off the log to form a pool on the ground. I seemed to be able to survey the whole scene dispassionately, I suppose my brain was anaesthetized by what had befallen. The Thai women covered their faces; my friends told me later that they thought I was like a chicken still standing after losing its head, and they were waiting to see me fall.

I am sure that when some of the Japanese lose their tempers they are quite beside themselves, and do not know what they are doing; neither can they control their actions. This one slowly regained his composure, and instead of setting about me again, he curtly ordered my comrades to lift the heavy log off my shoulder and sent me back to camp ahead of the others. I must have looked like something from Madame Tussaud's by the time I entered the camp and passed the guardhouse. I had continued to bleed profusely all the way back and I was covered thickly in congealed blood, I was also beginning to feel light-headed, and was unable to walk straight. I was well known to the guards on duty, since I always passed out of camp with the funeral parties, and I think most of them liked me. The duty guard stopped me and called his friends out; they gathered round looking at me in disbelief, and making their sympathetic clucking noises. For some strange reason I now for the first time felt sorry for myself, and an overwhelming desire to weep came over me. It was nothing to do with the pain, but just the effect of a little sympathy. Not wanting them to see tears in my eyes, I turned and tried to run away across the open space to our lines, but could not run straight. Luckily by this time some of our men were coming over, and a couple of them helped me to Major Moon's hut.

The doctor removed my hat and an orderly brought a bucket of water; between them they first of all cleaned up my head, and the worst of the wounds were sewn up. I was feeling better now, and they showed me my hat; in three places the sword had cut cleanly through both crowns. 'Sergeant' said Major Moon, 'if you head isn't solid bone it can't be very far short of it! You're not half as bad as you looked, your hat saved you from a fractured skull.' I knew also that had I fallen the Jap would probably have killed me on the ground. I was ordered to rest for three days, and then went back to work.

Strong rumours began to circulate that most of us were going to be moved to Chunkai, and on the twenty-third of November a load of sick men boarded barges and moved off by river. Two days later I spent my last day in the best camp in Thailand, having been informed that I was to move off with a party of men to Chunkai in the morning. We held a 'Farewell Tamarkan' concert that evening; the Japs all turned up at the show and made it clear that they also were sad because they must leave with us. For the first and only time, one of the Japs arose and volunteered to give a 'turn'. He rose to his feet and went sedately up to the stage. After bowing to us he began to perform a strange dance. We tittered at first, thinking that perhaps this was a comic turn, but we gradually began to be touched as he sang a plaintive song on one or two notes in strange rhythm, and to hand and foot movements the like of which we had never before seen. His sad expression as he sang told us without need of word understanding, of the nostalgia in his Japanese heart for his homeland.

It was at ten a.m. therefore on the twenty-sixth of November that we fell in, ready, we hoped, to board barge or train. There was a large crowd of us, all the fit men left in Tamarkan. My kit seemed heavier than ever as I struggled out on parade with it, but I think that was mainly because I had not yet made up all the blood I had recently lost. To my dismay I found that it was to be 'Shanks's pony' this time as we moved out across the paddy fields; luckily Chunkai was not many miles away, and I made it without having to shed any of my gear.

I seemed to have been a very long time there, and left a little part of myself behind in Tamarkan. I even now think of the comradeship there with some nostalgia.

Chapter 8

'I keep thinking of the good old days of the past,
Long since ended.
Then my nights were filled with joyous songs.'

We immediately saw that Chunkai was now unrecognizable from what we could remember of our earlier sojourn there. First of all the graveyard was ten times or more the size. With a dozen or more deaths a day it was to grow much bigger. Compared with Tamarkan everything looked shabby and dilapidated. Attap does not last for long, and I suppose there were insufficient fit men here to maintain the huts properly.

I was put in charge of feeding arrangements, and taking the job seriously got out my tools and fashioned two ladles for dishing out. The rice ladle did not work very well, so I found a couple of pig's shoulder-blades, and these proved very satisfactory.

Nearly everyone in Chunkai seemed to have skin disease; huge ring-worm patches overlapping each other; pellagra, the vitamin deficiency disease which makes the skin the texture of brittle tissue paper, weeping between the cracks, and often forming ulcers. There were no supplies of calomine lotion or other medicines to relieve the terrible itching these complaints caused, let alone supplies of the vitamins which would quickly have cleared the trouble.

As soon as I was able I toured the camp to find our own lads, and was disappointed to find that Jimmy had moved out some time before. There was one of our officers, Mr Oliver keeping a record of known deaths in our regiment, and when he was able to add those from my list the total reached one hundred and eleven. After a few days with no work to do I began to think that I was in danger of 'letting myself go' as I could see so many had already done in this camp, so I saw the camp RSM and asked if I could be given a full time job. Somewhat enigmatically he said 'Wait and see!' so I had to leave it at that.

Chunkai was still plagued with rackets, and after a few days one of our Corporals reported that a thousand Tickels worth of stuff had been stolen from his kit. I wondered how under our conditions any prisoner could legitimately have acquired such a huge amount of booty. Very few working parties were being sent out, and half the fit men seemed to be engaged in some business venture or other. Every few minutes of the day and evening someone would pass through the huts shouting his wares:'Come and get it! Hot and sweet, five cents a cup'. This was a 'coffee' made by burning rice on a shovel and then grinding it up with a bottle on some hard surface. By now we all called the 'Stang' 'cents', as there were a hundred to the Tickel. Other men came round with peanut toffee, sambals, and many other things. There was also a thriving industry in cigarettes, these fashioned on home-made machines from the black local tobacco, and they looked very professional although the thick paper, mostly torn from books, could not have tasted very nice.

On the eleventh of December, without much notice, we were told to pack up and parade to board a barge for Tamarkan. I could scarcely believe my ears or my good luck. It would be good riddance to dirty thieving Chunkai, where a good dose of Col Toosey was what was really needed. Thrilled to bits, I climbed aboard the boat and arrived at Tamarkan an hour or so later; but Col Toosey and Capt Boyle the interpreter had left the previous day.

The Japs lined us up to tell us why we had come here. The railway had been completed with the diligent help of the prisoners. As a token of appreciation of the work done by The Imperial Japanese Army, and out of respect for the lives laid down by the prisoners, we were to build a shrine under the guidance of Japanese soldiers. When finished it would be dedicated to all races, whatsoever their religion or colour.

We commenced work immediately, forming human chains

from the river bank to the hillock two or three hundred yards away where the monument was to be erected. Baskets of sand were filled and passed back to be emptied in a heap at the top. The guards regarded the work in exactly the same light as before, and every now and then there would be the inevitable shout of 'Courra!' perhaps followed by a blow as someone was spotted not working hard enough. On the second day it was decided that we had enough sand for the time being, and we were put to collecting shingle. We had to crawl along the beach selecting stones as near an inch in diameter as possible. One of the men picked up a stone, decided it was too big and tried blindly to throw it far away behind him. I heard the usual Jap scream of rage, and saw the nearest guard clutching his nose in furious agony. He laid about the unfortunate prisoner for a minute, but luckily his stick was not a heavy one, and no injury was caused.

None of my men had a watch, and the Japs refused to tell us when it was mid-day, so that we could eat. Our task was so many cubic metres per day, and when we had accomplished hat we could go home. So I rigged up a sundial on the beach. Sun was one thing we had plenty of, and if primitive peoples could rig up a sundial, then so could I. However I was wrong, my sundial never worked properly although I tried it at many different angles, adjusting it each day. Later on I wondered if he Japs moved it every night after we left for a bit of fun.

When we had gathered all the shingle they required, we were sent over to the foot of the Ack/Ack hill to gather small ocks. These we were told were to be built into a plinth which would form the base of the shrine. We carried them back by he hundredweight in barrows and on stretchers, and at last here was a big enough heap of these.

Lastly, as far as materials were concerned, the Japs gave us ozens of old marble table tops; they must have raided every afé in Thailand to find them all. Every one was badly stained nd our immediate job was to clean the faces up ready for ames to be carved in them. Although we tried everything rom soap to sand the stains refused to budge.

In addition to working on the shrine, we had to find work arties daily carrying stores and water to the top of the

Ack/Ack hill. This was the most hated job; there was no shade, the hill was very steep and the guards would allow no rest half-way. Our wooden buckets weighed as much as the two gallons of water they held, and if the Japs had not used all their previous day's supply they tipped it out on the ground in front of us.

Back to the shrine, and our next task was to clean up a big heap of old timber which was to be used as formwork in which to pour the concrete. The timber was full of nails, and very rough-sawn. We had no tools like planes or scrapers so I told the guards that it was not suitable but was just told to get on with it. In fact when they said that they were satisfied, the timber still looked pretty awful and it was clearly going to be unsatisfactory.

The Japs had to 'stand to' nearly all the night of the twentieth of December as a continuous drone of Allied planes was heard passing over the camp. I was on Ack/Ack fatigue the following day and found the tired guards particularly evil tempered, especially as we were unable to avoid a certain cockiness in our manner. For years they had been telling us that there were no Allied planes left as they had blown them all out of the sky. To get their own back they made us fill their bath to the brim, and when I protested that the precious water we were carrying would overflow when they got in if any more were added, I received a cuff for my trouble.

Parties of sick from up-country had been arriving in camp ever since we started work on the shrine. Many of these men were Aussies, and very sick, often with dead and dying among them. They mostly arrived during the night in barges, and when we heard the 'Poof Poof' of the boats stop at the camp we used to turn out to help carry bad cases into the huts. During the night of the twenty-third we were carrying a bargeload of very sick men in when the Jap gun opened fire on planes flying over the camp, and we were lit by the flashes of exploding shells as we walked. One Aussie died in our arms as a friend and I tried to life him out of the barge.

The Japs now issued us with wood saws and told us to make batch-boxes for measuring the ingredients of concrete. I was surprised to see that Japanese saws work in reverse to ours, cutting when pulled instead of when pushed. They are shaped something like a large butcher's cleaver, with the teeth starting small by the handle and gradually getting larger towards the further end. Two hands are necessary to hold the long handle, so the wood has to be held with a foot or by a comrade. None the less they seemed to work very well.

We were allowed a day's rest on the twenty-fifth of December but we scarcely noticed that it was Christmas, and I did not even mention it in my diary. This was the only occasion as POWs that we made no effort at all to celebrate Christmas Day.

Three days later we started mixing concrete. Two men at a time were required to do the mixing, working at breakneck speed until relieved. The mixers had to keep in front of the measurers who had to pile up the cement sand and stone on the end of the wooden staging. The staging stretched right up to the memorial itself, and as the mixers were required to turn the mix over four times in all, at the last turning the concrete went straight down into the formwork. This proved a very efficient way of working and I think the concrete went in faster than if we had had mechanical mixers. The pace set by the Japs was so fast that after a couple of days only a private soldier named Mooney and I could stand up to it, so we got the job full time. I did not really mind, especially as we knew that at least we were not assisting the Jap war effort as we had been on the railway work.

Fifteen days after our return to Tamarkan the Japs told us that their rations were now so bad that they were going to leave us for a time while they went upstream to blast the river for fish. As they disappeared round the bend in the river, I took a friend and waded out to collect any stray fish that might elude them. We were lucky, collecting and stowing away about ten pounds of fish before the guards came back. We had far more than many of the Japs. That evening we cooked them up and had a grand fish supper. The following day a plane came over in broad daylight, again attracting Ack/Ack fire and the guards had to 'stand to' all afternoon, which meant that we had the afternoon off.

On the first of January 1944, New Year's Day, the Japs told

us that this was a feast day in Japan, and celebrated by decorating the camp with palm leaves and green bamboo. Everyone had the day off, and I made use of it by sewing up the sword cuts in my Aussie hat. I also took the opportunity to insert some packing between the two thicknesses of crown as cushioning should further blows be struck. While sewing I heard the drone of planes again, and the ineffective staccato of the Bofors on the hill.

Out on the shrine the Japs were in a bad mood now and set us bigger tasks to complete. The first day back at work they gave us thirty-six bags of cement to mix with nine times the volume of aggregate, and we had to stay until the work was done. Mixing that lot in the blazing sun, by hand, with no respite, was almost too much for me, and I thought I was tough. To make matters worse they made us find hut pickets every night to make sure no-one got out of the camp. Every time a man left the hut to go to the toilet he had to collect a numbered tally from the duty picket, and hand it back when he returned. Woe betide any caught outside the hut at night without a tally, and the Japs collected the tallies in the morning to make sure none was missing. We were worked so hard for the next few days that it seemed likely that the shrine would be followed by another in memory of those who died on the shrine, and so on . . .'

There was a full moon on the night of the tenth, and as we heard the Japs being rousted out of their beds to 'stand to', and heard the sounds of our planes overhead, we began to feel that perhaps it was not all quite so one-sided now. We talked among ourselves, some voicing aloud the question that had bothered us all; what would the Japs do if our parachutists landed nearby and tried to free us? The general opinion seemed to be that we should all be shot before they had the chance. As we lay chatting, for the first time we heard the sound of distant bombs exploding. From the direction and distance we decided that the attack must be in the vicinity of Bangkok.

Our shrine was now beginning to take shape. It consisted of a cubic base or plinth with a tapering 'needle' rising from it; all cast from very rough concrete. We went down to Kanburi by barge to fetch a load of rocks; these and the smaller ones from the Ack/Ack hill were to be used to build a wall round the site. The marble tabletops were going to be stuck on; it seemed to me that it was going to look a very scruffy monument. However, I was never to see the finished job, as next time I returned to Tamarkan I was too ill to go out on working parties, and the shrine was outside the camp boundary.

On the seventeenth I was given by third stereotyped postcard to complete for sending home. I now saw that I had an opportunity to let the folk at home know that I had received their mail. One part of the card read: 'Please see that . . . is taken care.' On the dotted line I wrote 'Jennifer Jane' the name of my new niece. My parents did receive this card about a year later, and that was the first intimation they had received that I was alive. In spite of this my mother wrote me a long letter each week until the day of my return, learning to type as she had been told that typed letters would be more likely to be passed by the Jap censors. I believe that it was because of this I received letters when many of my friends received none. When, on the twenty-first of January I received another twelve letters from home my cup of happiness was full, let the Japs do what they might.

A new phenomenon now appeared in camp when one night Japs sidled up to a group of prisoners asking if any had pound notes to sell; up until now they had told us that Sterling was worthless. I guessed that the Thais were offering big money for our pound notes, and the Japs were trying to make a profit; I cannot think that they wanted to save them in case they lost the war. In fact they had changed their tale of late, telling us that the war would probably go on for ever; before they had always spoken of the imminent total victory.

For some days I had been developing an ulcer on my heel and it was not responding to the treatment I was giving it, probably because I was standing on it for such long hours while working on the shrine. In the end I had to show it to the doctor, and he took me off work at once. On the second of February, I was sent back to Chunkai, and arrived there at one p.m.

At sick parade the doctor told me to rest my foot up for seven days, and I spent practically all that time bathing my heel with salt water. When I was not doing that I was de-bugging my bed-space; the place was practically alive with the beastly things. Most days I heard planes fly high over the camp, and often heard them open fire at Tamarkan.

The Jap in charge ordered all prisoners to write an account of the fighting leading up to their capture, and to finish up by saying who they thought would win the war and why. He probably thought he would learn more from us than from his Japanese one hundred percent propaganda newspapers. For my part I enjoyed writing an entirely fictitious account of my part in the battle for Singapore.

A few days later volunteer blood-donors were called for to help certain bad cases in the sick bay. I had a sample taken but mine was A2 whereas they required O4 blood. However the next day a Pte Butler, a consumption case, had a bad haemorrhage of the lungs, and I was called upon to give blood to him. Blood was not stored in bottles for use later as in Britain, but I lay on a table above the patient, and a tube ran from a vein in my arm directly in to the recipient's. The poor chap rallied for a week or so but died before I left the camp.

A public highway ran through Chunkai, the Japs were unable to close it as there was no other thoroughfare in the area; until now we had been allowed to walk on this road when going from one end of the camp to the other. The order was now given that prisoners might no longer approach it; we took this to mean that there must be good news about and that they did not want us to hear it from the Thais. A rumour began to circulate at the same time that fit men in the camp were to be shipped to Japan, and a few days later this was corroborated when a list of men scheduled to go was published. My name was not on it, so as my ulcer was just about healed I saw the RSM and asked for my name to be added. He said I was too late, but put my name on reserve.

Now I was fit again I went out with work-parties every day, mainly gathering bamboo for hut-building, and firewood for cooking. Some days I was on hut-building, and this was what the Japs called a 'Speedo job'; we had to pull a hut down and try to rebuild it the same day so we really had our work cut out, as each one was fifty metres long.

When I awoke on the morning of the first of March I discovered that Jimmy had arrived in camp during the night with a couple of hundred men from Tak-a-Nun. During a very long chat I heard of all that had befallen him since we parted. It was only now, as I heard of the terror of those cholera camps, that I realized how fortunate I had been, safely in dear old Tamarkan while my friends suffered and died. As Jimmy had our cash when we split up he insisted on giving me half his Thai money now, anyway he said, he was going to Japan in a few days, and it would be of no use there. I gave him half my bedding, as he had lost all his.

Working long hours on the hut building party for the next few days I saw little of Jimmy, but he was issued with new clothes to wear in Japan, and on the tenth of March they left Chunkai on the first stage of their long and hazardous journey. I heard later that the ships on which they embarked carried no Red Cross or other distinctive markings, and many had guns mounted on the decks. They were bombed and torpedoed with our boys battened below deck. Jimmy was however one of the lucky ones to make the journey safely.

Someone told the Japs that I had been a builder back in England, and they ordered me to draw plans for the huts we were building. All they provided was pencil and paper. So during the following days, using my tools, I made myself an eighth inch scale rule, a protractor, two set squares, and a tee square. I bought a compass from a Pte Jennings; he had carried it around unused since he was captured. I quite enjoyed drawing the plans, and it made a nice change from the 'Speedo' hut-building party.

There was a Dutchman in our hut named Bruder. He asked me if I would draw him plans for a (pseudo) English Tudor house, as he wanted to build one in Holland if he ever returned. It took me a month of evenings and Yasume days to complete the plans, and then only roughly. However Bruder seemed quite pleased with them, and assured me that he would convert them to bricks and mortar if the opportunity arose.

We were given a radio message form on the nineteenth, and told to write a short message each to broadcast to England.

None of us believed there was the slightest chance of it being sent, (neither were we wrong), but we all wrote that we were well and hoped those at home were also.

The Japs at this time became very scared of catching cholera, and we had to build them new huts further from the river. They also decided that the river water was only good enough for prisoners to wash in, and imported Chinese well-diggers; two of them started work on rising ground not far from the river.

Watching these men work during our lunch break was, I found, an enlightening experience. Although I thought I knew a lot about excavation and the different methods of preventing earth falls, I was to learn a completely new technique. The only tools needed were two joss sticks! No timber whalings, simply joss sticks. One man worked at a time, excavating round and round with a short-handled chunkel and basket, and as he went downwards the man on top pulled up the basket of earth with a rope. Most important of all he tended the smouldering joss sticks, as without the smoke to keep the demons away the sides would be pushed in. With a simple faith like that, a Christian's life would become so much more straightforward.

The well sides went down perfectly straight and circular without gauge or plumb bob, and water was struck about fifty feet down. Concrete rings were then cast between two rings of sheet metal, pieces of banana stalk being let into the concrete to rot later, and allow water to percolate in. They did not seem to worry about germs from the surface water, perhaps the joss sticks took care of them also. Only three rings a day were cast so it was a long time before the well was ready to use. The men spent the rest of the day, when not making rings or lowering them down the hole, smoking opium in the canteen.

On the twenty-fifth of March we saw our first really heavy daylight air-raid, as literally dozens of aircraft flew over the camp. A few days later I was shocked to hear that a British officer was engaged in the medicine racket. Together with some other men I was told, he stole the precious life-saving quinine from the hospital hut, and sold it to the Thais for money. Thirty pieces of silver for sure. The next day two

Dutch sergeants, by name Pas and Lightman, were caught red-handed selling quinine, and they were interned in the Jap 'cooler'. This consisted of bamboo cells built out in the sun, each one too short to lie down in and too low to stand up in. The inmates were kept short of water and beaten from time to time. It was more a form of torture than imprisonment.

Soon after this I made friends with a Scot named Cpl Willox. He was an excellent fellow of the old school, sincere, kind and very proud of his nationality. He was also a piper and he had kept his pipes. Every evening he would unwrap them and lovingly clean them. Then he would march up and down behind our huts near the camp boundary piping old Scottish melodies. At times the pibroch would be slow and sad; at others Willox would be thinking of better times as he marched gaily to a jig or to a military air.

He told me that at one time he used to teach Highland dancing and asked if I would like to learn, to pass the time away. Having always loved to watch the Scottish dances I was pleased to accept, and within a week or two I could do The Sheen Trews, Highland Fling, Schottische and The Sword Dance. He told me that I had taken to it like a duck to water, and should have been born a Scot.

I seemed to be more sensitive to bug and louse bites than most of my friends, and would often get my behind bitten when sitting on someone's bed only to be told that I must be imagining it as they had killed them all; but I had never seen so much vermin as here, and since the dry season was now upon us I took to sleeping outside as the nights in the hut were intolerable. My black shorts wore out at this time, and I put the remains of them away to take home as a souvenir of the Chinese lady who gave them to me; later however I got so short of rag that I had to use them.

When I finished drawing plans I worked on making tools. From a piece of teak salvaged when the Jap quarters blew down I made a plane, and this was the best of all my tools; with its blade cut from a cleaver it worked really well. I also made handles for my chisels, and bound them on with wire as I had no ferrules. One of our men dug up an old axe head; it had been used as a hammer and the eye had been bashed in.

During the next few evenings I managed to straighten it out and fit it with a handle; it was to become my most useful tool.

A week or so later we were re-formed into a group and told that we should be leaving shortly for Burma. Then we were told that the Burma trip was cancelled and that we were to be known as No. 35 Japan party. This changed suited me very well, as at that time I felt that the nearer we were to civilization when the end of the war came the better chance we would stand of escaping murder at the hands of our captors. I did not know of course that the Allies were to drop on Japan the weapons which were to start a chain reaction which might end civilization for the whole world.

We went to work as usual on the morning of the nineteenth of April, but were brought back post haste and given two hours notice to pack up our kits ready to leave for Japan. Then we were paraded (they told us it was to receive warm clothing for the Japanese climate), but after hanging about for a long time we were dismissed, sans clothes. Looking back on events, I guess that the Japs were being forced to change plans almost daily with reverses in Burma, and the ships which should have taken us away being sunk or needed for other purposes. That night instead of being on my way to more temperate climes. I went to a camp concert organized by a professional actor named Leo Britt, and entitled 'Wonder Bar'.

Having just unpacked my kit and seated myself on the ground waiting for the show to begin, I was aroused from my reverie by the guards rushing round in a tizzy, calling us back on parade. Stuffing all my gear into the various haversacks as quickly as I could, very disorganized, I marched out past the cemetery with the others. We knew not whither, as far as we had been told we were still No. 35 Japan party, but as we were still clothed in our rags it was unlikely the Japs would parade us in front of civilization looking like this. As for Chunkai, I felt no regret at the parting, in fact I was glad to see the back of it. At ten-thirty that night we marched into Kanburi camp, and I lay thankfully down in the bed-space I was allocated, and for the first time for months slept 'til morning.

Kanburi was now a staging camp, only enough fit men being kept there to unload supplies from barges, and to load them on to trains bound for up country. Our first day there was spent in unloading rice out of barges on to a jetty. The river was outside the camp boundary, and water for camp use still had to be drawn from the well. Our guards at that first working party were some of the best we ever came across, and treated us more like comrades than captives. The second day out on this job the rickety bamboo jetty started to collapse under us. The water was deep and many prisoners could not swim; when I pointed out the danger to them the Japs asked me if I could strengthen it, but had no tools to offer. As they were so friendly I took a chance and told them that I had tools back at the camp, and they took me back to collect my 'illegal' things. They took considerable interest in what I did, and stayed watching until I was satisfied my repair was safe, and made to join the others unloading. However, they told me to wait, and brought out the office table for me to repair. For the next few days I was kept busy on interesting furniture repair work.

During my stay in Kanburi I was also to earn myself quite a lot of cash by doing jobs for those prisoners who had more than I did. One of my best money-spinners was collecting empty pea-tins from the Jap cookhouse, and making them into mugs by cleaning off the rough edges and riveting a handle on. I sold them for ten cents each.

I was also able to get a few leaking four-gallon tins thrown out by the Japs, and salvage enough good tinplate out of them to make them into buckets. I became quite proficient in joining smaller pieces together by folding the edges over, and some buckets were made from five or six separate pieces. I had made a mandrel from a length of teak tree-trunk about nine inches in diameter, and used this for forming the buckets on, and turning over the seam round the bottom edge. They were watertight without solder.

The wet season now came in and the camp soon became a sea of mud again; all fit men set to digging trenches in the hope of draining off the flood water to avoid the huts becoming flooded once more; and the trenches worked.

On the sixth of May at seven-thirty in the evening we moved out of Kanburi, and I was quite sorry to leave. Especially as we found out that we were destined for Chunkai once more, where we arrived at ten-thirty that night.

However I need not have worried as we were only to stay for one day, and during that day were issued with Red Cross parcels. These had been opened by the Japs, cigarettes and other items they fancied removed, and the remains issued at the rate of one parcel between six men. There should have been one parcel per man, so there was not really very much to share.

At three o'clock in the afternoon we boarded open rail-trucks in pouring rain, and travelled up country in the deluge for eleven hours, arriving at what we were told was Kinsio camp in pitch darkness at two o'clock in the morning; we could not have been wetter had we just emerged from the river. As dawn broke we were able to see that the camp was derelict, and had not been occupied for many moons. Most of the huts had fallen in, and this included the erstwhile cookhouse, where there were now no cooking facilities at all.

The CO sent for me and asked if I would take on the job of organizing repairs to the camp, starting by building a new cookhouse, so I started work immediately. As everything was so filthy and the camp looked as though it had been left in a hurry through disease, I thought to make a priority of providing a sterilizer for mess tins and eating utensils. I 'won' a steel forty-gallon drum from near the Japs' quarter, and started to cut round the top with one of my chisels and my axe. Nearly round, I tried to pull the flap up but my hand slipped on the oily surface, and I made a nasty jagged cut across the ball of my left thumb. I went to see Dr Gotla who had accompanied us, to try to get it sewn up, but he said the wound was too ragged and dirty to sew and I just had to keep it bandaged as well as I could. To my surprise the wound did not fester, and the piece of flesh (half my thumb) which I had nearly severed, grew back again with only the scar as a souvenir.

The next few weeks I worked pretty much alone putting the huts and cookhouse back into shape, and making utensils, as most of the men were out on daily work parties maintaining the track. One day the guard saw a wild pig running through the camp, and took a pot shot at it with his rifle. He only injured it, and the animal twirled round on its behind snapping fiercely when we approached it. I ran over to the cookhouse and collected my axe and a knife, and returned to tackle the task of pig slaughter, something I had never done before. I put on a confident air to impress the guard; first of course I must render it unconscious to put it out of pain, and to stop it biting me when I cut its throat, so I started to hit it over its head with the back of my axe as hard as I could; but no matter how hard nor how many times, the poor animal refused to lose consciousness, and in desperation I hit it between the eyes instead of on the top of the head; it went out like a light. I later saw that a pig's skull is over two inches thick at the spot I had been attacking.

The next job, that of cutting the jugular artery would, I thought, be comparatively easy, but how wrong I was. I fiddled about with the knife waiting for the stream of blood to tell of success but none came; and at last, when the pig began to stir, in desperation I cut off its head. The guard said that if I prepared the carcass our cooks could have half, and as this arrangement seemed too good to be true I left my other work and got cracking straight away before he changed his mind.

I had not so much as drawn a chicken before, so I cannot pretend that I made a very good job of scalding, scraping and dissecting that pig, but I did eventually finish up with two heaps of bruised flesh, one for us and one for the Japs. Our cooks complained at all the bone splinters produced by my axe, but the men at their boiled pork with gusto that evening on their return from work. As we had no butcher in Kinsio, after that many other beasts of different kinds passed through my hands, and learning from my mistakes I was to become a fairly proficient slaughterman.

The rations were as bad as I encountered anywhere and consisted of rice, dried greens and 'stinkfish', the last two items having been rejected as unfit for Jap troops' consumption. They were full of maggots and dropped to powder and string when we tried to get them out of the boxes. The fish had been something like kippers during early life, now like little Bo-peep's sheep they left only their tails behind them. There were, however, usually a few fish in each box that had not quite reached this stage of maturity, and if we grilled these on a piece of tin many of the maggots would wriggle out, and those that stayed behind would at least be sterilized. The fish themselves tasted so foul that many could not eat them, and the maggots that were eaten probebly tasted better than the fish. I ate my share, not willing to miss out on my necessary protein requirements.

I was asked to build an oven for the cookhouse, so that we could have baked rice-balls or 'doofers' as we called them. Although only made from boiled rice, they made a change and were much in demand from the cooks. When I looked round the camp to see what materials were to hand, there seemed to be nothing suitable for oven building. Well, one step at a time, I could at least start off by making a heap of sun-baked bricks, and accordingly made a wooden mould. Next I dug a hole and by treading earth and water together produced some nice glutinous mud, and soon I had a nice row of bricks drying in the sun. The following day however, when I tried to stack them, they dropped to pieces in my hands, and I realized that something must be wrong with my technique. Yet they used sun-baked bricks in biblical times and the sun must be hotter here. Yes, the Israelites in bondage to the Egyptians had to make bricks without straw, and found it difficult; that must mean that it is easier with straw. I looked round the parched camp with absolutely nothing growing in it. Then I saw the useless boxes of dried greens the Japs had issued; they were just string and powder, surely they would do for straw. My next batch of bricks were perfect and within a few days I had made more than I would need.

During the following days I searched every inch of the camp trying to find something to use for the inside of the oven, but without success; but outside the camp boundary the railway line ran, and in the distance I could see a heap of empty four-gallon tins and a six foot length of railway line. By next morning they were safely concealed under my heap of bricks.

Now I was able to start building, and mixed up another lot of mud to use as mortar. I built a long fire-pit with a low wall each side, and built in the oblong tins resting crossways over the fire, all the open ends facing the same way. The fire was to be drawn up the far end of the tins, and back over the tops, and

I was to build the chimney over the front end to draw the heat and carry the smoke away. I used the railway line to form the lintel which carried the top brickwork and chimney, and completed the effort with the oven door made from flattened tins and fitted with a handle. The final job I thought, as I surveyed it with pleasure, only requires a few wheels to look like Puffing Billy. I had been forced to build it much longer than necessary in order to conceal the end of the railway line I'd pinched.

'Let's try it!' said the cook, so I laid a fire in the trench, and after fanning it for a minute I was delighted to see the smoke rising beautifully from the chimney. As the clay began to dry out the oven heated up, and I had to push the damper in to stop it from becoming red-hot. The cook made a batch of rice balls and they came out as brown as berries; the oven was declared a success. Before I was able to eat my first 'doofer', three Jap engineers came stalking in, and searched the cookhouse. One barked at me 'You see Nippon line, so-ca?', and he held out his arms to indicate the length. Looking as innocent as I could I pointed to all the line running past the camp. 'Bagero!' (fool) he shouted, 'Smoroo (small) line.' We all commenced helpfully to look under the sacks and boxes on the cookhouse floor, but the Japs turned impatiently to go. Wait though, one of them caught sight of our new oven and he turned round to give it a closer look; Japs do not use ovens in their cooking. With much curiosity and murmuring they walked round it, and seeing the door handle one of them took hold of it; his yell would have awakened the dead. We then saw one of the others pick up a piece of sacking and lift the door off. Seeing the next batch of 'doofers' already nicely brown, they demanded one each, but when they tried them and found only plain rice they threw them on the floor in disgust.

The Thais do not use ovens either. They do make a kind of cake the texture of crumpets. They make these with a batter of ground rice and water, and bake them in earthenware 'bun-tins' with lids, which they heat over their charcoal fires. These buns only took five minutes to cook, and were delicious.

Men returning from outside work parties told me that there were camps of Tamils nearby, employed on maintaining the permanent way, and that they appeared to be treated worse than us by far, like animals in fact; and at this time the Japs were pumping propaganda into India about the wonderful all-embracing Nippon plan for an enlightened Greater East Asia. Less than ten per cent of the Tamils press-ganged by the Japs in Malaya were still alive when the capitulation eventually came.

Our captors were now printing very crude Thai money on what looked like their toilet paper. When we first came to Thailand only the Tickels were of paper, lesser denominations were all in the form of zinc coins. The new Jap money was in paper right down to ten Stang (or cents).

At about this time a party of men, clearly a nomad people, came walking past our camp accompanied by a herd of skinny goats. Very short and stocky, these fellows had bright red hair and looked more like Europeans than Orientals. I asked our guards who they were and was told that they were a tribe of Indians who came through Burma and Thailand each year, taking their goats with them and carrying goods to trade. There were no women with the party, and their skin was as fair as ours. I have since been unable to identify the race of these folk, and have often wondered who they were.

Two of our men broke into the Jap food store shortly after this, and helped themselves to a 100 kg. bag of sugar. The next day, as so often happened, word flew round that the Japs were starting a search. One of our first tasks on arriving in a new camp was always to prepare secret hiding places for one's forbidden articles. Within minutes of the warning the two miscreants came staggering into the cookhouse with their huge bag of the best Jap sugar, and being half-starved they weakly dropped it on the floor and stood panting helplessly. We looked blankly at the sack; there had been none of this stuff issued to us in Kinsio and if the Japs caught us with it it would mean a beating up, and a spell in the cooler at best; at worst . . .

One of the cooks was a short red-headed Welshman, very strong; I had never hit it off with him. He was the first to wake up; 'Give us a lift Sarge!' he said as he grabbed two corners of the sack. With a lift and a swing the hundred kilos was on his back, and in the twinkling of an eye he was trotting out of the back of the cookhouse. Thirty yards away the path crossed a ditch, and we always had to jump when we walked that way. Our cook threw the sack of sugar in the ditch and it was just about level with the path. We trod it well to flatten it out, and kicked dirt over the top for camouflage. As we ambled back in to the rear of the cookhouse the Jap search-party was coming in from the front. After searching for ten minutes they left the back way, up the path we had just left; but they did not notice that they did not have to jump over the ditch now. We left the sugar there for a week, daily expecting a visit from the dreaded Kempi-ti. We need not have worried as our guards could not report the loss since they had themselves filched the sugar from rations passing through on their way to the front line in Burma. When we felt safe we retrieved the sack, and I made a special measure to share the sugar fairly between everyone in the camp.

We now had two working parties leaving the camp daily, one was raising sunken parts of the embankment, the other was repairing wooden bridges. These abounded in this part of the country, where many ravines had to be traversed. On the twentieth of June one of our men fell off one of these bridges and suffered a very bad leg injury. He was carried back into camp, and on a table in the medical hut Dr Gotla operated without anaesthesia, there being no analgesics in the camp by this time.

On the twenty-third our CO and Sgt Pitkin (our medical sergeant) were ordered to go down river by barge to Chunkai to draw wages and rations for us. They returned four days later with nothing but a sack of soya beans. We had none of us ever seen these before, but someone said that they were very nourishing, and would provide some of the vitamins missing from our diet. No-one knew how to cook them, but they looked somewhat like haricot beans, so we cooked them for about half an hour. They were still harder than boxwood, and the best teeth in the camp could not crack them. After some experimentation it was found that by simmering for twenty-four hours they became just about soft enough to scrunch up. We cooked them in this way as and when firewood was available. I discovered later that the Thais did not cook them whole, but ground them up with water in small stone mills, and the white paste that came out was cooked as a batter. Some of our cooks later found a way of soaking them, and then grinding them into flour which they made into sour bread.

Rations began to improve slightly with the issue of a small amount of meat brought in by barge from Chunkai. The worst of our sick went down to Chunkai by barge, and fit men came to replace them on the return journey. These barges were hired from the Thais who also manned them. They had obviously been made originally to be pushed through the water by the big 'T' handled punt poles, as indeed some of them still were. The ones hired by the Japs all had paraffin engines, but in the swiftly flowing parts of the river skilful use of the pole was still needed, as the engines were not powerful enough to drag these heavy boats, often loaded down to the gunwales. Each boat had a running-board along each side; the boatman walked along this to the front of the boat, dropped his pole into the water, and walked back along the board, 'T' piece to his chest 'walking' his boat upstream; very hard work it looked too, and they kept it up all day. Those boats with no engine had two 'pushers', one walking along each side, and keeping the craft straight with no-one at the tiller must have taken quite a lot of skill.

On the fourth of July we were informed that there was to be no more meat sent up from Chunkai, instead we would be issued with beef on the hoof. I was still working as camp tinsmith, carpenter and general handyman. The CO asked me to add 'camp butcher' to the list, and never having been short of confidence, I of course accepted. The next day I was told to bring one of the cooks with me as we were going down the line a couple of camps to collect two oxen.

After a few kilometres we arrived at a Tamil camp, and outside this we found our oxen tied. They were very ancient beasts of burden with most of their hair worn off where plough and cart had rubbed during the years. They were not without sores either. The ropes they were tied with were far too short to lead them by, and we only had one piece of string between us. The cook and I agreed that the only thing we could do was to kill one of the animals then and there and carry it back, while the Jap led the live one back on our string. After some demur, our guard agreed, and I asked him if I could go in and ask the Tamils to lend me a knife and axe or hammer. He said he would go himself, and left us outside the wire, unguarded. Later he signalled for us to bring one of the animals into the camp, and we found him standing by a post with a hook in it where he could tie the ox while we killed it. He had a knife and hammer in his hand, so we dragged our reluctant charge to the post and tied it up.

Until now the camp had appeared to be deserted, but suddenly we were aware of dozens of furtive figures appearing from the nearby huts. Some were staggering on fleshless legs, most were crawling on hands and knees too weak to stand. We were soon completely surrounded by these poor Tamils whose shrunken lips, but still white teeth gave them the appearance of walking dead. Eyes and cheeks were sunken, bodies fleshless. Belsen could not have looked worse; I shall never forget them.

Our treatment of the Tamil workers on the Malayan rubber plantations before the war may have left much to be desired for all I know, and they may have been justified in welcoming the Japs as their saviours. Now in these forced labour camps they were quite unable to cope. Having been told exactly what to do all their lives, they were incapable of organizing themselves in the way we could. Japs only issued food rations to those who could do a full day's work. We shared ours out between the fit and sick. The Tamil each ate his own, the sick man starved. Since sooner or later all fell sick, inexorably they nearly all died, if not of their sickness, then of starvation. I was told that the Japs had written this camp off and left them to starve, and sent lorries in periodically to collect the dead and burn them in the jungle.

After the experience I had already gained in killing a pig, I managed much better this time, finding that both animals 'worked' more or less the same. The skinning proved the most awkward, and I was unable to avoid getting the carcass smothered with dirt off the ground. As I worked, every movement was followed by hungry eyes, as the Tamils squatted in a circle around us. They were waiting for the skin and entrails of this old-age pensioner we had slaughtered. I cut the skin into as many pieces as I could and gave them one each. We tied the ox's legs together, and slinging it on a bamboo pole we moved off with our load. I looked over my shoulder and saw two Tamils squabbling over a piece of skin from the head with the horns attached. It gives an indication of the condition of these animals that we arrived back in camp not unduly tired, though having carried the equivalent of a side of beef each for a distance of about three kilometres. The cooks found it necessary to cook the flesh until it separated like string from the bones, and every man received a tablespoonful of beef broth with his evening rice for three days.

A week later I killed the second ox, but after going to the trouble of killing and skinning it, I found its lungs were eaten away by disease, so we had to bury it.

I suppose the reason that there are no horses in Thailand is that there is hardly any grass. During the rainy season some coarse grass did spring up here and there, but this disappeared completely in the dry season. The oxen and water-buffalo however seemed to be able to exist on rice straw alone; no wonder they were so thin. The carts these animals pulled were long, but only three feet wide, so made for traversing the narrow jungle paths. The two wheels were untyred, the four felloes tied together with rawhide. As they wore they became nearly square as the softer long grain in the middle of each felloe wore away more quickly than the end grain, and they would rock crazily from side to side as they went.

The drivers would not carry a stick or whip to urge their beast on; instead they sat on the front of the cart, hand on the tail. If the pace slackened from the usual dead slow to nearly stop, then a twist of the tail would liven the animal up. These same beasts pulled the ploughs, which did not look to be much more than pointed branches to be dragged through the mud under water.

In our camp was the Jap office covering the whole area. On the eighth of July the Japs who worked there brought some native spirit into their quarters, and at nightfall they moved out of their huts the worse for drink and evidently looking for trouble. Experience had taught us to keep out of the way when they were like this; however to our surprise they made for the huts where our Korean guards slept, and started shouting what to us sounded like nasty remarks at the Koreans. Several of these left their quarters and started to scrap with the Japs, and the fighting continued until the NCO in charge of the engineers came over and sorted them out. These squabbles became fairly frequent from now on, as the hitherto latent dislike which had always existed between Japs and Koreans, broke through to the surface.

As camp handyman I was kept very busy with jobs which included making stretchers for the doctor, baking tins for the cookhouse, sharpening gramophone needles for the Japs, and mending their torches. These contained a small dynamo which was ratchet operated by means of a lever on the side. A Dutchman brought his ring for me to remove the diamond for him to sell. He wanted to keep the ring itself as it was given to him by his wife.

On the tenth of July I received two more letters, one from my sister written in June 1942, and one from my mother dated the following November. The rainy season had started a week or so earlier, and the rain was now falling in ceaseless torrents. The river was soon in full spate as it roared down from the mountains in swift, muddy and un-navigable flood. We had to stop washing in the river, not only because it was so muddy, but mainly for fear of being carried away. Instead we washed in the continual stream pouring from the eaves of our huts.

During the hours of darkness in Kinsio we could often hear tigers roaring in the jungle. The Japs kept their meat ration in the form of live pigs in an enclosure on the edge of the camp, and the tigers now started leaping the fence at night and running off with pigs. After losing three or four in this way the Japs erected a bamboo tower with a platform on the top, overlooking the pigsty, and on the night of the nineteenth they lay up there waiting to ambush the unsuspecting tigers. In the middle of the night we were awakened by a noise sounding like the opening barrage of the Somme. Next morning we heard that the bag had been one tiger, and that it was to be shared by all the Japs in the area. Our four guards share was one leg and a portion of the brain, which later they ate raw, dipped in sugar!

The leg they stewed and had for supper. One of them brought the bones out of the foot to me and ordered me to make them cigarette holders out of them. I made them all right, and was so pleased with them that I decided to keep one for myself for a souvenir. When the Jap came to collect them a day or so later he spotted at once that one was missing. When I explained that one had been no good and that I had thrown it away, he clearly did not believe me, and yelled and waved his arms about for a while; but no blows were struck, and he eventually left muttering. Our four Japs were pretty good as Japs went; the working parties on the railway however worked under the Jap engineers from the next camp, and they were a savage lot, and not a day passed without tales brought back of someone beaten up.

Not only did I have to kill the very few animals that the prisoners were given but as camp butcher I had also to kill the Japs' pigs and cattle. On my own it was quite a problem holding the animal still while I clubbed it unconscious. In the end I hit on quite a satisfactory expedient. I tied the animal to a tree with a fairly long rope, then chased it round and round the trunk until it was jerked to a stop head against the tree, and I landed my blow before it could start to unwind.

As I have indicated before, the Thais seemed to be an independent and brave race. A day or so later one of our work parties came across a dead tiger with a knife in its side, and not far away on the jungle path lay a dead Thai. Thais did not lick the Japs' boots as did most of the Oriental races, and although like all peoples there were plenty of rogues, I left Thailand with a very soft spot in my heart for them. It is one of my life's ambitions one day to return and see that country and people through a free man's eyes.

Early on in our stay at Kinsio a trainload of Javanese and Sumatrans had stopped at our station on their way up country. Some of the Dutchmen went over to speak to them but were hissed and spat at. They spoke to us however, and one of our boys who spoke Malay was told that the Japs were giving them virgin land for them to colonize and each would have his own farm.

On the twenty-fourth of July a Javanese lad in his early teens staggered into our camp and collapsed. When he regained consciousness he told us that he had walked without food from Moulmein, about a hundred miles as the crow flies, but probably twice as far the way he had come; with no-one to share the terrors of the jungle nights, it was a miracle that he survived the journey. In fact he was the only one who did.

He told a Dutch interpreter that the trainload of them had been dumped in the middle of the jungle without supplies, and expected to scratch a living without help to get them started in their cultivations. Cut off from everything that was familiar to them, and without food or medicines, they were dying mainly of starvation. The boy said he had left while he still had the strength to walk. The guards came over and told us not to talk to him but leave him to die where he was. Needless to say we ignored this (with impunity, to our surprise), and laid him in our hospital hut. He had nothing but the rags he was wearing, so many of our lads brought him presents from their meagre kits. I made him a set of mess-tins.

Looking more like a sick child than a young man he hung on only for a week or so, but our doctor said that the will to live had gone. The terror of the solitary nightmare journey, together with the shock of losing all his family had proved more than he could take, and he died peacefully among our sick; we buried him with our dead. We all mourned him as one of our children.

One of our boys had a narrow squeak two days after the Javanese lad arrived. Out on a working party, he had gone a hundred yards into the jungle to relieve himself when, hearing a rustle, he looked round and found himself looking into the face of a large tiger. He hoisted his shorts and ran for his life back to the protection of our armed guards. It seemed to him that there were worse things than Japs. Especially when on the twenty-eighth a Japanese general visited the camp and left a present of a Tickel each for every prisoner. Never having heard of anything like this before we wondered if the war were approaching its close and the general was trying to curry favour.

The river was getting frighteningly high now, and tales filtered back from up country of bridges inundated by the raging torrent, the Japs not having made proper note of the high flood marks when they surveyed the route.

In camp, one of the guards obtained an old Burmese sword and proposed to take it home with him as a souvenir. However, it was badly bent, and be brought it over for me to straighten for him. It was just what I had been looking for, with enough steel in it to make a slaughtering knife, a spokeshave blade, and perhaps even a sheath knife. I bent the blade backwards and forwards until the metal broke, then I pulled the handle off and threw it on the rubbish heap. In the evening I went over to the Japs' hut and told of the terrible accident that had befallen the sword; it had just come to pieces in my hand. Although the owner exploded in rage and unbelief, his friends laughed uproariously at some huge joke. There was clearly a tale behind that sword. However the mirth of his friends I think saved me from the bashing for which I had been prepared, and he simply asked me for the broken pieces; I took him to the rubbish dump, and after raking it over for a while managed to find the handle. He let it go at that, to my great relief. I worked late that night over my charcoal furnace, transforming the metal so that it would not be identifiable in the event of a search.

I had not been feeling well now for several days, and one of the symptoms was constant pins and needles in my arms, gradually becoming worse until on the night of the second of August I collapsed and was taken into hospital with a high temperature and a rigor. I remember little of the next week as I had the worst malaria attack I had experienced up to then. The next day a Pte Wilcoxon was carried back from the railway, and laid beside me; he had the same complaint and died two days later. Eleven days after becoming sick I had recovered enough to sharpen the doctor's scalpels and scissors. A friend told me that someone else was managing to butcher the animals satisfactorily. It is always a little disappointing to discover that one is not indispensable. I was still in hospital when a trainload of wounded Jap soldiers passed through the station on their way down country; we had never seen or heard of wounded Japs up until then, and as our last news had been that they were still attacking on the Indian border this was a most encouraging sign. It almost certainly indicated that fighting must be taking place much nearer to Thailand. What, we wondered would our guards do when their front line was pushed back here?

To aid my recovery I bought a pint of gula-malacca, a kind of sugary treacle the Thais obtain from a palm tree, one of the tallest out there. They cut off the stalk which bears the fruit and suspend a bamboo bottle under it to catch the sweet juice. The water is evaporated to produce the product which is a cross between brown sugar and syrup.

On the sixteenth of August the doctor said I was fit to return to work. Things had not been progressing too well of late on the external work-parties. The Japs in charge of bridge repairs had a difficult job to do, and they were often impatient and brutal. Our CO decided that I would be better employed in charge of the bridge repair party than as odd-job man, so Dusty Miller took over my job. The next day a load of Aussies, nearly all of them sick, arrived from up country in the pouring rain, and we all mucked in to get a hut ready for them.

I was surprised on my first day back on the railway, to find that we had 'bolshie' guards who did not seem to care whether we worked or not; I'd never come across this situation before. We were taken to Rin-Tin, a few kilometres up country, supposedly clearing away undergrowth where the jungle was creeping back and encroaching on to the line. After an hour's work the Japs took us into an old hut, and we all spent the remainder of the day talking and singing.

A few days later we started with the engineers, on what was to be our regular job, bridge repairs. First they told us to dig a deep trench round their site hut. They were at pains to explain this was for drainage, but as it was five feet deep we guessed that it was for use during air-raids. We had been hearing for some time that the railway up country was getting regular attention from our bombers, and we had seen that traffic on the line through our camp was now moving mainly by night. On the way back that evening one of our men was severely beaten because the guard did not see him salute as he passed.

The bridges we were repairing were simply constructed from timber baulks, cut straight from the jungle, and held together with metal dogs. The baulks had been cut from trees irrespective of quality; some were of good hard timber, others were soft and pithy, easily and quickly eaten away by the omnipresent termites. Now, as the trains passed over, the unserviceable beams could be seen being compressed like sponges with the weight. Our job was to cut sound teak trees down perhaps a hundred yards away in the jungle, square them by hand into baulks, and drag them to the site of the bridge.

Our only tools were blunt cross-cut saws, blacksmith made axes, and ropes. As we felled each tree, we first cut it to length, then cut a series of slots across each side in turn with our cross-cuts, then flattened them out with our axes. It would have been a painfully long job were it not that there were so many of us, working like the ants whose ravages we were repairing.

Sometimes there would be no suitable trees close at hand, then we would travel up to half a mile into the jungle to find them. Elephants with their mahouts would then be hired or commandeered, one with a chain to pull at the front, and the other to push the timber from behind. Two of these animals could manage far better than the hundred prisoners heaving on ropes with sticks waved over them. The Japs sometimes tried riding the elephants themselves, and worked themselves into terrible paddies when they would not do as they were told; but it is no use getting cross with these incredibly intelligent and gentle beasts, as they know themselves, better than their masters, how to cope with their work.

Each fresh log an elephant is given to move is first assessed, it is gently rocked to and fro with head or tusks, or if chained to it, gently pulled from side to side. If he feels the log is too heavy, or if the ground is too soft, neither blows, cajoling nor shouting will move him until more help is provided.

The actual process of exchanging new beams for the faulty ones in the bridges was far more difficult. Handling heavy timbers weighing a ton was difficult and dangerous at the best of times; it was made worse by the fact that our engineers spoke little English, and thought that we could be made to understand their incomprehensible orders with screams and blows. Many of the replacements were fifty feet up; we had no winches or derricks, and each one had to be hauled up with ropes, and levered into position with crowbars. Sometimes when a train was heard the Japs would get excited and lash out at the men pulling on the rope that was preventing the baulk from falling on the men trying to push from below.

After one particularly dangerous episode, when a Jap told the wrong men to pull, and a dozen of our men narrowly escaped falling to their deaths, I stuck my neck out and ordered the men to lower the baulk to the ground. I paraded them in two lines, and ignoring the shouts of our engineer, I marched over to the Jap in charge. I made him understand I was suggesting that if he would go for a rest under the trees with all the other Japs, I would supervise our men and get the job done. Since we always had to finish a replacement job once we had started it, no matter how late we finished, I could see no harm to our cause in what I was offering to do; getting our men killed would help no-one.

'Bagero!' shouted the Jap, 'Engerisoo soljah no good.' His cronies gathered round him and for five minutes they argued and gesticulated. At last, without speaking, I was waved back to my men, and the Japs moved a little further off. I think that none of them would take the responsibility for letting me do what I wanted but they all wished to see what would happen. I called our gang together, and we discussed our plan of campaign. Smaller gangs were split off, each with a leader, and with a specific job to do, and we all moved back to the bridge. Without a shout or a blow, the beam moved into place with military precision, and in less than half the usual time. Never again on that working party did we get any interference, and in fairness to the Japs it must be said that however quickly we replaced our beam, no more work was ever added.

With our new system working satisfactorily, our guards became more friendly; during meal breaks they would come over for a chat, and sometimes offered us some of their food. Some of us would be asked how long we thought the war would last, evidently realizing at last that their propaganda had misled them, they thought that we had more genuine information than they. More and more they would reiterate that if Japan did lose the war it would be the duty of every

Japanese man to kill his wife and children, and then to commit the hara-kiri, giving us a practical demonstration (without knife of course) of how the ceremony was performed. When the end did come I was to see no-one carry out this gory deed.

We had one guard who spoke some English, having been a schoolmaster. Seeing some of our men elbowing one another out of the way to get at some of the left-over food, he said to me 'At school we teach all English gentlemen.' I replied, looking towards a Jap bully, 'At school we teach all Nippons polite.' After thinking awhile, he said 'War change all!'

Although we had no regular source of news at Kinsio we knew that things must have been going badly for the Japs. Apart from the trainload of wounded and the air-raids, their manner had undergone a change from their earlier arrogant and boasting attitude.

The twenty-eighth of August, we left camp for Rin-Tin bridge soon after dawn. The bridge was a long curved one, and very high; we were working near the centre of it later in the day when I heard a plane, and looking up saw it approaching straight down the line at us. I yelled 'Run' at the top of my voice, and Japs and prisoners alike legged it over the sleepers for the end of the bridge over fifty yards away, every moment expecting to hear the whine and crash of bombs. We took cover in the jungle, and knew that it was not to be as the plane passed overhead, down line in the direction of Kinsio. At intervals of about two minutes several other planes passed over, and towards the end of the raid we heard a stick of bombs explode. 'No far down the line, hope they haven't got our camp!' said someone.

When it all seemed to be over, our guards held a hasty conference, they seemed to be arguing whether to take us back to camp or carry on with the work. After a time one of the Japs hurried off down the line, and the rest of them took us back to work, albeit with many an anxious glance skyward from us all; no-one's mind was on the task in hand. An hour later a diesel engine came up the line with the Jap on board who had gone off earlier, and as he gesticulated and excitedly told his tale to the others we knew something serious had occurred. We were hastily fallen in and marched back in the direction of our camp.

As we approached Kinsio station everything was in turmoil, dust still hanging in the air, and Japs running about everywhere. We entered camp and learned from our comrades what had befallen. A stick of a dozen bombs had been aimed at the station, but none had hit its target. Before the raid the Japs had dispersed into the jungle, including the station-master who had taken refuge over a hundred yards away. The nearest bomb to the station scored a near direct hit on him; he would have been safe had he remained in the station. They burnt what they could find of his body that afternoon, and put the ashes into an eighteen inch cubic box, covered it in white paper inscribed with Japanese characters, and held a funeral service in the evening. The ashes were then sent off down country, ostensibly destined for Japan.

After tea we were ordered to dig trenches round our own huts similar to the ones we had dug for the Japs, and these saved lives later on.

We left camp as usual on the first of September, initially to repair a bridge. However we were diverted to what we were told was an emergency, and about a hundred of us piled into a diesel train and moved off down the line. The emergency proved to be in the shape of a steam locomotive which had left the track and ploughed its way down the embankment pulling six trucks after it. Fifty yards of track were torn up, and the locomotive's nose was deeply buried in the soil. The only tackle we carried was a few jacks and ropes. The engine was heavy; I asked our engineer if a crane was coming, 'No crane' was the curt reply. One of the boys was an ex-railwayman; 'Quite impossible to put that back with this tackle.' We all agreed. The monster, boiling hot and steam squirting from every nook and cranny, would have to be hoisted up, the embankment restored, sleepers and lines replaced, and engine and trucks replaced on the line.

In spite of all that, by twelve-thirty that night, working by the light of acetylene flares the Japs had all back on the line, steam up and ready to move off. I cannot recall exactly how it was accomplished. We cut down trees to make sheer-legs, others to make long levers and fulcrums, we were yelled at, pushed out of the way to let the Japs, running round like maniacs, do the work themselves. They worked like men possessed, some dropping from exhaustion and being replaced by others. I caught odd glimpses of a Jap face straining in the light of a flare. Never have I seen men more determined to complete a job. Complete it they did, but I never knew whether they were driven by patriotic fervour or fear of what would happen to them if the next train could not get through.

We spent the next few days digging trenches beside the railway station, and several trainloads of troops went by in daylight; these were the first we had seen as they had previously travelled only by night. They always stopped for a while at Kinsio, and often tried to speak to us. They were crowded in similar trucks to those that had brought us up from Singapore, although they travelled with the sliding doors wide open. We saw that the floor of each truck was covered with upturned forty-gallon drums, and one soldier sat on the end of each drum; the roof was only a little way above their heads, so they were unable to stand up.

The Jap in charge of this section of the railway was changed, an officer named Konoye taking over. He proved not to be very nice, and our tenth day, Yasumi day, hitherto sacrosanct, and highly necessary for de-bugging, washing etc., had to be spent digging his garden. He came along just as I was giving the men a rest, and he beat me up with his stick.

Two days later I was put in charge of a small party of men in the Jap sweegy-bar (cookhouse) and we managed to help ourselves to a bottle of highly prized soya sauce each. One man's loin-cloth was so brief that he was spotted as we left. He only had his face smacked, and the remainder of us were not searched. I was unable to understand why.

For the next week or so my party was on engine firewood fatigue, and our task was to cut firewood in the jungle, cart it to the embankment, and stack it beside the rails between two stakes which we had to drive into the ground. While doing this work I received my first scorpion sting while picking up a log from the ground. I staggered back feeling as though I had touched a live electric wire. As the shock seemed to affect my whole body I did not realize what had happened until my hand swelled later. It was about an hour before I recovered sufficiently to carry on with my work.

When we returned to camp that night our CO told us that he had heard officially that forty prisoners had been killed and many injured in an air-raid on Non-Produk, a camp some miles farther up country. We sat on our beds late into the night discussing the latest turn in events.

On the ninth of September our CO sent for me and told me that he was appointing me Acting and Unpaid Company Sergent Major to take charge of our company. He gave me no reason for this but I guessed that no-one else wanted to take on the job, as not many relished being in charge of working parties, and therefore having to carry the can when things went wrong and be punished by the Japs; and although blows could be expected, there was never praise or reward for a job well done. However, it was true that I always preferred to be in charge, knowing that if things went wrong I had only myself to blame for any errors of judgement; so I could not complain at my promotion. At one time I had two warrant officers and a colour sergeant working in my gang; although senior to me they had removed their badges of rank.

The next evening, by the feeble glow of my oil-lamp, I read the first official news of our captivity. It was a small slip of newsprint headed 'Victory News' and was being passed from camp to camp, having been dropped by an aircraft farther down the line. I cannot recall the exact message, but broadly it said that help was on the way to us, and the best thing we could do to help our country was to stay where we were. I was later to see thousands of leaflets dropped by our planes, but none in English. All the others were in Chinese or Thai, and we had no interpreters with us at the time. It is a wonder the Japs did not notice the radiant faces of their captives during the next few days. Not many days later we heard that a stick of bombs landed right in a camp down country killing nearly two hundred and fifty of our boys.

On September the twenty-seventh one-hundred and four Aussies marched into the camp, which made us so crowded that we had to close all the bed-spaces down to make room for them. In the evenings I spent much time chatting to them, some of whom were real 'old timers', tough old nuts reared with sheep on outback farms. I found them very good company and made some good friends.

At Hindato there was a very long bridge, more of a curved viaduct that swung round, skirting a cliff, over a deep ravine. On the ninth of October a troop train similar to the one previously mentioned, with men sitting on oil drums, was passing over this bridge when part of it collapsed; the train fell off and landed upside down in the ravine. We were never told how many men died, but from the mess we saw it must have been several hundred. The Japs made no attempt to salvage the train as it was too badly damaged and the gory mess remained there until we moved away.

Chapter 9

'My health is broken and my heart is sick,
It is trampled down like the grass and is withered.
My food is tasteless, and I have lost my appetite.
I am reduced to skin and bones . . .'

We were now to be given an insight into the way our enemies had been educated to treat those of their own race who were no longer of use to their Emperor, and this enabled me to appreciate even more the way we were treated by them. My party was working at a station a few kilometres along the line. The time was mid-day, and we were eating the cold rice we had carried out with us from camp that morning. A train of closed steel cattle trucks, such as we travelled in from Changi, pulled into the siding about twenty-five yards from where we were sitting.

A party of Japs appeared from the station hut, carrying buckets of rice which they placed beside the train, one to every third truck. They went back and reappeared with buckets of water which they set down beside the rice, then walking the length of the train they slid open all the doors.

There was no platform so there was about a five feet drop from the cattle-truck floors to the ground. As we watched thin legs pushed out of the door openings and weakly reached for the ground. One emaciated creature fell out and remained in a crumpled heap on the ground, quite still. The station Japs returned to their hut without a glance at their comrades in the train. Our own guards had not seemed a bad lot as Japs go, and I looked at them in disbelief as they carried on laughing and joking among themselves as though they had not seen their fellow countrymen dying a few yards away for want of a little help.

I asked one of our guards who spoke a little English why he was not helping his sick mates. He blithely explained that a good Japanese soldier neither became a prisoner, nor allowed himself to be sent back wounded. In either event he must commit the hara-kiri, and not become a liability to the Fatherland. For a moment or two we looked at one another. How many times had we said what we would like to do to the little yellow so-and-so's. How wouldn't we like to see them suffer. Now, almost to a man, we got to our feet and moved to the train, the guards' laughter still ringing in our ears.

We were greeted by a terrible stench as we approached the trucks. Those poor chaps must have been shut in without food or water for several days. Some were only boys, most under twenty-two years. Nearly every truck contained several dead; many had terrible wounds, undressed and covered in flies. Others had amputations only covered by field dressings put on in the field. None had been through a dressing station before being bundled into the train. The first truck I looked into had two above knee amputations, yet any of these men who wanted food or water would have to drop to the ground or be shut in that iron hell again without either.

Our men, their prisoners, walked the length of the train, lifting out those who were able to stand, and filling mess-tins and water bottles for the others. When we had done all we could, we returned, nauseated, to our guards. About ten minutes later, after we had started working again, a Jap drove up in a lorry; Tamils piled out and commenced loading the dead from the train into the back of the lorry. As it drove off into the jungle we could see that the bodies were piled up higher than the sides, and the Tamils were sitting on top of the load. We soon saw smoke rising from the jungle as the bodies were burned. Our guards told us that they were the lucky ones, troubles finished.

Yet we were tolerated and fed for nearly four years. During the time they were losing ships in huge numbers and finding it difficult to keep their own people fed, they provided for us, and indeed sent many prisoners back to Japan where they were looked after as well as their own people. It is all very difficult to understand. In later years friends told me that the Japanese civilians were always friendly to them, and none tried to avenge even after the horror of Hiroshima and Nagasaki.

By now I had got to know the Aussies who were sharing our hut quite well, and a great lot of characters I found them to be. Generous to a fault, thorough individualists, ready to take offence and offer to fight one minute, and the next give you half their blanket; quarrel with one and you quarrelled with all the others in his gang. They loved to tell the naîve, tall stories about their tough life in the Australian outback. To tackle a difficult or dangerous job choose an Aussie for a partner; need a company of men to have to try to organize? Stay well away from these chaps. I do not remember seeing one of them as prisoner still wearing his badges of rank.

In particular I made friends with a tall slender young Aussie named Lloyd Stennett, who had in peace-time worked for the Post Office in the Sydney area. We had lots in common, both being useful with our hands, and having a collection of tools, some of which we exchanged. In the evenings we would swap yarns, and discuss politics and world affairs. When I was sick he brought me a boiled egg; knowing he had no reserve of money, he had spent half his ten days' Jap pay on me.

I always supplemented my rations by boiling up any kind of weed or leaf that I found growing in the vicinity, usually first trying a small piece of anything unfamiliar before eating much of it. By now, therefore, I was becoming quite an authority on the edible flora, and comrades often brough new plants for me to try out. Not that I was an infallible judge of these things, I just happened to have a strong digestive system. I still made plenty of mistakes. During the dry season some potato-like tubers were dug up by the embankment and brought for me to try. There was no top left on them to indicate the kind of plant which produced them, but as they looked and smelled harmless I boiled them up in my mess-tin during the lunch break. They cooked soft and floury, and as I chewed a mouthful they tasted not unlike real potatoes, so I swallowed. Even as the mouthful went down I began to feel pins and needles in my mouth, and soon mouth, throat and stomach felt as though they were on fire. I put my fingers down my throat but nothing happened. I said nothing to my friends during the next couple of hours as I endured a kind of fever. However I suffered no permanent ill effects, and warned my friends not to eat them. Later I was to find that a plant like our 'Lords and Ladies' grew from these tubers.

I was to have a similar adventure from the local fungi. There were the remains of an old cattle stockade in Kinsio, and where the posts were rotting in the ground I found growing what was not unlike the European Champignon or 'Fairy Ring' mushrooms, which I knew were edible. Taking a chance I picked a mess-tin full instead of the usual precautionary sample, and stewed them over the fire we kept burning in our hut to help keep mosquitoes away. Our evening meal was of plain rice, and I poured mushroom stew over it.

My recollections of the next few hours are some of the clearest of all my POW days. When I had eaten most of my meal, looking down I saw a regular and almost pretty pattern of bright pink blotches on my hands as I dipped my spoon in for another mouthful. My friends were always 'taking the mickey' at my omniverous habits, and I raised my eyes apprehensively to see if any had noticed what was happening to me. I suddenly felt ridiculously self-conscious, and although I could catch no-one's eye, I felt that everyone was staring at me. Looking back at my body I saw the strange pattern spreading up my arms. At last, as my friends had so often foretold, I had poisoned myself, and thoughts raced through my brain of the fatal cases often reported in the newspapers back home. I looked around me again; whatever happens the lads must not know about it yet; as I looked the faces of my friends took on a strange air of fantasy, and my blotches became brighter. Although I was able to think very clearly, I still did not realize that the colours appearing on my skin were really a product of my mind, and that it was really something akin to looking at a white object through a prism, and seeing the colours of the rainbow.

Under my bed was a rusty tin containing half a pint of the local rock salt. With slow deliberate movements I descended from my bed staging, tipped all the salt into my homemade pint mug, and filled it with cold water from my bucket. Walking down the centre aisle of our hut I had a job not to break into a run as I felt thousands of imaginary eyes boring into my back. I hurried over to the latrine trying not to spill my salt and water; my legs began to feel wobbly, and by the time I reached my destination I had to lean on a post as I stirred my potion and then tried to swallow it. The cold water had not melted any of the salt, and the gritty mixture scratched my throat as I swallowed it: all the willpower I could muster was needed to force the last spoonful down; but I did not feel the slightest bit sick. I put two fingers down my throat in the accepted manner, but still to no avail.

Every moment I felt dizzier, my throat more sore as the salt worked on the scratches it had made; yet I was still determined not to see the doctor and have everyone know of my discomfiture. After trying to vomit for about ten minutes in vain, another man entered the latrine, and seeing me holding on to the post he asked me what was wrong. Opening my mouth to speak I found that my tongue would not obey me and my words came out mixed up and slurred. The man drew my arm around his neck and half carried me to the doctor. One of the strange facts about the incident is that I remembered every part of what took place so clearly.

Dr Gotla said 'And what have you been up to, Sergeant?' I tried to form a word but could only slobber. 'You're drunk!' he said crossly, having been called out from his meal. I remember how indignant I felt at his accusation, and how frustrated at my inability to refute it. He lay me down and sent the man who had brought me to fetch two medical orderlies. When they came and took an arm each I seemed to float up without effort, and my seemingly weightless body glided over the ground to the hospital hut. My feet did not feel the ground. The path along which I was passing was in fact a depressing sheet of brown dried mud with the odd piece of rubbish clinging to it here and there. Now, to my eyes it had 'suffered a sea-change, into something rich and strange'. Everything had become symmetrical, and all was edged with Technicolour patterns. More perhaps like a bright and beautiful mosaic design, in place of the chaos of reality. We passed several men

I knew, walking up from the river in their loin-cloths. As I looked, each man became a caricature of his former self; one looked like a fat pink pig, another I can still see in my mind's eye, as he assumed the appearance of one of Bruce Bairnsfather's grandfather monkey characters. As I looked at each of them in turn I burst into peals of uncontrollable laughter.

Before we reached our destination my ego seemed to detach itself from my body, and I was able, I felt, to travel along beside the poor orderlies who were dragging my ridiculous form between them. As I was guided into the hut and laid on a bed the pain of my sore parched throat brought soul and body together again, and I called for water to assuage the unquenchable thirst I was to endure all the coming night.

In between long drinks of water I sang at the top of my voice. My thoughts were pervaded by a feeling of universal love, I felt so happy that I wanted to tell everyone how stupid it was to fight and quarrel; I had to be restrained from trying to go out and tell the guards that I even loved them. The orderlies had to sit on my head as the Japs patrolled past the hut, lest they hear my uproarious singing and think I had been outside the perimeter and got drunk with the Thais. Had it not been for my poor throat constantly bringing me to a state of reality this would have been one of the greatest experiences of my life. Next day I was told that I emptied a two gallon bucket of water during the next few hours, before dropping off to sleep at about one a.m.

Surprisingly perhaps, I had no trace of a hangover the next morning, and apart from the ever-present thirst I felt perfectly normal. However, the doctor refused to allow me to go out that day working on bridges. 'Tell no-one about it,' he said when I told him the cause of my 'trip'. 'Your system has coped with the poison as a narcotic, someone else could die after taking half of what you ate.'

The Japs asked my boys the whereabouts of the 'Gunzo' who was usually in charge, and some of them reported with glee that I had poisoned myself with mushrooms. When I was once more out with them, every few minutes one of the Japs brought me old pieces of toadstool pulled from the rotting wood and suggested I cook and eat it, keeping the while a straight face. Although I got a bit fed up by the time we finished work, I had learnt for the first time that the Japs do have a sense of humour.

A few days later one of my men, Keyhoe by name, fell off the bridge on which we were working, and by a miracle he only had bruises to show for it. The real surprise however was that our guards showed real concern, and told him that he was awarded two days rest on full pay; nothing like that had ever happened before. That night we were called out of bed at two-thirty and boarded a train to collect a load of firewood for the locomotives. The Japs admitted that the night journey was to avoid air attack. Ten kilometres down the line our engine came off the track, and it took twenty-four hours to get it back on again.

On the twenty-sixth of November the Japs conducted a major search of the camp, collecting all tools, razors, pencils and paper. Mine, fortunately, were too well hidden to be found. That evening I was asked to try my hand at writing a sketch for a camp concert, and agreed to try. Just as I was putting the final touches to my first literary effort I had a sudden attack of malaria, and was taken into hospital.

During the next few days, for the first time the fever caused me to lose a lot of weight. For a while I was delirious, and during that time a bundle of Red Cross blankets arrived in the camp. There were only a few, so it was decided to cast lots among those in hospital to determine who would receive one. When I recovered consciousness a couple of days later I was surprised to find myself wrapped in a soft fluffy cotton blanket. My legs were very weak after this, my worst attack so far, and it was some time before I recovered my strength.

I managed to preserve one presentable set of clothing right through all the days of our captivity. I had an obsession that I must at all costs, when we heard the war was over, be able to march smartly on parade and let the Japs see the loin-clothed figure transformed once more into a British Sergeant. The clothes then that I had been wearing when we were captured, lay always under my blanket, clean, neatly folded and with scarcely a square inch of trousers or shirt not neatly darned. I wore it only to go to Church or on special occasions, in order to ensure that it did not drop to pieces before we were freed.

On the seventh of December after we paraded for work as usual the Japs dismissed us without our leaving camp, and they had to 'stand to'. The next thing we knew was that a big party of guards marched in and herded us into an open space. They surrounded us, some mounting machine-guns, others holding hand-grenades. It was clear to us that they were expecting a parachute landing to attempt to free us; what measures would they take to abort such an effort? However, at nightfall they all 'stood down' and we were allowed back into our huts.

The next day we experienced our first air-raid as direct targets. We all took refuge in the trenches dug round our huts as we were machine-gunned and bombarded by four-engined planes flying low over the camp.

In the weeks before this a siding had been built into the camp terminating in what we called a sporry, which was a short earth-covered tunnel built above ground to house and protect one locomotive. We guessed that the planes were after this. Bombs and bullets landed in every other part of the camp, the Dutchmen's hut was blown completely to bits; the sporry was not touched. Although after the raid all our huts and the cookhouse were peppered with holes, lying in our trenches none of us were killed, although two were injured. The Dutch started to look through the rubble of their hut, to try to find any of their personal possessions not destroyed; I saw one clutching a photograph, but virtually nothing else remained.

The raid showed us for the first time that the Japs were not the supermen that we at times had believed them to be. While the raid was on we were frantically waving to the planes, most of us quite unafraid. We saw the Japs nearby, manifestly terrified. It is amazing the difference it can make to be on the winning side. When the Stukas dived on us in Singapore it was we who were terrified. I never felt quite the same about our captors after this, and took their brave talk of hara-kiri rather than capture with a pinch of salt.

When it was clear that the planes were not going to return, the guards started to shout at us to regain their confidence. 'Courra! Oroo men in hut speedo speedo!'

Two days later while working on a bridge there was another

raid, and the guards allowed us to disperse into the jungle. Half a dozen large cartridge cases fell on the ground near me as a plane machine-gunned the railway line. I took some of them back with me as they appeared to be made of copper, hoping to make one of them into a soldering iron.

Some time earlier I had purchased a pewter mug from a comrade with the idea of using it as solder, but so far I had been unable to find the copper to make into a 'bit'. These cartridges were not the answer however; I think they must have contained some zinc, as although I was able to gather plenty of resin for flux, my new soldering iron would not solder.

We now noticed a pronounced reduction of trains proceeding up country; instead Jap troops marched past the camp, pulling hand carts stacked with weapons and stores.

On December the thirteenth I had another relapse of malaria, and went back into the sick bay. While there news came through that a trainload of prisoners was machine-gunned from the air the other side of Rin-Tin resulting in forty-three being killed. It was becoming clear that travelling by rail was now a very risky business. Most days we heard at least one flight pass over, and the crunch of bombs exploding in the distance.

I now had a period of almost continuous fever, and by Christmas Day had become so debilitated that the doctor told me that I would have to return to Tamarkan with the next party of sick. I tried hard to kick against the pricks, but to no avail. Christmas Day was my last day in Kinsio. I had got to know all the guards with their peccadillos and they knew me. Although Kinsio food was terrible, I knew all the other prisoners, and had made many good friends. Dutch, Australian and British. It would be all strange again in Tamarkan.

Feeling very despondent and weak, I turned my kit over, half intending to dump all my illegal items rather than endure the constant strain of hiding them from the Japs. Once again however a comrade offered to hold on to them while I was being searched, and then he smuggled them to me on the train. We moved off at midnight, very glad not to be travelling in daylight, arriving in Tamarkan at eight a.m. after an uneventful journey.

Although feeling ill, I was not too bad to notice that this was no longer the same dear old Tamarkan of yesteryear and Col Toosey. It had become untidy and dirty, much like any other camp. There was a Japanese 'doctor' nominally in charge of the sick, but his job was just to tell our doctors how many men they were to send up country as 'cured' and fit for work. Our people therefore often found themselves being told to turn a hundred men out of the hospital camp as fit for work, when they knew that there were none.

When this happened the 'doctor' would call all men who were strong enough to get off their beds on parade, and walking along the line he would push out a man here and there until the required total was found. According to reports, the Jap MO had been a vet's assistant before the war! Once he made up his mind and pushed out a man from the ranks, it mattered not if our doctors explained that he were dying of TB, the Japs would see no reason. After the parade therefore our doctors would hold another one, and exchange any men that were too bad so that the Japs still had the same number.

Tamarkan was now run entirely by the Australians, and although my first impressions of it had been depressing, I soon began to realize that it was being run much better than I thought. The camp authorities were not getting the same co-operation from the Japs, now that the war was not going well for them, as Col Toosey had received. In spite of this a laundry had been organized to wash clothes and bedding for the sick, and I had never seen that done before. The cookhouses were also very well run in spite of the very meagre rations. I had to revise my idea of the Aussies and their organizing abilaity.

I was even given a blood test, and my complaint diagnosed as ST malaria. I also had pus in my stools, which indicated that I had not completely recovered from my last attack of dysentery. The quinine situation in the camp was so bad that only sufficient was available to give to patients who would otherwise die. Therefore blood counts of patients were taken in order that the quinine should go to those with the greatest need. I really cannot speak too highly of those Australian doctors, they must have saved hundreds of lives by their dedicated efforts. Our doctor sent for me and told me that in spite of my infections my body was standing up to the strain incredibly well, as I still had a blood-count of 68%, much better than most of the other chronic malaria patients. As there were only four doses of quinine allocated per day for the whole of our ward, needless to say I did not have any. There were fifty patients in each ward.

On the following day, the ninth of January 1945, I was feeling very low, and was very lucky indeed to escape with my illegal gear during a surprise Jap search, as I had not hidden it with my usual care. I felt unable to face the risk again, and asked one of the orderlies to take all my tools to the cookhouse for the cooks to bury for me. I never saw them again, the product of thousands of hours of spare time work, and much ingenuity. Next day the quinine ration was reduced even further, and it was now only three doses per day for the fifty men. However, after twenty-four hours with a temperature of 106 degrees, I was given a dose the following day.

During the next two months I had constant malaria and it is quite certain that only the constant devotion of the Aussie doctors and medical orderlies kept me alive. Before we were captured we called our army doctors everything from butchers to quacks. It seems to be a tradition, probably due to the unending battle waged between them and the lead-swingers trying to escape parades. Throughout the days of our captivity both the doctors and our medical orderlies lived up to the highest standards of their tradition. They fought a ceaseless battle against filth and disease with very little, and sometimes nothing, in the way of medicines; yet I heard of none ever giving up his thankless task.

On the twenty-ninth of January I received nine postcards from home, all over two years old, and older than my last batch of letters. Seeing neighbours die every day, I became very depressed. I had myself weighed on the cookhouse scales, and found that I had shrunk from my last reading of eleven stone to a present four stone. In spite of this I was determined to get away from this camp of sick men as soon as I could, lest I also lost the will to live.

On the third of February at three o'clock in the afternoon, we endured a very heavy air-raid. The steel bridge over the river, with a smaller wooden one a little way off, and also an Ack/Ack gun on a small mountain overlooking the camp, have been mentioned before. The steel bridge on its concrete pillars was only a few hundred yards away, and that was to be the target of the ensuing attack.

Our first intimation that something was afoot was when we heard the drone, and saw a solitary aeroplane flying high over the camp; this was quickly followed by the sounding of the camp air-raid alarm. As I watched the plane I saw what looked like a great swarm of bees leave its belly; this descended, growing ever larger as it fell towards the Ack/Ack position. The Bofors gun opened up on the plane, and we saw the shells explode far below it. Suddenly we saw the mountain-top illuminated by thousands of flashes, followed by the crump of small anti-personnel bombs exploding around the gun position. During the following raid not another shell was fired at the planes.

A minute or so later the first plane of the main bomber force appeared, low in the sky, making a bee-line for the bridge. Machine-guns on the mountain opened fire on the plane, which was so low that we saw the bullets raise dust on our parade ground, heard them click through the roofs of our huts. Several of our men were injured by these but none killed. We had a grandstand view of all that followed.

When the alarm had sounded our guards ran around the camp shouting that we must stay under cover or we would be shot. However, we got between the huts where they could not see us and waved Jap-happies or anything we could lay our hands on at the planes as they came over. I saw a huge bomb leave the belly of the plane, saw it fall towards the bridge, and after a few seconds time-delay, heard the roar of the explosion. When the smoke cleared the bridge remained intact. The next plane approached within seconds of the first explosion, and this one dived on the Ack/Ack post, guns blazing. The first pilot must have warned this one of the machine-guns up there, and after this we heard no more of them.

There seemed to be seven planes in all, and they came round

and round, follow my leader style, each time dropping one bomb on the bridge. The attack lasted all afternoon; every now and then one of the planes would release a burst of machine-gun fire as the gunners spotted targets. Our guards fired not a shot but remained in their trenches, heads down until it was all over. No bullets or bombs fell on the prisoners. On the previous raid, which took place on the twenty-eighth of November, eighteen of our lads had been either killed or injured.

This raid lasted for three hours. When the all-clear sounded and we were able to get a good view of the bridge we were amazed to see every span still intact. Three hours non-stop virtually unopposed bombing from low-level, and not one direct hit? But when work parties left the camp next day they found that the concrete piers had been undermined to such an extent that they were three feet out of upright in places. The purpose of the operation had not been to knock out spans which could be replaced fairly easily, but what they did was made sure the bridge was never used again. Our men also found out that three direct hits had been made on the wooden bridge, and from this time forth there was always to be a working party repairing it; and as soon as this was done it would be bombed again.

From now on there was also a party of prisoners on the unenviable task of salvaging unexploded bombs from the river bed. There seemed to be hundreds of these, mostly five-hundred-pounders, and before long we saw them in rows along the river bank. At first our officers told the Japs that it was against international law for prisoners to do this dangerous work, but the first work-party detailed to do the work was told that any man refusing to do as he was told would be shot, so the lesser of the two evils was the bomb retrieving.

On my birthday, the sixth of February, I marched out of Tamarkan for the last time, never even to see it again, destination Chunkai, where we arrived at six o'clock that evening.

The RSM sent for me the next day and asked me if I would take over the job of group canteen purchaser. This consisted only of purchasing two eggs per day for each sick man from our regiment in the camp, and giving them out personally. I had no money of my own and found the practicalities rather awkward. I therefore borrowed twenty Tickel from Sgt Horrocks, who seemed to be one of the favoured 'permanent residents' of Chunkai, and in business in quite a big way. This loan enabled me to buy eggs in bulk, and more cheaply than the hand to mouth system I had originally been expected to operate.

Now the Japs decided to take the remaining officers, and send them all to Kanburi further down the line.

Officers had been looked upon as 'they' by most other ranks up until now. This was partly because they received money from the Japs which they were in theory to pay back after the war out of their officers' pay. It was also because the officers lived always in separate huts and ate on their own, that we always thought they were living better than they actually were. In fact I am quite sure that our officers did all they could to help us at all times, and allocated some of their cash in the larger camps like Chunkai to the welfare of the sick.

When we realized that the last of our officers were really going to be taken right away from us they suddenly became 'we's' for the first time. As they moved out of camp it was a sad parting. We all knew that the end of the war could not be all that far off, and many believed that the Japs would shoot us all when they realized the end was approaching. They knew our officers were our leaders, and were probably removing them because leaderless men would, they thought, be easier to dispose of. It was with sadness therefore and with many a moist eye that we said goodbye.

I was still having one relapse of fever after another, and soon had to give up even my little canteen job. A blood-slide showed both ST and BT malaria, and I was able to do little other than rest.

On the twentieth of February I was told to be ready to move out of Chunkai, to go further down country, and the next afternoon we marched into Kanburi. Before they would allow us in the camp we had to unload a trainload of firewood. In the camp we sat by our kits all night, awaiting a train to take us further on our way. Next morning we were told to stand down, and I got two hours' sleep. Going to the well to fill my water-bottle, I saw that since our last sojourn someone had made a big set of bamboo pumps with great ingenuity, and water was now pumped up from the well in bamboo pipes and stored in big tanks. After spending yet another night awaiting our train, at four a.m. on the twenty-third we climbed on board at last. After a wait of three hours we steamed slowly off, passing through Banpong (our first port of call when we came to Thailand), and on to Ratbury, where we saw that another bridge of steel and concrete had been blown up. Here we spent the afternoon carrying sacks of tapioca for the Japs, many of us so weak that we needed four men to a sack.

That evening we crossed the river by barge (the bridge being destroyed) and were made to mount the roofs of cattle-trucks similar to thse in which we had arrived from Changi. We were given a dollop of cold rice each on the roof, and then the train moved off on what was to prove a very dangerous journey. We should have used our rice ration to stick ourselves on those roofs. As it was we linked arms and hung onto each other like grim death as the train bumped and swayed over the uneven track, and we steamed South towards Malaya.

We all considered ourselves very lucky to arrive safely at our destination at ten o'clock that evening. We dumped our kits by the railroad and sat on them until one a.m. before being marched away by our guards. We knew by the stars that we had been travelling South, so we could be in either Southern Thailand or Northern Malaya. Another thing we were not to know was that we were marching to our last POW camp.

Chapter 10

'He brought the exiles back
From the farthest corners of the earth.'

Arriving in our new camp after a long march, in my debilitated state I felt about all-in, and from seven in the morning when we arrived until mid-day, I lay more or less out for the count. I was brought round by my friends at mid-day to receive a plate of rice with sugar sprinkled on it. For the first time I became cognisant of my surroundings, and saw that there were no huts for us, and that I had been lying in the open.

Luckily we were in the dry season, although for those of us with fever and almost continually recurring rigors it was not much fun to be sleeping on the ground outside. Our first job was to be hut-building, but I was unable to help much, as I was now entering into a three-month period of virtually untreated malaria, often delirious for days on end and remembering little about it all. One thing I remember clearly. A week or so after completing it, we were all lying in our new hut when a frightening and oppressive stillness descended over everything. Gradually we began to hear a strange rushing sound coming as though from afar. Louder and louder, until it became a roar, and all at once hell broke loose as with an unholy din our hut was wrenched from the ground, and it sailed high up into the sky never to appear again. Men were lifted into the air as the bed stagings went up, and were dumped on the ground yards away. Just as suddenly the wind ceased and rain came down in torrents. We had experienced our first hurricane. I hope it is my last. I found a piece of attap about two feet square and held it over myself to keep off the worst of the rain. Nightfall had been approaching when the catastrophe commenced, and I stayed under my 'umbrella' until morning.

With the dawn we were able to see the extent of the devastation. Not a stick was left standing in the whole camp. There was no cookhouse and therefore no breakfast. Most of the men's blankets had disappeared and everything and everyone was soaked; we looked a very sorry spectacle. The work of replacement was put in hand at once, priority being given to hospital and cookhouse huts, and before another week had passed everyone had a roof over his head again. Not however before many of the fever cases developed pneumonia, and over half the population of the camp became too sick to work.

When the huts were completed for the second time the first outside work-parties left the camp. When they returned they told us they were clearing the jungle five kilometres away to build an aerodrome. They had a rough lot of guards, and several were beaten.

This camp was called after the nearest village, Pechaburi (although none of us was sure of the correct way to spell it). It was without a water supply, and those able to walk that far were escorted by guards once a day nearly a mile into the jungle, where water was bailed out of a muddy stream and carried back to camp. Those of us not well enough to go were dependent on comrades for their water. I was able to lend my bucket (very precious in this camp) on the understanding that I had half the water, so I was able to wash myself down every day, even though I only used a pint of water in my mess-tin. Another sick man would always use this after me, so its consistency by then can be guessed.

A party of Aussies started to dig a camp well near the cookhouse. Well might they be called 'Diggers'! Working like Trojans, and in shifts, twenty-four hours a day, they gradually worked downwards into the rock-hard wall. I have never seen our men work so hard. They dug it like a big square mine-shaft, and there was soon a big heap of soil. Within three weeks they were over thirty feet down and had reached water. It came up yellow as mustard for the first few days, and the cooks had to leave it to settle before it could be used.

The well did not provide enough water for the whole camp, so a party of 'Pommies' volunteered to dig another one in another part of the camp, and when that was working we just about managed by rationing the water carefully.

Pechaburi was the first camp during our stay in Thailand where there was no river for miles around. Kampongs and the camps themselves, all threw their refuse into the river, and as we began to recover our health in Pechaburi we wondered whether our sterile well water was a factor. As the months went by there were fewer and fewer deaths, and our health generally did improve greatly. After three months in the camp I at last shook off my malaria, and had no relapses. Looking back I feel that it was little short of a miracle that without medicine and adequate diet I could have recovered at all from the very low state I was in only a few months before, as it is said that malaria cannot be cured without drugs. The bones that had bulged in my knees, hips, shoulders and ribs gradually became covered with flesh again as I regained my ability to eat.

Not that I had ever given up. No matter how many of my friends I saw carried out feet first I never seriously considered the possibility of my joining them. A confidence from outside helped make me feel that somehow I was different from the others who were dying: although time seemed to be standing still I was quite sure I would return home in the end. By this time it seemed as though we had been in captivity for untold years; visions of home became more and more difficult to conjure up, and then only as a dream. Where we now were was the only reality.

While I had been so ill my diary had gone by the board for the first time since our capture, so I do not have the date of the day in May when at last I was pronounced fit to go back to work. I had always hated staying in camp, so even though it meant working under the Japs again, I was delighted to be detailed for work on the aerodrome party the following day, and confidence returned. I wondered how they had managed without me to look after them!

Arriving at the site, I was surprised to see that hundreds of acres had already been cleared and roughly levelled, and that a modern American bulldozer was parked at the edge under the trees. It was spotless and shone like a new shilling. I asked a neighbour if it had to be cleaned up after work every day, and with a laugh he told me that it was never used, the work being done with picks, rakes and chunkels, all by hand. The bulldozer was started up every morning to make sure it worked, then polished and left. It was the only bulldozer they had, having been captured in Singapore at the same time as us; now no-one was going to risk breaking it and incurring such wrath as would probably entail being flayed alive. This machine could have done more work than all the prisoners in the camp put together, but it remained a museum piece.

There was, however, one sop to progress in the shape of two ancient British steamrollers with fireboxes enlarged to burn wood. They were lubricated with pure castor oil, and lots of this had already been smuggled back to the camp for our doctors to use. The runways on the aerodrome were being made from rocks which parties of prisoners were breaking up with sledgehammers, and the steamrollers were being used to level and consolidate these.

We had to walk five kilometres to work carrying our tools, and then spend all the day in the sun working like ants on the aerodrome levelling the ground with our picks and chunkels; then there was the same journey home again. After the months of inaction the first day had been a gruelling one for me, and I was glad to put my feet up on our return that night.

However we did not get our rest without first experiencing some trauma; on the usual roll call which took place before we were dismissed it was discovered that one of the prisoners had escaped from the working party. The Japs threatened reprisals in the form of dire punishment should anyone else escape, and our own camp authorities asked us not to attempt to, as the sick in camp would be the most likely ones to suffer. In any case the end of the war could not be far off now. Nevertheless it was not to be long before three more British and then two American prisoners also escaped.

I soon toughened up out on the site, and for three months worked sometimes on levelling and sometimes on stone breaking, always in charge of one of the working parties. One day, soon after my return to work I saw a crowd of about a hundred men come running towards us from the other side of the ''drome'; they were waving sticks and yelling. This is it, we thought, the war is over. We left our guards and ran to meet them, but as we got closer we saw that there were Japs in the crowd, acting as excited as the rest, and finally we were close enough to see what the fuss was really about; a snake going for its life followed by hordes bent on its destruction!

The fauna here was somewhat different from that up country. We were eating our mid-day rice a few days later when I met my first bulldozer beetle, and found it a most interesting little creature. He had been disturbed from his earthy home and was doing his best to rehabilitate himself as quickly as he could. About an inch long, beautifully made, black rounded and silky, he carried a perfectly made bulldozer blade in front. When I picked him up he feigned death. Looking closely at him I was surprised to see no sign of eyes or feelers, and wondered how he knew where to dig, so I put him down about a foot away from the nearest soft earth. After a minute the blade slowly lifted to reveal two beady eyes and a pair of short feelers, and within seconds he was at the heap and digging himself in. Quite the most perfect creature I have ever seen.

There were also blue velvet covered spiders with bodies an inch and a half across, poisonous we were told. They lived in holes in the ground, each one lined with silky cobweb.

Then there were pale green semi-transparent tree-frogs with strange stary eyes. The first time I saw one I reached to pick it up but was stopped by my Dutch companion. He told me they could squirt blinding acid from their vents and were best left alone. Although I found this difficult to believe, especially remembering our childhood belief that British frogs could spit fire, I left them alone. They clung to the leaves with little suction pads on their feet.

The prisoners were organized into companies, and each company comprised three working parties. Our company consisted of one Australian and two British working parties. I was in charge of one of the British groups. The Aussies were breaking rocks with sledge hammers and my men were carrying broken rock on to the runway, where the third party was laying it in position and ramming it down. No-one of course ever worked harder than was necessary to keep our guards quiet, and one day I noticed one of the Aussies tapping gently away at the same rock without breaking it, all the time we were loading up. His guard was some way off and he thought he was unobserved. However there was another one watching him from the trees, and in the usual way he came rushing out with a roar, clouted the culprit round the head, and kicked his shins. Then he made him stand to attention with a fourteen pound hammer held over his head. When we returned some minutes later for another load of rocks, I saw that the poor chap was still there and on the point of collapse; every time he attempted to lower the hammer the Jap threatened him. As the sun blazed down and the man began to sway no-one tried to help him from his own group, so I left my lot and ran over to the Aussie; snatching the hammer out of his hands I yelled at him without ceasing for about a minute. Then leading him over to a big rock I told him to get stuck into it if he valued both our lives. The Jap had said nothing while this took place, and turning to him I made him understand that I would see to it that the bad boy did his share in future. That evening back in camp a delegation came over from the Aussies and asked me if I would take charge of their party as well as my own, which I agreed to do.

Buckets were in very short supply in this camp, and now I fashioned myself a few rough tools to enable me to resume tinsmithing again; before long I was turning out a bucket or some other item most evenings.

I was now becoming really fit again. On my way to work I tripped and fell with two heavy picks on my shoulder. Somehow or other I managed to get my little finger caught between them as I hit the ground, and it was so mangled that an inch of bone was exposed. However I drew the flesh together and kept it bound up with a piece of rag for a couple of weeks and it healed without becoming infected.

Occasionally my work party was taken down to the small town of Pechaburi to collect goods for the guards. The first time I went our guard told me that the correct name of our actual camp was 'Katchu Mountain Camp'. In the town we passed a long line of Thais celebrating some event. Each one was dancing individually with the strange and beautiful hand movements of the country and thin strains of music came from the head of the line. Men and women had bamboo bottles slung over their shoulders, and now and then I would see someone stop and take a swig from over his shoulder.

The second time we went a plane dived at us as we were passing a stream, and I jumped in for protection. I heard an explosion, and climbing out of the water saw thousands of leaflets falling from the sky. Our guards searched us for these leaflets, but they did not find mine. When I got it back to the camp I found that it was printed in Chinese and no-one could read it.

A few days later the Japs brought in a group of Thais they had caught, we were told, stealing blankets. They held them in the guard-house all night, and every now and then we heard them scream; apparently they had been tortured by having hot water poured up their noses. The next morning, after being kept kneeling in front of the guardroom for a long time, they were eventually taken away somewhere.

The wet season set in now, and as usual the camp became a sea of mud. Drawing the tools for my party from the tool store one day, I dropped an axe on my bare big toe. I was saving my boots to wear on our release, and I could not keep sandals on when it was muddy. My toe was gashed too badly to go out to work for a couple of weeks, so I got a temporary job in camp tinsmithing. Again, in spite of having been inundated with mud many times, my flesh healed completely with a simple dry rag dressing.

On the fifteenth of August 1945, an exceptionally strong rumour swept through the camp that the war was over; although of course it had to end some day, I did not believe it. However, something was in the wind as we did not go out to work that day, and the guards were standing about in groups talking with worried countenances.

The following day again we were not called out to work, and to our amazement the Japs unlocked what we had until then believed to be one of their ration stores, and we found it to contain Red Cross goods which they had been sitting on for months. This consisted of mostly sports equipment such as deck tennis rings, tennis rackets and balls, and these were shared among the huts. We began seriously to consider the possibility that the war was indeed over.

I spent every spare minute I had working on tinsmithing, and turned out hundreds of mugs from the empty Red Cross food tins. I had to work to avoid thinking about what was happening, as for some strange reason I felt extraordinarily unsettled instead of relieved at the thought of imminent freedom.

We had no officers with us, as they had all been separated off at Chunkai, but had a British RSM in charge. The camp was strangely quiet all day on the eighteenth, and late in the afternoon the RSM called us together to tell us that at last the war was over. We responded spontaneously with a deafening cheer, and then gathered in little groups of friends to discuss the news.

How can I explain what it felt like to be told that a bad dream of nearly four years' duration was at last ended? It was a most complex reaction. Try as I might I seemed to be unable at this stage fully to realize the implication of the message we had just received. Why was my soul not soaring with rapture at the thought of the fast approaching freedom? 'Rejoice and be exceeding glad' I told myself. 'Suffering and privation is over, we are all going home.' I was talking to myself aloud I suddenly realized, and looking quickly about me saw the same dazed look on the faces of my friends in place of what should have been rapturous anticipation.

I felt terrible as my tummy turned over with an unidentifiable fear; where was the joy our release was to bring? All the hitherto unanswered questions as to how the Japs would react to defeat were now known; they had made no attempt to kill us and commit hara-kiri as they had threatened, but were taking it all very calmly. I did understand all these things, but I was in a state of shock and could not appreciate them.

That evening meal was the best since we had been captured, the cooks surpassing themselves with the aid of Red Cross rations. I collected mine, but sitting down felt sick at the sight and smell. Can't waste it I thought, and called out 'Any one for buckshees?' A day or two ago fifty voices would have sung out, today there was not a sound as everyone fiddled with his own helping.

The nineteenth found Japs still guarding us. They had told our RSM that the Allies had sent them a message to the effect that they were to remain armed and in charge until someone came and took us over. One of our men passed a guard and did not salute him, thinking it unnecessary now that the war was over; but he was knocked down in just the same way as he would have been before.

Still unable to rid myself of the nameless fear I was experiencing, I spent all my time working. Our lives had been ordered for us during the last few years, now I would need to make many major decisions for myself. It had been said that after our privations we should be impotent for the rest of our lives. After living the way we had, everyone would think we were a bit 'peculiar' when we got home. I could not keep these and other thoughts from my mind as I worked.

Some of these fears were far from groundless; I had left home a lad, but to use my sister's words, I returned 'a queer old man'. Later they told me that for the first few months, among other things I never walked, but ran everywhere. I can now remember hardly anything about those first few months at home; but years later my family told me they found it hard to hold back their tears in my presence.

During the next few days I kept thinking I would wake up and find I had been dreaming, as the camp looked the same as usual with the Japs still in charge. However, we were issued with more Red Cross stuff, including tins of fruit, and American shirts and trousers. Men now began to discuss the possibility of breaking out of camp, so all NCOs were called together and asked to ensure that the men were kept under control to avoid mob rule taking over. There was also the possibility that if a breakout occurred irresponsible elements might cause trouble with the Thais. I realized that this was quite right, we did not want any trouble now that we were soon to be free.

On the twenty-first of August some Thais called through the wire and told us that we were going to be evacuated on the twenty-eighth of the month. It seemed strange that none of our people had communicated directly with us, and that all we knew was coming from either Japs or Thais.

Just outside our camp was a large cemetery, containing the remains of all POWs who had died in the area. On the twenty-sixth we held a memorial service there, attended by all the prisoners and the Jap camp commandant and his staff.

On our return to camp one of the Americans who escaped a few months earlier, drove a truckload of Red Cross food into the camp just before mid-day. We heard that he had been living in the jungle with a party of Allied guerillas who had been dropped by parachute. The following day, a paratroop officer drove into camp.

He mounted our earthen camp stage, and we all gathered round for what should have been one of the most dramatic moments of our lives. Tommy-gun in his hands, and dressed in camouflaged clothes, he looked as though he had just fought his way in to the camp. I sat down on the earth and waited to hear about all the exciting things that had happened in the world leading up to the capitulation of the enemy. Up to now we had been told nothing. His 'news' was that while we had been prisoners, scientists had discovered a wonderful new medicine called penicillin. It cured many diseases, but especially all forms of venereal disease. No longer need we worry about associating with girls out there as at the first sign of trouble a couple of injections was all that was necessary!

Later on that same day another Red Cross lorry came in, this time the load included a small radio set. It was put in position on the stage, and we all gathered round waiting for news time. As it was not loud enough for us to hear, one man listened and then shouted the items out as they came through. I had my first 'pukka griff' for four years.

Still later a party of our officers arrived, having journeyed from a distant officers' camp. They brought with them the news that we were all to be flown out from the aerodrome we had been building.

Just before dusk a party of free Allied troops came in after travelling up from the Malayan border, and they were to share with the Japs the job of guarding us. They hardly seemed to speak to us, and we were clearly regarded as not 'one of them'.

That evening we were each given pencil and paper and told we could write a message of not more than twenty words to be cabled home. I spent the whole evening trying to compose a reassuring story in so few words; I later found out that my parents never received it.

Next day, as we were all gathered round the stage listening to the radio news, an American paratrooper drove into camp, stalked on to the stage, and held up his hand for silence; at last we heard what we had been waiting for. 'You will all be flown out by the United States Airforce within a few hours.'

When he could again make himself heard above the squeals of excitement, he told us that his regiment had been operating in the jungle only a few miles away. Had the war not ended abruptly his job would have been to release us in a few weeks time. Those who had escaped from camp earlier were all safe with his boys. Thais had co-operated in getting a message to individuals asking them to escape and leading them to the paratroopers. They had been needed to supply details of the camp layout when the time came to attack.

Our camp began to fill up with hundreds of ex-prisoners, arriving to be flown out from 'our' aerodrome. By evening no more could be crowded in, and there were still hundreds waiting in the local town.

The first Yankee plane landed on the twenty-ninth of August. When the doors opened a ramp was lowered and a tiny truck drove out. The driver told us that it was a 'Jeep' and that they had thousands of them. We also learned that the plane was a Dakota.

The worst sick cases were loaded on the plane, and it took off safely from our bumpy runway with the first of our boys to be really and truly released from their captivity.

An American camera team had flown in with that first plane and they began filming the camp. I carried on throughout this time, making tin mugs; I had orders for hundreds, they were wanted to take home for souvenirs.

From now on the planes were landing at the rate of about

one an hour, from dawn to dusk, first ferrying out the sick and hospital staff, then taking loads of fit men. I made my last tinware on the last day of August as I was told to be ready to leave the next morning.

I tipped all my kit out to go through it and decide which items should accompany me out of Thailand. As I gazed at all my bits and pieces, from my tiger toe cigarette holder to my recently made soldering iron, I was overcome with a feeling of nausea as I thought of the dead friends and other unhappy memories that nearly every piece recalled. In the end I dumped everything apart from my diary, clothes and a set of sergeant's stripes I had made to use as an armband when I was not wearing a shirt.

We marched out of camp with scarcely a backward glance, and arrived on the 'drome just as our plane landed. It had originally possessed double doors, but these had been removed. We were packed tightly in, and as we climbed into the air I saw our American 'conductor' leaning nonchalantly against the door post looking out of the door opening, and chewing gum just as I had seen them do on the films four years earlier. He looked likely to fall out any minute, as we climbed over the mountain range separating Burma from Thailand. Had there been a window in the floor I might have taken a farewell look at the railway line, every sleeper of which represented a man's life.

'When Jehovah brought back His exiles to Jerusalem,
It was like a dream.'

THE END